ASTROLO(
MAGI(n

To:
Caroline

Happy Birthday & Many Happy Returns

Mary.

ASTROLOGICKAL MAGICK

ESTELLE DANIELS

A guide for magickians who are not necessarily astrologers and for astrologers who are interested in magickal psychic indicators in astrologickal charts.

SAMUEL WEISER, INC.

York Beach, Maine

First published in 1995 by
Samuel Weiser, Inc.
P. O. Box 612
York Beach, ME 03910–0612

Library of Congress Cataloging-in-Publication Data
Daniels, Estelle
    Astrologickal magick / Estelle Daniels.
        p.   cm.
    Includes bibliographical references and index.
    ISBN 0–87728–826–7
    1. Astrology.   2. Magic.   I. Title.
BF1711.D36   1995
133.5—dc20   95–3723
EB   CIP

Typeset in 11 point Palatino
Printed in the United States of America

00 99 98 97 96 95
10 9 8 7 6 5 4 3 2 1

The paper used in this publication meets the minimum
requirements of the American National Standard for Perma-
nence of Paper for Printed Library Materials Z39.48–1984.

TABLE OF CONTENTS

Foreword ix
Introduction xi

PART ONE. THE LANGUAGE OF ASTROLOGY 1
The Basics, 3
A Little About Astrology Itself, 6
Esoteric and Exoteric, 7
Tropical, Siderial, and Heliocentric Astrology, 13
Brief History, 14
The Language and Alphabet of Astrology, 15
The Words, 16
The Planets, 18
The Mundane Wheel, 23
The Houses and Signs, 30
Planets Again, 33
Aspects, 38
Magick and Astrology, 41
Houses, Signs and Planets in Magick, 46
The Twelve Houses in Magick, 50
The Signs in Magick, 53
Planets in Magick, 57
Interpretation in Brief, 58

PART TWO. MAGICKAL TIMING TOOLS 61
How Timing Works, 63
Waxing/Waning Moon, 74
Avoiding a Void-of-Course Moon, 76
Retrograde Mercury, 79
The Moon in the Signs, 82
Planetary Hours, 88

The Moon in Houses, 100
Secret Timing Tools, 101
Last and Next Aspect, 103
Last Aspect, 104
Next Aspect, 105
Aspects, 106
Rulerships, 108
Mutual Reception, 110
Other Planetary Aspects, 113
Other Methods, 116
Summary, 124

PART THREE. MAGICK AND YOUR NATAL CHART 125
Introduction, 127
Magickal Nature of the Signs and Houses, 128
The Final Signature, 130
Sign and House Definitions, 148
Magickal Natures of the Planets, 154
Planetary Definitions, 160
Sun, 162
Moon, 163
Ascendant, 165
Mercury, 166
Venus, 169
Mars, 170
Jupiter, 171
Saturn, 173
The Outer Planets, 176
Uranus, 178
Neptune, 178
Pluto, 180
Mutual Reception, 181
Final Dispositor, 183
North and South Nodes of the Moon, 192
Esoteric Rulers, 211

PART FOUR. ADDITIONAL STUDIES AND
ASTROLOGICKAL RULERSHIPS 223
Introduction, 225
Birthstones, 226
Caduceus, 227
The Three Major Astrological Systems, 227
Cookbook Astrology, 229
How to Start a Fistfight Among Astrologers, 230
Transits, Planetary Stations, and Eclipses, 232
Syzygy, 235
The Uranus-Neptune Conjunction and Outer Planet
Cycles, 240
Constellations vs. Signs, 247
Fixed Stars, 253
Asteroids, 264
Chiron, 278
Eight Moon Phases, 281
Rulership in Astrology and Magick, 294

PART FIVE. AN ASTROLOGICKAL RITUAL 309
Introduction, 311
The Ritual, 315

Afterword 321
Resources 325
Bibliography 329
Index 333
About the Author 336

To my Mother, who got me into all of this in the first place. Thank you for your support and encouragement over the years.

And to Paul, who uttered the fateful words, "Why don't you write a book about it?"

FOREWORD

This is a book about astrology written especially for the craft and other practitioners of magick. There are hundreds of astrology books that help teach astrology, let you know what all those hieroglyphics mean, give you some insight as to why you can't be as personable as your rotten little brother, why your significant other is hopelessly straight in bed while you like things to be kinky. There is no book out there which tells you how to use astrology to increase the effectiveness of magick, charms, spells, workings, or ceremonies. Well, there wasn't until this one.

In the craft, most traditions and teachers and books insist each student have some passing knowledge of astrology. This ranges from the basic, "What's your sign?" up to Buckland's requirement, "cast and interpret your own chart thoroughly with predictions derived from transits and progressions." Yeah. Right. Get real Buckland!!!!!!!!!!

In order to bridge the gap between the two extremes, I wrote this book. An alternate title could be "Horary and Electional Astrology for Magickal Practitioners Who Are Non-Astrologers," but nobody would buy that book because it would sound incomprehensible (Horary?), and dull (like a masters thesis or a lost volume by one of Crowley's lesser pupils). But—surprise! That is really what this book is about. Hopefully if you've read this far, you've already bought the book. Otherwise I urge you to ignore the last paragraph and buy this book anyhow. It's more useful and fun than that title sounds. Really. I promise.

And fun. Fun? Yes, FUN! I love astrology, but I wouldn't love it nearly as much if I couldn't have fun with it.

This book is written for people who have little knowledge of astrology beyond, "What's your sign?" For people who are not practicing astrologers, or even students of astrology, but people who do have a passing knowledge of the possible benefits that applying astrology to magickal workings can bring. And always remember that important astrological aphorism:

> "Sometimes the magic works, sometimes it doesn't."
> —Chief Dan George, *Little Big Man*

You thought it would be that old chestnut, "As above, so below." That one's nice, but this one has more down-to-earth immediate applications. And it works in other areas, too. Try it, with my permission (and apologies to Robert Penn Warren). Nothing is guaranteed, especially when the God/desses decide to get involved. But you already knew that from the study of magick. (You say your teachers didn't mention that part??? Oh well, another trade secret divulged, all for $14.95.)

There is another Great Secret here which I will divulge. These techniques work as well in the everyday world as they do in magick. You can also use this stuff for buying a car, or asking for a raise, or going out on that important first date. The techniques adapt themselves for whatever purpose you might have. Really. Just be careful they do not take over your life. Save it for the important stuff. The little things can take care of themselves.

INTRODUCTION

How do you do? My name is Estelle Daniels. I would like to introduce myself. Isn't that what the introduction is for? I am an astrologer and a practicing Wiccan. The astrology part came first, sometime during the spring of 1967. My mother read Joseph F. Goodavage's, *Astrology: The Space Age Science*,[1] and thought I might like it. I did. We both read more and became very interested in astrology. We took classes in astrology together in the Chicago area in the late 60s and early 70s. Since then I have been self-taught for the most part, and I do attend conferences and seminars and talks now and then. I practice astrology professionally, for money, but it is not my main vocation, it's more of a sideline. Mom wanted me to be a professional astrologer, but I just didn't think it would be a secure enough living, so I opted for something else for a bread and butter career, but I have never stopped studying and practicing astrology. That way I can be more mellow about who I read for and if I feel like not reading for a while, I just kick back and do other things. The areas I specialize in are natal astrology, synastry, horary and electional astrology. I also have been a consultant for a Pagan organization and I also have done horary and electional work for them.

The Wiccan part has a shorter official history. Unofficially I have been studying about mythology and occult and mystical things since childhood. I have been reading and collecting comics since about 1961 (comics have a lot to do with modern mythology and archetypes). I have read lots

---

[1](West Nyak, NY: Parker Publishing Company, 1966).

of fairy tales and folk tales from many cultures. I have read SF and Fantasy all my life. I have studied and tried most every divinatory and mystical discipline a fairly inquisitive person could learn about in books. I read a lot.

In the summer of '89 I hooked back up with some old friends and became more actively interested in alternative religions. I had been in the A.R.E. (Association for Research and Enlightenment—the Edgar Cayce Foundation) for some years, but was not totally satisfied with their methods or teachings, specifically how very Christian their outlook was. Not that I'm anti-Christian, I was given a nominally Protestant Christian upbringing and education, but I really felt there was a lot out there not being addressed. Some of those old friends I met again were Wiccan, and through them I was introduced to Wicca and Shamanism, and there I found what I was looking for. It was the typical feeling of homecoming that so many Wiccans/Pagans feel. I am an initiate in the Eclectic Wiccan Tradition (isn't that an oxymoron—eclectic tradition?) and a member of a local Pagan church. I teach locally about the craft and astrology and attend several Pagan Festivals every year. Now that you know a bit about me, it's time to get introduced to this book.

Nowadays, natal astrology—the astrology of personality, character, and destiny—is the most common and familiar. "What's your sign," is a cliche, and something like 96 percent of all Americans know their birthsign. Many have had their charts cast and read. There are many good astrological services that calculate birthcharts by computer for a nominal fee. There are services where you can find out where 250 interesting asteroids are in your chart, and other fun and esoteric astrological computations and delineations. That is a wonderful and useful application of the astrologers' arts. Many people make their living doing this type of astrology. That is not what this book is about. There are plenty of good books out there on that type of astrology already.

My personal philosophy (that is to say, the philosophy which is MINE) is that if you can't do or say something new and different, don't bother just rehashing all the old stuff and dressing it up in a new wrapping. That is not to say that there is nothing more to be said on the subject of standard natal astrology, it's just that I can't think of anything new at the moment.

I had never contemplated writing an astrology book, much less an astrology book dealing with magick. To do an astrology book I would need an astrological topic which has not been done to death. Or even maybe one that was relatively unexplored. Or best of all, one which hadn't been written about at all yet. Finding an untouched astrological subject seemed a bit far-fetched, and certainly smacked of hubris. Goddess forbid I should be guilty of hubris! But I was just minding my own business and studying the craft and reading Buckland's big blue book (*The Complete Guide to Witchcraft*) when I came across his section on astrology.[2] I had been really enjoying the book, really getting into it. I read his big five pages and got quite upset. After the book landed on the floor across the room after making contact with the wall. (My book flies across the room. All by itself? Oh no, I fling it!) I thought about his introduction to astrology, and I was not happy. Apart from the recommendation that students cast and interpret their own natal charts, oh and by the way, also include predictions based on transits and progressions, there was NO mention on how to use astrology in magick. I looked further, and everyone I read or talked to said, "Oh yes, become familiar with astrology because it is important to the craft," but then didn't say what to DO with astrology after that. Apart from the obvious character interpretation aspects, astrology is very useful in everyday life, quite apart from one's natal chart.

---

[2]*The Complete Guide to Witchcraft* (St. Paul, MN: Llewellyn Publications, 1986).

There are many methods, from planetary hours, to planting guides, to the secret power times, and other really neat stuff which can add effectiveness to magick (and life in general). I mentally listed eight or nine ways to aid magickal effectiveness—things to do or not do, which are easy and readily learnable, all without math. Well, I quickly determined that I knew this, but there was no one place a person could go to tie all the various tricks and techniques together. I thought of lots of different books to read to look for parts of this information, but most of those books are for advanced practitioners of astrology, or out-of-print, or need math, or are just plain couched in weird old language.

I thought about all this for a few days, and became more and more weirded out. That is a technical term which describes the state one attains when one thinks something which should be simple and elementary and easily accessible, is none of those things. Kind of like how the little kid felt before he blurted out, "The emperor is naked, can't you all see that???" It's obvious to him, but the rest of the world is acting strangely about it. Massive confusion concerning basic life issues. Well, then the Cosmic Sledgehammer hit. A "Boot to the Head" as celebrated in the song. Hey stupid, if you think it's so elementary and easily accessible, and you understand it so well, why not write it all down yourself? Wow!! A cosmic homework assignment—a mission from the Gods.

After I had picked myself up off the floor, metaphorically speaking, I thought, yeah, right. Me write an astrology book about that. There has to be something out there about it already. I just haven't looked enough. So I looked. And looked. And looked. And I asked around, and read a lot and got lots of neat ideas and more techniques and thought of new ways of using old things, but I never did find that arcane tome which had covered this stuff already.

The upshot of it all was that in my searching and research, somewhen in that process, I eventually accepted the inevitable and ended up writing this book. I had indeed discovered that golden topic on which nobody had written comprehensively. Some days I feel more lucky about it than others. But I have had astrology as my companion in life since 1967. I love it, really, actively. I love astrology, the elegance of it, the universality of its applications and uses, the comfort of its explanations, the limitless facets of its branches and areas for study, the deep mysteries and endless surprises it holds for the seeker. Ok, ok, that sounds like mush, but occasionally I get mushy. I'm a Cancer, it's allowed. Mush aside, astrology has given me so much in life, that now it is time for me to give back. Here it is.

All this stuff did not spring full-blown from my fevered brain. I have researched and read extensively to get information and inspiration. I have drawn heavily on the techniques and rules of horary and electional astrology. I have used planetary hours, basic Moon sign transits, natal interpretation techniques, esoteric astrology in natal applications, and other weird stuff. I have not hesitated to use old techniques in new (and some would say perverted) ways. There is some stuff which did spring full-blown from my poor brain. Or maybe it was just the mental mixmaster which ground all this stuff up and spit it out in new configurations.

There is also quite a bit about magick and the natal chart. This is technically natal astrology, but it is especially slanted for the person interested in magick and spiritual development, and what in the natal chart addresses these issues. Where some of this material is available, it is, again, scattered around and not easily accessible to someone who wants to learn some, but doesn't want to become an astrologer. And the material about signs and houses that seem to relate to magick doesn't appear anywhere in any sort of a cohesive form. Some of it is new and some is intuited or borrowed from old sources.

The fourth part—additional studies—is a collection of strange and interesting topics that relate to magick and spirituality in an astrologickal way. Some come from the questions I have been asked, some arise from perceptions about astrology in the craft, some address astrological issues that I think should be disseminated to educated non-practitioners, some are just neat and relatively unaccessible, so I included them. I couldn't resist using syzygy. Read that section and you should be able to amaze your friends, at the very least in knowing what that weird and wonderful word means.

This book addresses a new area of astrological study, specialized though it may be. It will never be a best seller. That's ok. I hate talk shows. Being new there is a lot yet to be said. That's good. If you, gentle reader, read this and use these techniques and find them to be useful, or not useful, or problematic, please let me know. I have experimented with these ideas, and there are people who are trying their hands at it also, but nobody claims to be an expert in these techniques with respect to magick. Well, nobody currently alive that I know of. By reading this book and trying these techniques you are participating in an astrologickal and magickal experiment. Keep notes, if you feel like it. However, I will not grade your efforts. You will. The final test is: did it help? Are things better? Are your workings more effective? Then this book has done some good. Are you no worse off or just as effective (or ineffective) as before? That's ok, too. At least I've done no harm.

PART ONE

THE LANGUAGE
OF ASTROLOGY

THE BASICS

In the craft, astrology is considered a "high magick." Wiccans are encouraged to have a familiarity with astrology, know their own birthcharts and so forth. Yet there is little available in the "craft manuals" to allow average Wiccans access to astrology as it pertains to magick. Wiccans must be astrologers—and more specifically astrologers with moderate understanding of natal, horary, electional and possibly mundane astrology—to use the art as recommended by many well-known Wiccan and magickal writers and teachers. This book is meant to fill that void—to make this type of astrology accessible to all who are willing to study, but not interested in becoming astrologers themselves. With this book, and an astrological almanac (or calendar), and an ephemeris (often included in the almanac), you can tailor the timing of rituals so as to maximize the effect or desired outcome. Technically this is a horary/electional astrology book for non-astrologers, who are magicians.

There is a lot of strange stuff out there which calls itself astrology. But what most of the "regular" astrologers deal with is called natal astrology, also called *genetheliacal* (which just means "natal" in Latin or some other language—it just sounds more mysterious and important.) Most astrologers don't even qualify the kind of astrology they practice if they mean natal, as if that is all there is. I will discuss some aspects of natal astrology that are useful. You can get your chart calculated by computer, or you can have a real live astrologer calculate and interpret your natal chart for you. Your choice.

But you don't need a natal chart for a good portion of this book. I will also NOT teach you how to cast or interpret a chart yourself. Too many other good books out there which do that. I will expect a minimal familiarity with astrology: I will give brief descriptions of the signs, but from a magickal perspective, the "plain ol'" interpretations are also widely available. I have enough to cover without starting with basics. If you are unsure you can benefit without the basics, don't worry; fully half of the techniques in this book require little or no math and a third don't even require you have a copy of your natal chart.

This is the ancient astrology, used by "wise ones" everywhere since time immemorial, part of the ancient sacred teachings passed down over the centuries. It is used, in part, to compile the predictions in The Farmer's Almanac. It's that kind of old-weird-Auntie-over-the-hill folk wisdom which is much too basic and simplistic for our modern technological society to bother with. It's part of the stuff the AMA has been trying to stamp out for years. It's so basic and easily accessible that even presidents have denied its efficacy while secretly using it slavishly for decades. (Well, one President in particular—I'll get to that part later, under Void-of-course-moon.)

Many of the concepts and rules applied here are those of horary astrology—the astrology of divination, and its sister branch, electional astrology—which is just picking a favorable chart for a future event. Because of this, some of the rules and rulerships set forth in this book are different from those a regular (natal) astrologer would use. The tools are the same—planets, signs, houses, aspects—but their use is slightly different and more precise and time-critical.

Because this book is based on the principles of horary and electional astrology, which are more conservative and somewhat more archaic in scope and outlook than regular natal astrology, some things your everyday corner astrologer may use will be absent. There is little mention of Chiron or the asteroids (the big four are Ceres, Pallas, Juno, and Vesta;

while there are hundreds of minor asteroids). These have influence in natal astrology, but the effects (if any) have not been widely researched or accepted in the horary community. Some horary astrologers do not even use or consider Uranus, Neptune, or Pluto. But horary still works, and works well, so the fuddy-duddy old-fashioned ways must still be correct. We will deal with dual rulerships, mutual receptions, fixed stars and other more obscure and old-fashioned astrological concepts. But if you follow these rules, you will be able to add power and effect to your magickal workings. Really.

There is an appendix for Chiron, Ceres, Pallas, Juno and Vesta. These planetoids are not used in horary astrology, but they do pertain to many issues and archetypes which are vital to the Craft today. Rulerships—still highly controversial—things governed and archetypes addressed will be covered in brief, mostly with a magickal slant. Many Astrologers include these entities in natal charts, and there is a small but good pool of information available. However, few seem to have considered the magickal aspects of these bodies, so it will be addressed here.

What we'll be dealing with mostly is Horary Astrology (not Hoary or Horrid, though both adjectives have been used in connection with Horary) and its (evil) twin, Electional Astrology. Electional isn't really evil, you just have to have an insane self-abusive bent to practice it for a long period of time. In both Horary and Electional, there comes a point in time when the astrologer is gripped with the insane desire to move the planets around to more favorable positions to get a desired result. DO NOT ATTEMPT THIS YOURSELF, AT HOME! Even professional astrologers do not do such things because:

1) they are impossible, no matter how big a lever you come up with,

and

2) they are wrong and will disturb all the other astrologers and

3) if one person does it, then everyone will want to do it and then there goes the order in the universe and wouldn't that be a big cosmic mess.

You just have to live with the planets as they are and make do as best you can.

A LITTLE ABOUT ASTROLOGY ITSELF

It's old. Really old.

Evidence indicates that a rudimentary form of astrology was being formulated and practiced ca. 5000 B. C. E. in Mesopotamia. And, if you buy into the theory, Atlantis used astrology lots. Esoterically, many believe astrology is left over from Atlantis, the only really "advanced" learning left over after the deluge, fall of Atlantis, etc. Prove it ain't so. Conversely, prove it is so. One thing you can't deny, it makes the whole idea of astrology being really old a lot more romantic and new-agey.

Astrology has evolved and changed in focus and direction over the centuries. Out of this has arisen the many branches of astrology. Yes, I know you thought astrology was one big homogeneous discipline. No, it isn't. Is Magick????? Tell a Gardnerian and a New Reformed Druid that just because they both practice a form of magick, they are doing the same thing in the same ways. Yeah, right. Astrology is the same. Try that same schtick on a tropical, siderial, or heliocentric astrologer, and they will tear you apart.

In the past, the ancient, medieval and renaissance worlds, the common and familiar astrologies were horary and electional or mundane astrology—the astrology of nations and world events. These are the astrologies of Nostradamus, Paracelsus, John Dee, Hermes Trismegistus and others. Until modern times and the standardization of time zones (which came about with the intercontinental railways) most individuals did not have accurate birth times, which is critical for a natal chart. Shakespeare's birth date is a matter for conjecture (though presumably not to the Bard himself). Nostradamus' prophecies are just mundane astrological predictions, couched in flowery, deliberately archaic and obscure language.

ESOTERIC AND EXOTERIC

These are the two main subgroups of the branches of astrology. The words esoteric—hidden or spiritual, and exoteric—open and mundane—pretty much describe what the subgroups are all about. The esoteric stuff deals with karma and reincarnation (if you buy into that trip), the soul's journey through the signs and the other stuff which is not really provable. It is the secret doctrine type stuff, the greater mysteries of astrology, like the tarot trumps, which also have esoteric astrological meaning and applications. Exoteric astrology is the everyday working astrology which people use to decide when to buy a car, or marry the guy, or why Cousin George can't get a date. This is the astrology which is trying to become respectable and scientific. Don't be fooled, it comes from the same roots as the other stuff, it is just dressed up more formally and is wearing a tie. It is ashamed of its weird cousin from down home. But you can't pick your family, so you might as well live with them and love each for their own unique qualities, warts and all.

Esoteric Astrology is more spiritual, it is the realm where astrology links with kabbalah and other mystical doctrines. It is less concerned with individual chart interpretations as with the philosophy as a whole. Charts can be interpreted esoterically to ascertain the spiritual paths chosen by a soul to follow in this life. However the main thrust is on the meanings and roles of the various planets and signs, as they relate to spiritual progression, the evolution of the soul as it passes from one sign to the next. Also the study of the precession of the equinoxes and the various world ages which arise (the Age of Aquarius), and how astrology links with various other mystical disciplines and how they interrelate.

Uranian Astrology is based upon the teachings of Alfred Witte of the Hamburg Astrology School in Germany. It is considered an esoteric branch because it deals with hypothetical planets and interprets birthcharts in terms of soul growth and karmic debits and credits. It calculates charts (called planetary pictures) using midpoints, cardinal points, dial analysis, antiscions. Uranian astrologers use fewer aspects than regular astrologers, and their charts often look incomprehensible to a non-initiate.

In many ways, esoteric astrology is where astrology and magick are most closely associated. Many astrologers never really have much to do with esoteric astrology. It has strange rulerships, it addresses the symbology of the glyphs for the planets and signs, Alice Bailey invented it, and nobody can really read her books. Besides, in today's world of Jungian archetypes and Gauquelin zones as they relate to statistical analysis, astrology has little to do with magick. Well, astrology is trying really hard to be accepted as a real science, like psychotherapy or graphology. And if the real world is going to accept astrology as a real science, it has to drop those mystical and magickal roots like a hot potato. Something about being "politically correct" in the eyes of the real world.

Exoteric Astrology is the more familiar nuts and bolts astrology, applied and used as a tool to make everyday life easier. There are many branches of exoteric astrology. Some are more respectable than others, but few are as strange and offbeat as the esoteric doctrines. Some take more time and training to master than others.

Natal Astrology: the astrology of individuals. This is where most people start when they begin studying astrology. It has been around for a while, but has really come into its own in the last century or so. And this is the branch most earnestly touted as the astrology which will become scientifically accepted by "those in charge" of such things. Most of the published astrology books are about natal astrology in one form or another. After all, people like to hear about themselves, and for the "me" generation, self-help and personal fulfillment are the big goals in life. Natal astrology deals with casting birthcharts and reading them. Using astrology to help define personality, character, aptitudes, and predicting future trends, all based on the birthchart. It is the basic astrology in sun sign books, newspaper columns, and your average astrology class. There are subclasses of natal astrology, among which are *Vocational Astrology*—using the birthchart to determine vocational aptitude and abilities; and *Astrocartography*—which plots planetary lines of influence on the globe and shows where it would be fortunate or unfortunate to relocate based on the lines of influence.

Michel and Francoise Gauquelin did a statistical study in the 1950s which used natal charts of successful or prominent people in certain professions and found significant statistical correlation between planetary placement in house areas (Gauquelin zones) and profession and character traits. This was the beginning of the race to get astrology accepted in the scientific community. This is not a bad thing in itself, and certainly this type of scientific analysis does help get respect for what is at best currently considered a pseudo-science. However, there are some things which people are meant to take on faith. Certain aspects of astrology end up in the faith category. They work, but they defy statistical analysis or categorization. If it works, is it really necessary to be able to explain exactly why? There are those who count results, and I am one of them.

Synastry—the astrology of relationships; comparing and/or combining birthcharts of people in relationships to see where the rough and smooth areas are. Synastry is used for people in all sorts of relationships—love, marriage, committed partners, business, parents and children, roommates, co-workers—any relationship where two or more people interact closely over a period of time. Mostly though it is used for love and personal relationships. "I'm a Sagittarius and my sweetie is a Taurus and we want to get married, but all the books say it will never work out. What do we do?"(Whine, moan) In the end, no matter how the charts compare, it all depends upon the two people involved and how willing they are to work to make the relationship successful. But few people want to hear that, so there are a lot of astrological books for people in relationships out there. And you still can't predict absolutely what causes people to fall in love with each other. (There goes another sacred cow.)

Horary Astrology—the astrology of divination. A querant (person with a question) asks a question and the astrologer casts a chart for the time and place the question was communicated to the astrologer, and then reads the chart according to specific rules and finds the answer therein. More archaic and exacting than natal astrology. Has all sorts of strange picky rules and archaic terms, but when you do it right, the damn thing works. But it takes a thorough grounding in natal astrology before you can start learning horary, and then it can take a couple of years to get comfortable with it. If you like rules and like to zone in on minutiae, this is for you. You don't even have to look at the whole chart, you usually just use two or three planets and houses to get your answer. There is no rational scientific explanation for why this one works, but it does. Drives the statistical analysis crowd bonkers (snicker). The Jungians refer to synchronicity, and leave it at that. You can even use it to bet on the horses. Picking a winner is easy, it's the betting strategy which can be confusing.

Electional Astrology—the astrology of planning events. Kind of the reverse of horary—the two are practiced together as a rule. A person decides what end is desired and the astrologer looks into the future and finds a time when the event will go according to plan if started at a particular moment. It is used for house closings, weddings, store openings, contract signings, mailing resumes, etc. If you thought horary was kinky, this one can drive you insane. You are often gripped with the desire to move the planets around to suit your purposes. It won't work, trust me. You have to be pretty familiar with horary to be a successful electional astrologer. These are the charts where you end up worrying about every planet and point. And you want not only to have the cake, but to have the icing on it as well (those extra astrological frills which make a really wonderful election). There are about three or four golden days every year when anything you try will turn out wonderfully. Otherwise you have to compromise and take the best you can get. And in the end, it depends upon the person initiating the thing. You can set up the most wonderful, favorable electional chart and if the person doesn't have it together about the matter in hand in the first place, it probably won't work out. All the chart does is optimize conditions. It does not make up for deficiencies or stupidity. Remember this. We will come back to it later.

Medical Astrology—the astrology of health and wellness. The birthchart is interpreted to determine disease, its cause, and possible ways to alleviate medical problems. Most medical astrologers are health professionals or work closely with them. It postulates alternative philosophies as to the causes of disease and approaches to wellness. Horary charts are also used to help determine cause and the actual systems which are under stress. The prevailing opinion is that you need some sort of Medical degree to practice medical astrology. There are certainly more diseases and conditions than there were just a hundred years ago, when medicine and astrology were both simpler. And malpractice being what it is, most health professionals who do use astrology will never admit it. Psychologists and psychiatrists do use astrology as a diagnostic tool—to pinpoint the areas of possible psychological dysfunction so as to cut to the root cause for analysis, saving years of therapy getting to the causes of emotional distress. After all, Jung made astrology acceptable for the analytical crowd, or at least the Jungians.

Mundane Astrology: the astrology of non-people. Uses birthcharts of businesses, nations, events (like ingresses, equinoxes, and eclipses), disasters. Also the astrology of the masses, using transits in the sky and the charts of nations and national leaders to gauge happenings in countries, or the mood of the people, or societal trends. Some subclasses of mundane astrology are: *Financial Astrology*—investing using astrology and business charts; and *Astro-Meteorology*—predicting weather and climate using transits; and *Natural Astrology*—predicting earthquakes and other natural disturbances; *Agricultural Astrology*—planting by the Moon.

Natural Astrology is really being studied for earthquake prediction. That guy who has been predicting earthquakes with some success reportedly uses this branch of mundane astrology as a tool. One man who worked for AT&T for decades with overseas communications, in the days before satellites, used astro-meteorology to predict cable breaks and magnetic interferences (along with sunspot activity). It did work and he even published a few articles in the scientific press about his methods. They were ignored.

As for financial astrology, tycoons and financiers have been using it for a century or more. But they either do not admit it, or are rich enough to not care if people know. Evangeline Adams had lots of business astrology clients. You do need to know about business and finance and the stock market to do well. But strangely, in the pursuit of the

Almighty Dollar, anything which works is ok. After all, it's the bottom line of profit and loss which is the ultimate measure of success or failure, not how you arrived at your decisions.

TROPICAL, SIDERIAL AND HELIOCENTRIC ASTROLOGY

Technically these aren't branches, but are styles of astrology.

Tropical Astrology is the standard Western version which everyone uses. The Vernal equinox is the 0 Aries point and everything is figured from there. It does not correspond to the constellations in the sky due to the precession of the equinoxes and Earth's rotation on its axis. But it works, so people don't bother worrying about the differences.

Siderial Astrology is the Hindu version which does correspond to the constellations. It is currently about 24 degrees behind Tropical. So when we are at 0 Aries, they are only at 6 Pisces. It works, too, for Hindu astrology. This is one reason why there is a bit of resistance to the acceptance of astrology in the scientific community. Still, if light can be particles or waves, depending upon the need, this can't be too far a reach to deal with.

Heliocentric Astrology is based upon a Sun-centered chart. Both Tropical and Siderial imply that the Earth is at the center of the chart. We do live on the Earth, so this is not as strange as it may sound. But there are those who, when it was discovered that Earth was not the center of the solar system, decided that Earth-centered astrology was wrong, and heliocentric astrology was invented. It also works. As we move out into the solar system and away from our home planet, some feel this will be the astrology we take with us. Maybe. But what happens when we move out of the solar system altogether? Fear not, there are astrologers working on that also.

These are the most common branches of astrology. The list illustrates how rich and varied a field it is. You can spend a lifetime studying and not run out of new material.

BRIEF HISTORY

Originally, people had little access to accurate birthtimes, so natal astrology wasn't feasible for most people. In some cases people didn't even know the exact day of their birth. So astrologers used horary and electional astrology when dealing with the common people—for answering questions and planning events. They used mundane astrology when predicting national and world events. Nostradamus made famous predictions based upon mundane astrology. John Dee, Paracelsus, and Hermes Trismegistus also used mundane, horary, and electional astrology in their work. Since Victorian times, the rise of railroads and the standardization of time zones have encouraged birth certificates to include time, and this has made natal astrology accessible to most people. There was a renaissance of natal astrology around the turn of the century through the work of the Theosophists, Golden Dawn, Astrum Argentum, the Rosicrucians and other secret societies. Many older books were re-issued and new books written by people who were astrologers and also members of these secret societies. More recently—since the 1960s or earlier—astrology has sought to distance (some say divorce) itself from its magickal and divinatory roots. Nowadays we talk about the astrology of personality, Jungian archetypes, self-determination and making the most of your aspects and Gauquelin zones determined by statistical analysis. Positively, this has eliminated much of the fatalism of older astrology, but negatively it has made astrologers almost anti-magick and mysticism. Hopefully astrology can be secure enough in its newer outlook and image to be able to pay homage to its roots and reclaim the mystical and magickal heritage from which it arose to become what it is today.

THE LANGUAGE AND ALPHABET OF ASTROLOGY

Astrology is a foreign language, to most people.

> The lesser light, being co-significator of the querant is peregrine, besieged and cadent, and being that it partakes of no mutual reception and further is in its fall, and in the combust way in the house of sorrows and in the terms of Mars, it indicates that the matter promised will only come to pass through great difficulty, and not bring benefit to the querant.

How many really understood that sentence—be honest. I thought so. It is a foreign language. The terms here are specialized terms used in horary (see why people use the word "horrid"?), but we won't bother with them here. Well, except if we explain them first. For those who are wondering, I made that quote up. It refers to a Moon between 0 and 5 degrees 59 minutes of Scorpio, in the 12th house, within seventeen degrees of the Sun and between Mars and Saturn, and Mars is not in Cancer. I can and do on occasion speak that brand of "high astrologese." I'm not totally fluent, but having studied horary for years, and read lots of books written in such flowery archaic language, it comes naturally. High Ceremonial Magicians should also be familiar with the style but using different specialized terms.

The basis of language is vocabulary. So it is with astrology. The above notwithstanding, the basic vocabulary of astrology is not weird words like the sample above, but the signs, planets, houses and other basic building blocks of astrological knowledge. There are not a whole lot of "words" to learn in astrology. The strange thing is that each word means quite a few things, depending on context and outlook and how you choose to express it. In fact, each word is more of an idea or concept than a single word. Once you get the feel of each word, building sentences becomes easier. There are five basic word lists which help make up most of astrology.

7 Elements and Qualities;

12 Signs;

10 Planets (15 with Chiron and the big four Asteroids);

12 Houses (they share some characteristics with signs);

11 Aspects (but there are only 5 standard ones, and you can add lots more if you so desire)

---

52 basic words in all

What other language expresses itself with 52 basic words? Not even Spanish is so easy. (Yeah, you say, I can hear it now. Well if you know your sign you're familiar with one word already and only have 51 to go. See, it's easier than you thought—Nyaaa.)

THE WORDS

The main 12 words—the signs—are derived from seven other words—the four elements and three qualities. The four elements are fire, earth, air and water. Hopefully most of you have heard of these. Astrology defines the elements pretty the much the same as mainstream magick.

Fire—spirituality, fire, inspiration, enthusiasm, animals, spirit;

Earth—rocks and crystals, grounding, material stuff, present, now, body;

Air—incense, mental activity, words and communication, intellect, future, astral planes, humanity, mentality;

Water—oils, liquids, emotion, psychic, the past, plants, soul.

The three qualities are:

Cardinal—active, initiating, moving, irresistible force, leadership, goal oriented;

Fixed—fixed, grounded, stubborn, steady, immovable object, ending, reward oriented;

Mutable—changeable, goes with the flow, adaptable, following, hard to pin down, windsock, facilitating, process-oriented.

When you blend the four elements and three qualities (or three qualities and four elements) you get 12 signs, one of each element and quality. Honest, that's how it works. Each sign is defined by an element and quality, and signs which share elements or qualities have certain similarities and affinities. Furthermore:

Fire and air are compatible and complementary;

Earth and water are compatible and complementary;

And

Signs of the same quality operate in a similar manner, but may not get along with each other because though they may operate in a similar manner (quality), the styles (elements) may clash.

In these few concepts are contained 30 percent of astrology. Really. Sometimes it's tough to remember that it all boils down to these few basics, but it does. So blending fire, earth, air and water with cardinal, fixed and mutable you get:

♈ Aries—cardinal fire;

♉ Taurus—fixed earth;

♊ Gemini—mutable air;

♋ Cancer—cardinal water;

♌ Leo—fixed fire;

♍ Virgo—mutable earth;

♎ Libra—cardinal air;

♏ Scorpio—fixed water;

♐ Sagittarius—mutable fire;

♑ Capricorn—cardinal earth;

♒ Aquarius—fixed air;

♓ Pisces—mutable water.

THE PLANETS

Astrology was developed before anyone knew Earth revolved around the Sun (if you dismiss the Atlantis theory). So all horoscopes have Earth at the center (implied), and have an Earth-centered view—that the planets (including the Sun and Moon) revolve around Earth. (Except for heliocentric astrology, which is a whole "nother" can of worms—we'll ignore it.) This geocentric outlook gives rise to some strange stuff—retrograde motion being one of them. See figure 1.

Ok, Ok, those planets don't really move backward, it only looks like that. But it fooled a lot of people for a long

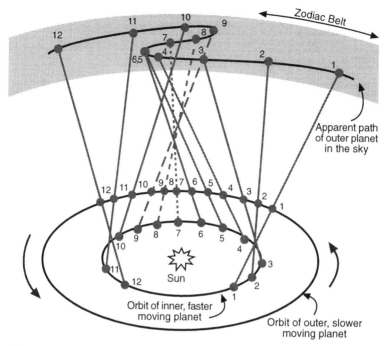

Figure 1.   Retrograde motion. Retrograding is shown by dashed lines 7, 8 and 9. Numbers refer to planets' orbital positions and the outer planets' "apparent" location on the zodiacal belt over a period of time. (Adapted from *A Spiritual Approach to Astrology* by Myna Lofthus.)

time, so don't be so quick to snigger at those "old fashioned" ideas. And astrology still works, in spite of the geocentric basis. Nor has astrology been invalidated by the discovery of new planets. In some cases, the astrological community felt there were those other planets out there and tried to put them in charts before they were actually discovered. (There are still "hypothetical" planets which you can get ephemerides for [tables of placement and movement] and place in your chart and use in interpretations.) Retrogrades have an effect on planets, in the natal chart, in transits and in horary. This will be covered later. Be patient.

The planets are Sun (☉), Moon (☽), Mercury (☿), Venus (♀), Mars (♂), Jupiter (♃), Saturn (♄), Uranus (♅),

Neptune (♆), and Pluto (♀). The Sun and Moon technically aren't planets. They are "the lights" because they emit (Sun) or reflect (Moon) light, and are much brighter than the other celestial phenomena. Still, in all of astrology, they are lumped under the group term "planets" because, people being what they are, would rather refer to "the planets" than "the lights and the planets." It's easier.

Sun through Saturn are referred to as the classical or ancient planets. These are the obviously visible planets you can go out on a clear night and (hopefully) see in the sky depending on where they are in the zodiac. Uranus, Neptune, and Pluto are called the modern or trans-Saturnian planets, because they were discovered through the use of telescopes and gravitational variances and other modern, scientific techniques.

Interestingly, Uranus is sometimes visible as a 5th magnitude star, and it has been retroactively discovered in quite a few star maps in various cultures. But it is not always visible, and it moves so slowly, that nobody put two and two together and realized it was another planet and not a star until 1781.

The things ruled by the modern planets used to be ruled by other of the classical planets, but as of their discovery the things ruled were re-assigned to the newer planet. From all of this you get dual rulerships—of signs, houses, and things. And some of the things ruled by these newer planets are things which did not exist before their discovery. Television is ruled by Uranus. Look at the glyph for Uranus and then think of a TV antenna. Unless you have cable, or are not old enough to remember the sea of houses each with its own antenna. (We baby boomers are getting older, and sometimes it shows.) In that case, you have to either ask your parents or take my word for it.

When these planets were discovered, each discoverer had a hand in naming it. Now you would think that scientists naming planets would have little sensitivity as to the importance of names, but the laws of synchronicity being what they are, the right names ended up on the right planets. And you find that the discoverers usually have that planet prominent in their natal charts. So they resonate to the vibrations of the yet-to-be-discovered planet, which helps them discover it. The cosmos takes care of its own. When a planet is inappropriately named (as in Uranus being known as Herschel—for its discoverer), and Sidum Georgius (for King George III of England—where one of the discoverers lived), those names end up being dropped and the "correct" names are used more and more widely. Then the astrologers take over and "fight about/decide on" the attributes and rulerships. It can take a while, and some interesting mistakes are made. The first rulership assigned to Pluto was Aries (can you believe that!!!). It took nearly a decade in which people observed the planet in natal charts and in transits so that the correct rulership of Scorpio was generally agreed upon. Astrologers are still fighting over and researching Pluto's Detriment and Fall.

Roman names are used to be consistent with the names of the classical planets, but the archetypes of the corresponding Greek deities (which the Romans mostly stole anyway) apply to the planet also. Even the original attributes of the deities—before the patriarchialists took over—work; as seen in the four main asteroids. In fact, the four asteroids seem to operate most effectively with the original Great Goddess attributes, rather than with the watered-down Greco/Roman Goddess attributes.

The way the planets work in astrology can be summed up in an analogy: Planets are the actors in a play, and the characters that they play. The signs are the costumes the actors wear, the houses are the stage settings in which the parts are played out, and the aspects are how the various characters interact. Or, planets are the WHAT, signs are the HOW, houses are the WHERE, and the aspects show IN WHAT WAY they interact with each other.

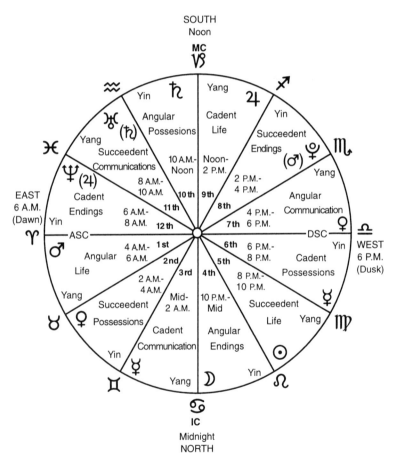

Figure 2. The mundane wheel.

THE MUNDANE WHEEL

The "mundane wheel" is the basic horoscope showing each sign and planet in its own house and rulership (see figure 2). It is astronomically impossible. For one thing, Mercury and Venus each appear twice, and without major cosmic disruptions, this will not happen (we hope). Theoretically, new planets will be discovered which will rule two of those signs with dual rulership and then there will be 12 planets for 12 signs and 12 houses. Numerically elegant. Even now, there is a considerable body of astrologers who are pushing to have Chiron be considered the ruler of Virgo. There are a lot of correspondences between the two. But it is by no means decided yet (no, we do not get together and vote on it), so Virgo is still under the standard rulership of Mercury, which it shares with Gemini. The old rulerships, which were in effect before the modern planets were discovered are also shown in parentheses. They also still work, especially in horary and electional astrology. I guess it's a mindset sort of thing.

To read this mandala, you think of a clock (which is supposedly based on a horoscope wheel). You start at the 9:00 position, which is known as the Ascendant, or cusp (beginning) of the 1st house. The little hour wedge between 9:00 and 8:00 is the house itself. Kempton[1] calls them slices of pie. You can call them whatever you like, so long as everyone knows that the word/phrase you choose means "house." The ancients decided to call them houses, so now that is the standard term. The next hour wedge in a counterclockwise (or widdershins) direction, between 8:00 and 7:00 is the 2nd house. The 8:00 line is the cusp of the 2nd house. You continue all around the wheel widdershins until you get to the hour wedge between 10:00 and 9:00 being the 12th house and the 10:00 line being the cusp of the 12th house.

---

[1]Debbi Kempton-Smith, *Secrets from a Stargazer's Notebook* (New York: Bantam, 1982).

The symbol and numbers next to the cusp in a standard chart is the sign and degree on that cusp. That sign is said to rule that house in the chart in question, which is not to be confused with the mundane rulership of that house. Think of the mundane wheel as the stripped-down basic car, and the placement of the planets, signs on the ascendant, and cusps of the chart in question as the paint-job and special options and features added to the standard model. It's still a car, but it's YOUR car, customized for you, if we're talking about your personal chart.

The sign on the ascendant or cusp of the 1st house (the terms are interchangeable) is said to be the "rising sign." This is the sign of the zodiac (which does NOT correspond to the constellation) which was on the Eastern horizon at the moment the horoscope depicts. This is an important point in astrology. The sign on the cusp of the 10th house is commonly called the midheaven. This does not hold true all of the time (in the Equal House System, the midheaven and 10th house cusp do not always correspond), but is common enough that only a real nit-picky anal-retentive astrologer will take exception to using the terms interchangeably. Most astrologers use the terms that way, anyhow. When in Rome. . . .

Now that I've opened the house system can of worms, I suppose I need to explain it. This will be the short version. Because Earth is tilted on its axis $23\frac{1}{2}$ degrees, the angle between the ascendant and midheaven is not always 90 degrees, as it would be if there were no tilt. If you are on the Equator, the distance between the two is pretty close to 90 degrees all the time. The further north or south you travel from the equator, the more warped the angle can become. The majority of Earth's population lives between 0 and 45 degrees north and south.

In all the various house systems (even equal house) the signs and degrees on the ascendant and midheaven are the same. Equal house does not have the midheaven and 10th house cusp correspond. The midheaven is shown as a separate point and interpreted by sign and house like any other planet or point. In all the other house systems (and there are something like twenty) the ascendant and midheaven are the same. To see how house systems can change a chart, refer to Charts 1, 2, and 3 on pages 26-28.) Where the various house systems arise is in the methods used to determine the signs and degrees on the intermediate (non-angular) cusps. Those are derived by spherical trigonometry and time-references and other strange and arcane spacio-temporal methods.

All astrologers have their pet house system which they swear by as "the one true and only accurate house system (accept no substitutes)." The funny thing is that all of them work. People being what they are, and house systems coming from books (or computer programs) and not growing on trees, it costs money (and time) to work in several house systems at once (not to mention being confusing). So astrologers pick one which seems to work for them and tend to stick with it. Then they become familiar with the one which they have chosen and become married to it and then they begin to believe it is the best and all others are false. But we know better because they all work.

I use the Koch system, (see Chart 2 on page 27), which I personally believe to be vastly superior to all other house systems, which any right-thinking astrologers will readily admit unless they have been blinded by the allures of some false and inaccurate system which is naturally inferior. (The reader will kindly ignore the previous sentence and diatribe contained therein. Think of it as a strange disease all astrologers suffer from, and give us your sympathy.)

Because the angle between the ascendant and midheaven can be from less than 60 to more than 120 degrees, you can get the phenomenon where some signs appear on two cusps and some signs appear on none. This causes an interception of the signs not appearing on any cusps (always a pair of signs opposite each other) and any planets contained therein. This is significant in natal and horary

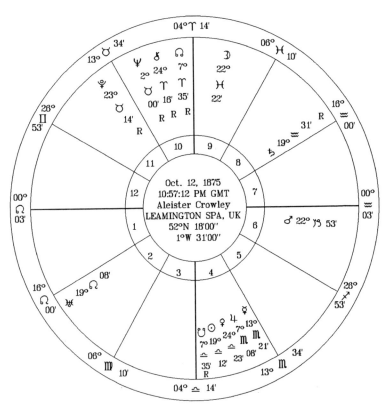

Chart 1. Aleister Crowley's chart using Placidus houses. As you read this section, you might like to refer to his chart and see how "Uncle Al" stacks up in terms of magickal/psychic potential. This is the chart Crowley used, so this one is included here. Born October 12, 1875, 10:57 P.M. GMT, Leamington Spa, England. (Data from *Magick*, revised edition, Samuel Weiser, 1994, p. 289, 717).

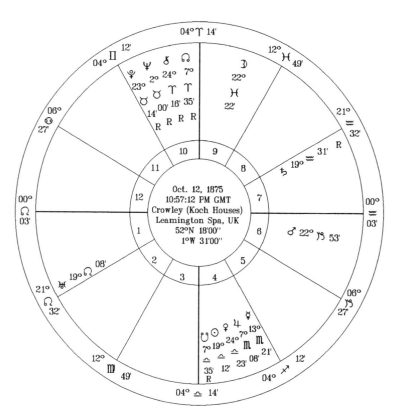

04° ♈ 14'

12'
04° ♊

♀ ♇ ♅ ♂ ☊
23° 2° 24° 7°
14' 00' 16' 35'
R R R R

☽ 22°
22' ♓

12° ♓ 49'

06° ♋ 27'

21° ♒ 32'

10 9
11 8

♄ 19° ♎ 31' R

00° ♌ 03'

12
1

Oct. 12, 1875
10:57:12 PM GMT
Crowley (Koch Houses)
Leamington Spa, UK
52°N 18'00''
1°W 31'00''

7
6

00° ♒ 03'

♂ 22° ♑ 53'

2
3 4 5

21° ♌ 32'

♅ 19° ♌ 08'

06° ♑ 27'

12° ♍ 49'

☊ ☉ ♀ ♃ ☿
7° 19° 24° 7° 13°
35' 12' 23' 08' 21'
R
♎ ♎ ♎ ♏ ♏

12'
04° ♐

04° ♎ 14'

Chart 2.   Aleister Crowley's chart using Koch houses. This is an example of how different house systems can change a chart. Born October 12, 1875, 10:57 P.M., GMT, Leamington Spa, England.

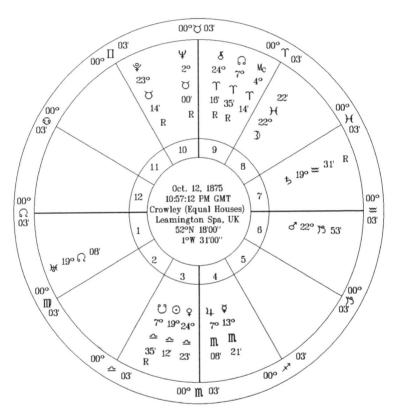

Chart 3.   Aleister Crowley's chart using Equal houses. Born October 12, 1875, 10:57 P.M. GMT, Leamington Spa, England.

work, but as we are not doing full natal or horary interpretations, it will be only mentioned here.

This mundane wheel has a number of applications, beyond the standard teaching aid. In interpretation, a planet which mundanely rules a house still has influence over it, regardless of the sign which occupies that cusp in the chart in question. So Mars always addresses 1st house issues, Jupiter 9th house issues, and so forth, no matter what cusps the signs of Aries and Sagittarius occupy. This can be used as a sort of second level of interpretation when looking for correlations between houses and signs in a chart.

For now, just try to remember the correlations between planets, signs, and houses. They are very important. These are the glue which unites influences and ties things together. In many ways, you can often "get to" something using the planet, sign, or house, whichever is most convenient for your purposes. In this way, having a planet in one sign and another house, you can blend influences.

For example, you want to consecrate a ritual sword which you have made yourself. You can use Mars for the sword, Virgo for the craftsmanship and the 9th house for the ritual use. Or Aries, the 6th house and Jupiter. Or the 1st house, Mercury and Sagittarius. (I refuse to go through all six possibilities. Think of it as an exercise, and try it yourself.) Each combination addresses the issues in different ways. And by using different combinations, you can adapt things so your need to wait for a particular planetary placement is minimal. Jupiter takes 12 years to go around the zodiac completely. If Jupiter is in Libra, and you need it in Aries, you will have to wait 6 years or so. (Now do you understand the desire to move planets about at will?) But Jupiter goes through each house once each day, so the maximum you would have to wait for Jupiter to be in the 1st house is 24 hours. Get the idea? One suspects this is one reason these correspondences were made so important.

THE HOUSES AND SIGNS

The houses are a circle, an evolution of experience and growth. The houses are divided in various ways by influence and activity. The houses on the bottom of the chart (1-6) are personal houses, they relate to the individual directly. The houses on the top half (7-12) are houses of "the other," the same as the personal houses, but as experienced from outside or projected onto others. This divides the chart in several ways. Bottom is personal and private, top is other-oriented and public. You can also divide the chart into a left and right half. The left half is considered to be self-determining and active; the right half is reactive and going with the flow.

The polar opposite sets of houses are directly related by function—1 is self, 7 is the other; 2 is possessions and values, 8 is others' possessions and values; 3 is neighborhood, lower mind, short distance travel, 9 is the world or far away places, higher mind, long distance travel; 4 is home and Mother, 10 is business/career and Father; 5 is children, lovers, and speculation, 11 is others' children, friends, groups, and associations; 6 is health, work, and servants, 12 is hospitalization, inability to work, and service to humanity. These are broad topics which relate to each house.

Then there is the division by quality—angular, succedent and cadent. The four houses on the angles (1,4,7,10) are angular, most powerful, active, initiating, leading, having to do with birth. The four houses which follow those (2,5,8,11) are succedent, next most powerful, solid, stabilizing, establishing, growth. The last three houses (3,6,9,12) are cadent, least strong, transitional, moderating, compromising, adaptive, coming to fruition. The cadent houses are bridges from one triad to another. The angular houses are the beginnings, the first establishment of energies, while the succedent houses have the most solid, most strong, expression of those energies. Then the cadent houses wrap up matters and prepare the way for the next cycle.

Angular houses correspond to the cardinal signs;

Succedent houses correspond to the fixed signs and;

Cadent houses correspond to the mutable signs.

All three sets share things in common, so you could say:

Angular and Cardinal are similar;

Succedent and Fixed are similar, and;

Cadent and Mutable are similar.

So using these similarities you could re-word the above paragraph to say that the cardinal signs are the beginnings and first establishment of energies, and the fixed signs are the most solid, most strong, expression of those energies. Then the mutable signs wrap up matters and prepare the way for the next cycle.

Another division of houses is by four sets of three.

1, 5 and 9 are the houses of life and correspond to the fire signs;

2, 6 and 10 are the houses of possessions and correspond to the earth signs;

3, 7 and 11 are the houses of communications and correspond to the air signs;

4, 8 and 12 are the houses of endings and correspond to the water signs.

And the correspondences indicate that the elements and house types address similar issues. Another correlation is between the signs and houses:

Aries is similar to the 1st house;

Taurus is similar to the 2nd house;

Gemini is similar to the 3rd house;

Cancer is similar to the 4th house;

Leo is similar to the 5th house;

Virgo is similar to the 6th house;

Libra is similar to the 7th house;

Scorpio is similar to the 8th house;

Sagittarius is similar to the 9th house;

Capricorn is similar to the 10th house;

Aquarius is similar to the 11th house;

Pisces is similar to the 12th house.

See how the words and phrases begin to come together?

Notice I am careful to use the words "correspond" and "is similar" and NOT "is the same as." There are distinctions, but those are best addressed by accomplished astrologers. For this book, knowing they correspond closely but not exactly will suffice, and interchanging them should not be a major problem, for the level of work we are doing herein. Trust me.

All 12 houses as a whole are a cycle of birth, growth, maturity, decline, and death of individuality. Or put another way, the path from pure self-oriented, to pure other-oriented, which then prepares for another cycle of birth to merging with the Infinite. This can be an actual cycle, or an allegorical cycle. As the planets move around the wheel, each person simultaneously experiences several cycles in various ways, from the shortest, daily cycle of the Sun moving around the sky to the longest cycle we know of at present, Pluto moving by transit all through the individual's chart (which takes 248 years and is currently longer then our average lifetime).

It is from the various "divisions" of houses that the varied meanings for each house arise. So one house (and by correlation sign) can "rule" such varied things as cars, siblings, the neighborhood, everyday life, lower education, speech and words, books, one parent's state of health, organizations an individual's children belong to, long journeys of a spouse. These topics may seem to have no relation to each other, but according to astrology, there is solid evidence and empirical observation over the ages that these things are related and do come under the rule of one specific house and sign, the 3rd and Gemini.

Astrology can be confusing when each "word" has so many meanings, and various words meaning almost the same things. And then one wonders how the astrologer decides which of these meanings to use when interpreting an individual's chart. This is the area where astrology moves from a science to an art. And why the language analogy works so well. Most good astrologers think in "astrology." Every action or situation or person is dissected and interpreted in astrological terms. "He's so Capricorn." Or, "That was a real Mars cab ride." Or, "I'm really feeling Void-of-Course." The really good astrologers are so fluent, they can translate from those statements to everyday English, "He's such a stiff authority type." "That cab ride was fast and dangerous." "I'm really feeling spacey and disconnected from the everyday world." Sadly, the only way a person can become fluent in this type of translation is to do it and do it and do it. There are no short cuts.

PLANETS AGAIN

The planets are the glue that hold a chart together. The signs and houses define the form of the chart, but the planets show how that chart functions. They are the actors in the play. Where they are by sign and house, how they interrelate by rulership and aspect, and how they bring change through transits, brings the basic chart into life. Without planets, there could be only twelve basic personality types, based upon ascendant placement. The planets add many and varied shadings of meaning and make each of us unique. If you take all the possible placements of the planets and also ascendant degrees (and I am assuming 360 separate degree placements) there are something over 500 septillion (5×10^{26}) possibilities of planetary placements. That's a lot of people. Even if you limit the three outer planets to something like a 40+ year period of degree possibilities, you still have 15.9 septillion (15.9×10^{25}) degree possibilities. That's still a lot of people. And I have not factored in the ascendant/midheaven possibilities based upon where on the globe you were born. So you see how the planets help add differentiation to the basic personality possibilities set out by the signs and houses.

As I have said before, the Sun and Moon are lumped into the group term planets, even though they are not strictly planets, but lights. In astrology we usually deal with ten basic planets. Sun, Moon, Mercury, Venus, Mars, Jupiter, Saturn, Uranus, Neptune, Pluto. Unless an astrologer is very traditional (or using Hindu astrology) they will not use any fewer than these ten. Some use more, adding Chiron and the big four asteroids (Ceres, Pallas, Juno, Vesta), some add other hypothetical planets (Transpluto and others) and/or other asteroids (there are ephemerides for almost a thousand others, but there are services which routinely track 250 and sell placement charts for a small fee). But for this book the "basic ten" will be quite enough for us. In Part Four there are sections on Chiron and the big four asteroids, for those who are curious. Many astrologers are routinely using these in their natal work. Horary and electional astrology do not use any more than the basic ten planets.

Each planet rules one or two signs and, through the placement of those signs on the mundane wheel—houses.

Planets also rule houses in a chart by virtue of ruling the sign placed upon a cusp, dependent upon what the ascendant and midheaven are. They also still retain a secondary rulership over the mundane house they would rule if Aries were on the ascendant and every house was 30 degrees (the mundane wheel). So with a Libra ascendant, Venus rules the ascendant because it is the ruler of Libra, and it also has secondary rulership of the 7th and 2nd houses, by virtue of having Libra and Taurus naturally on the cusps of the 7th and 2nd houses.

Through these rulerships and the planets interrelationships by aspect and other factors, the chart then becomes a web of interrelationships. If three planets are tied by aspects, it is as if they form a mobile. Tug on one and all three move, because they are tied together. This sort of interrelationship makes it difficult for people to totally "compartmentalize" their lives. If you have a trine between planets in the 2nd and 5th, then money and love will be tied (no money and you can't go out on a date with your sweetie).

Each planet has a nature and various attributes which help define its meaning. Hot and cold are attributes of energy movement—hot is greater than average energy movement, cold is less than average energy movement. Wet and dry are qualities of malleability—wet is highly malleable and changeable, and dry is static and fairly immovable. These four attributes combine to make up the elements: fire is hot and dry, air is hot and wet, water is cold and wet, earth is cold and dry. Spirit, the "fifth element," is pure heat, it initiates change and is unchanged. Earth is the least changeable, it ends change and is, itself, unchanged. All this is ancient Greek esoteric philosophy, but it is the basic philosophy from which modern astrology developed.

The reason for the above is that where signs are defined by the elements and qualities, planets are defined by these attributes. The correspondence of attributes and signs helps explain how planets and signs are tied, but it

Table 1. Planetary Correspondences and Rulerships.

Planet	Attribute	Action	Day	Nature	Manifestation	Gender
☉ Sun	hot dry	yang	Sunday	will	life	male
☽ Moon	cold wet	yin	Monday	emotion	instinct	female
☿ Mercury	convertible	neutral	Wednesday	idea	mentality	both
♀ Venus	warm wet	yin	Friday	attraction	love	female
♂ Mars	hot dry	yang	Tuesday	action	ego	male
♃ Jupiter	hot wet	yang	Thursday	increase	optimism	
♄ Saturn	cold dry	yang	Saturday	decrease	boundaries	
♅ Uranus	hot dry	yang		change	electricity	
♆ Neptune	cold wet	yin		spirit	formlessness	
♇ Pluto	converting	neutral		upheaval	transformation	

does not always work. For example, Mars being hot and dry, classically rules Scorpio, which is fixed water (which is cold and wet.) Yet the planetary rulerships have tested out over the millennia, so we know they do work. See Table 1 for planetary correspondences and rulerships.

The attributes of the outer three planets are debatable as are their actions. Warm is sort of half-hot. Mercury being convertible means it takes on the attributes of the sign it is in and the planets it aspects. Pluto converting means it changes the attributes of the signs and planets it contacts to their opposites. Male and female are indications that these planets archetypally represent male and female. Mercury is both, being hermaphroditic. Uranus is considered to be the higher octave of Mercury, Neptune is the higher octave of Venus, Pluto is the higher octave of Mars.

These attributes are not vital to understanding the planets, but show how the definitions are built. What is vital to understanding is the planetary rulerships. See Table 2. The rulerships in parentheses are the classical rulerships, which were in effect before the modern planets were discovered. Traditionally, it is believed that two more planets will be discovered which will end up ruling Taurus and Virgo, thereby having 12 planets for 12 signs and 12 houses. Numerically elegant.

Table 2. Planetary Rulerships.

Planet	Sign	Planet	Sign
Sun ☉	Leo ♌	Moon ☽	Cancer ♋
Mercury ☿	Gemini and Virgo ♊ ♍	Venus ♀	Taurus and Libra ♉ ♎
Mars ♂	Aries (and Scorpio) ♈ ♏	Jupiter ♃	Sagittarius (and Pisces) ♐ ♓
Saturn ♄	Capricorn (and Aquarius) ♑ ♒	Uranus ♅	Aquarius ♒
Neptune ♆	Pisces ♓	Pluto ♇	Scorpio ♏

ASPECTS

Aspects are the angular relationships that exist between planets (and points) which tie their energies together in various ways. Most aspects are based upon the various ways you can divide a 360 degree circle (that being the whole of the horoscope wheel). Generally, those aspects based upon a twofold division (and its multiples) are active and challenging, those based upon a threefold division (and its multiples) are harmonious and easy. There are other prime numbers you can use to create aspects (fivefold division has to do with mentality and creativity) but they aren't commonly used. We will concern ourselves with the basic five traditional aspects and six others which come up fairly commonly.

> Traditional—conjunction, sextile, square, trine, opposition;
>
> Also semi-sextile, inconjunct, parallel and contra-parallel, semi-square and sesquiquadrate.

I will also outline quick ways to spot some aspects (some you have to either figure or have listed for you) so you can use an ephemeris to eyeball them yourself. Do not be shy about counting on your fingers or around the mundane wheel, if that's what it takes for you to figure this out. Magick is best done at home, behind closed doors anyway, so nobody should see you. (Even if you work in a coven, your coven-sibs should know you well enough by now, so you will either not be intimidated, or have no illusions of reputation to be burst anyway.)

Anytime you talk about aspects, the question of orb comes up. This is the amount of slop which is allowed before an aspect is considered to not be in effect anymore. Sigh. This is another hotly debated topic among astrologers. Generally (and I will amend this statement later on in various sections) a leeway of 5 to 8 degrees is allowed. The closer to exact the planets are, the stronger the influence is.

And applying aspects are stronger than separating aspects. This concept is integral to horary and electional work. Aspects can either be applying—coming together, exact, or separating—moving apart. In horary and electional, only the applying and exact aspects count. This will be covered further elsewhere. The orbs indicated here are those commonly accepted for use in natal charts.

☌ Conjunction: 0 degrees, same sign. Fusion of energies for good or ill, coming together, union. 8° orb.

✶ Sextile: 60 degrees, two signs apart (complimentary elements). Opportunity for harmony and / or communication, no guarantees of success. 6° orb.

☐ Square: 90 degrees, three signs apart (same quality). Friction, incitement to action, stirring up of the status quo, obstacles to be overcome. 8° orb.

△ Trine: 120 degrees, four signs apart (same element). Harmony, ease of accomplishment, can be talents taken for granted, laziness. 8° orb.

☍ Opposition: 180 degrees, six signs apart (complimentary elements, same quality). Opposition, separation, polar opposites, self vs. other, doing one or the other, see-saw effect. 8° orb.

These are the classical aspects. There are others which may be useful to know. Here they are.

⊻ Semi-Sextile: 30 degrees, one sign apart (no correlation by element or quality). Growth, natural progression, process, helpful but not convenient or easy. 1° orb.

∠ Semi-Square: 45 degrees—half of a square (no special correlation or not) stirring up, mental activity, minor annoyances, little frictions which can drive you mad if you let them. 2° orb.

⛢ Sesquiquadrate: 135 degrees—a square-and-a-half (no special correlation), more mental activity, more frictions, visions or ideas which are not necessarily comfortable. 2° orb.

⊥ or ⊼ Inconjunct (or Quincunx): 150 degrees, five or seven signs apart (no correlation by element or quality) adjustment, compromise, accommodation, health aspect, need to meet halfway. 3° orb.

Two other aspects are figured differently and have no correlation by sign, only declination. These have to be figured or given in a table, but they work in Horary and Electional.

∥ Parallel: same declination—operates like a conjunction. 1° orb only;

⧤ or # Contra-Parallel: opposite declination—operates like an opposition. 1° orb only.

In some cases, it matters not what particular aspect is between two planets, only that the planets are joined by aspect. Hindu astrology does not consider the nature of the aspect, only that the aspect is there, and how the two planets which are in that aspect get along in terms of energies. A planet which is unaspected in a chart is a standout high-focus indicator, and the individual who has an unaspected planet in his or her chart will most probably have difficulty expressing the energies symbolized by that planet and the house (or houses) it rules. Remember, planets are the WHAT and aspects are the HOW do they interact. If a planet does not interact with any others, then it operates in a vacuum, so to speak. In natal astrology the nature of the aspect is less important than the fact that there is an aspect. In horary and electional, the nature of the aspect is highly important, as it helps determine how things will go, and what the outcome will be. This is one of the differences between natal and horary and electional astrology.

Whew! There they all are, the basic words which make up the language of astrology. If all this is still Greek to you, don't despair. As you go along with the various methods, you will use these concepts more and more, and eventually you will absorb them by osmosis. Not all techniques use all the words, and they are arranged from really easy to most complex. Be adventuresome and go on to the next section. I'll be gentle.

MAGICK AND ASTROLOGY

Now that we've covered the general basics of astrology and introduced the 52 words of the basic language, we need to get more specific as to our topic. Astrology and magick. Magick and astrology. As there are only 52 words in this language, how does each pertain to magick? Are some more "magickal" than others? Where do we look when we are talking about magick? All these will be covered here.

A word before starting. These correspondences are for the most part derived from inference, and correlation and astrological logic (no pun intended, well, not at first). There aren't that many references where you can look up "magic" and see a correspondence by sign or house. Rex E. Bills, in his *Rulership Book*,[2] lists Magic and Black Magic, and has planetary correspondences, but two lines does not a valid research pool make. Lilly mentions the 12th house[3] as pertaining to "witchery." That's about it. There is lots pertaining to psychic matters, and ESP and all that jazz, but as to the subject of magick (or even magic), it just doesn't come up. A paranoid person might find a sinister hand in all of this, but I prefer to think of it as a sort of indication of how much astrology has sought to "clean up its act" and impress

---

[2] A reprint of this book was published in 1993 by the American Federation of Astrologers in Tempe, AZ.
[3] *Christian Astrology* (Issaquah, WA: Just Us & Associates, 1986).

the empiricists. After all, magick can't be measured or proven or bottled, so therefore it doesn't exist. Right? If you really believed that, you wouldn't be reading this book.

Anyhow, what all this is leading up to is that there is a lot of stuff here which is relatively unsupported in mainstream astrology. You can certainly look up the element "water" and find it corresponds with feelings and emotions and intuition and psychic things. I have just gone one step further and tied all that together with magick. If at times the logical leap may seem far-fetched, put it down to many years of thinking in astrology and eliminating the intermediate steps. All this stuff has been thought about a whole lot, and studies have been done, in a limited way. I am under a geas, so to speak, to get these ideas out there and don't have three or five years to do correlative studies and collect 1000 charts and apply statistical analysis. A geas is a "Mission from the Gods" to paraphrase the Blues Brothers. More formally, a compulsion or assignment of divine origin which must be accomplished regardless of other life pursuits or interests. It sort of takes over your life until the task is accomplished. And this book did just that. And how do you statistically analyze magick anyhow? Especially in its many forms and styles and disciplines.

In the natal chart section in Part Three, there will be lists of things which may incline an interest or aptitude for magick. This does not mean that if these things are present in a chart, the person will be a practitioner of magick. He or she may come from a background that forbids such things. He or she may have an interest but no way to obtain the materials to begin study and practice, or may have other interests which take up time. And he or she may be totally materialistic, yet use "talents" in everyday life and not even know that it could be called magick. Think of the investors who act on hunches, the people who "follow their intuition," the people who have good gut-level instincts. All those things can be said to relate to magick. They are just expressed in more acceptable everyday terms.

So what is magick? Come on, you must have an idea. Is it the conscious manipulation of energies to affect a desired outcome? Is it an ability to attune oneself to the natural forces and make life easier by going with the flow? Is it an ability to tap into a cosmic reservoir of knowledge and come up with information about the past/present/future not attainable by normal material means? Is it the ability to go within and come up with resources which are deemed paranormal or supernatural? Is it the search for that metaphorical Philosopher's Stone which can transmute base elements into gold? Is it the study of arcane, hidden or lost knowledge which may be so dangerous that it is best left to only a privileged few?

However you define magick, most all definitions contain the element of being outside the realm of the ordinary. Which is really a shame, since all magickal practitioners are supposedly doing is tapping into natural cosmic energies which are already there, and putting them to individual use. Just because we cannot, as of now, measure and quantify those energies does not mean they do not exist.

So what does pertain to magick, astrologically? All good magicians know about the four elements, fire, earth, air and water. Then there is the fifth element, spirit, the ether which holds all the rest together. Astrology does deal with the four elements, and in pretty much the same way. The ether is also mentioned as the medium by which the influences of the planets and signs are transmitted to Earth and to individuals. Spirit could also be said to correlate to the concept of "free will" by which the individual can choose the way to experience the energies of the planets rather than just taking what comes.

The elements combine with the qualities to produce the signs. The houses come from the imposition of the signs on a spacio/temporal map of the heavens. And the planets are separate bodies, which operate in the arena of the signs and houses. Aspects are the angular relationships between planets and points which show how they interreact. We still can't quantify or measure the mechanism by which astrology works. Maybe gravity waves will provide some answers. But, in a sense, we don't care about that mechanism. All we care about is that it works. Magick is the same way. Magick focuses upon the "results" of a working and not necessarily the physical/chemical/electrical energies or processes manipulated to achieve those results.

So we go back to the elements. Fire is spirituality, and energy, and enthusiasm. Earth is material and solid and tangible. Air is mental and abstract and communicative. Water is emotional and unconscious and intuitive.

We can get more magickally oriented and say that if there is a preponderance of **fire** in the chart, the person will probably be an "energy worker," someone who wants to create and/or control lines of force, work with fire itself, engage in chakra work, create shields. Getting more abstract, fire deals with spirituality and so this fiery person may get into the philosophies behind magick, the spirituality of magick, the religions which use magick, the creativity and self-expression which magick can offer the practitioner, the fun and play inherent in good magick, someone who can be precognitive, someone who can "fire up" others with his or her energy and enthusiasm, a person who needs action in their magick.

With **earth**, we get a person who is concerned with working with items, tools, and objects, rocks and crystals, being a gardener—growing herbs and such, someone who studies the magickal effects of herbs and foods, someone who wants to use magick for tangible/practical ends, someone who may not necessarily be open to the energies and feelings during the working itself, but who will count results, someone who may use sex magick or Tantra, someone who wants to materially or socially better his or her condition through magick, someone who may work well with sympathetic magick, a person who may adopt a discipline/tradition and stick with it fairly closely—psychometry would be something to investigate—a person who is very good with practical ideas and things to do which will achieve results, someone who can sit still and be in tune with the Earth, use of music or silence can be effective.

With **air** the practitioner is interested in the world of ideas, words, and communication. This is the magickal writer—be it of books, or rituals, or spells; the person who uses clairvoyance/clairaudience, the person who likes tying various disciplines together, experimenting with mix-and-match rituals and ceremonies, a person who will probably want to be a member of a working group rather than being solitaire, a people-person who likes the talk and socializing (and gossip) of magickal associations, someone who may be in several groups or traditions, telepathy would be a subject of interest, a practitioner who might use auras and colors a lot, someone who needs words and talk OR vivid imagery and pictures for his or her workings, who is more abstract and intellectual, who needs variety in his or her workings.

Water is the basic element of magick itself. Water also deals with emotion and feelings that manifest in a magickal practitioner who is an empath, sensitive, mediumistic, mystic, works with liquids, oils and perfumes, is attuned to the feelings and nuances of magick, is into meditation and exploring the "inner realms," has an interest in past lives and reincarnation, who researches magickal subjects (particularly old traditions), can be a magickal historian, is very concerned with lineages, is highly sensitive to the feelings of the people around, and needs time alone to rest, recharge, and recoup, someone who has a wonderful imagination and works with visualization, scrying is a possible talent, works well near lakes, rivers, streams, oceans, wants to feel deep inner change and regeneration.

Taking the qualities and exploring them, gives us more clues as to how a person might operate magickally.

A person with strong **cardinal** emphasis wants to be a leader, start things, is an irresistible force, is into innovation and experimentation, relates to the holidays of Oestarra, Midsummer, Mabon and Yule, is more into "peak experiences," is very concerned with intent, has good ideas and wants to try them out and see how they work, wants action.

With a **fixed** emphasis, the practitioner of magick likes routine, doing the same ritual the same way each time, is an immovable object, is more conservative in action and outlook, can be tough to get going but once started will stick with a thing until the finish, relates to the holidays of Beltane, Lughnasadh, Samhain and Imbolc, is good at grounding and centering, wants results, takes a wait-and-see attitude, has strong will, likes to see things finished, wants things to stay as they are unless they are impossible or unbearable, will not change unless the person thinks it is his or her idea.

The **mutable** magician goes with the flow, is changeable and adaptable according to the circumstances, can be a mediator between the two other qualities of expression, likes compromise, thinks movement is important, likes the magickal journey itself, not necessarily dependent upon the intent or results, is looking toward the next working with an eye to the past and making it better, is a reformer, will go with the wishes of the group, wants to make the world better in a way described by the element of the sign, is more into the process of how things work rather than the results.

No person will be a pure expression of any of these energies. We each have all the signs and planets and houses in our astrological makeup. With work we can operate in any of these ways; it's just that some ways are more easy or natural for us than others.

HOUSES, SIGNS AND PLANETS IN MAGICK

There are four houses which seem to relate specifically to magick, and by correlation the signs which rule them also have influence. The houses of ending (4, 8, 12) correspond to the water signs—Cancer, Scorpio, and Pisces—and the 6/12 axis which corresponds to Virgo and Pisces. The 6/12 axis is related to work/service, health/hospitalization,

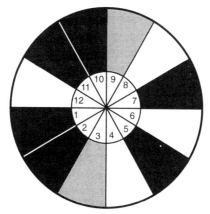

Figure 3.   The four houses of magick.

individual/group magick, low magick/high magick. Lilly specifically mentions that the 12th house pertains to witchery. See figure 3.

Two other houses relate peripherally to magick—3 and 9—corresponding to Gemini and Sagittarius (the other two mutable signs along with Virgo and Pisces). The mutable signs do express themselves by "going with the flow" and adapting and changing to circumstances, and magick is a way to either adapt yourself to the world or adapt the world to yourself and your needs and desires. But these two houses are not really as integral to magick as the four mentioned above. Houses 3 and 9 are of mentality and mind, and they have relevance to a magickal practitioner, but only in a way that the other six houses not already mentioned also relate to magick. (You could see how they tie into your chart and try to prove me wrong. I make no claims to omniscience or perfection.)

Realistically, all 12 houses and signs relate to magick in some way; by rulership of a magickal practice or technique or through derivational houses. My findings are that 4, 8, 12 and the water signs (Cancer, Scorpio, Pisces) relate to your internal makeup, your inborn magickal potentials and how you use magick. The 6/12 axis and Virgo/Pisces relates to the actual performance of magick, what systems you use and how you practice, and what you do with the magick. Other signs and houses have relevance to magick and its practice, but these four are the main ones.

4th House: The basis for magick. Your inherent abilities and inclinations for magick and how you operate magickally. Also the 4th can indicate any inherent psychic talents, which can either manifest naturally or be cultivated. The element of the sign on the cusp, and element of the planet ruling the sign on the cusp, and the Moon sign, can all show the mode of psychic ability. Look at the sign on the cusp for the style of magickal expression, and the sign and house placement of the ruler of that sign for more information on how and in what way you practice magick. Any planets in the 4th house will also add their influence. Also the sign and house placement of the Moon (which naturally rules the 4th house) adds another level of interpretation. Generally, if you look to these indicators you will find something which relates to the way you "got into" magick in the first place. One person with Sagittarius on the 4th cusp started in martial arts (sports) and from those disciplines and philosophies moved into magick. One with Aquarius on the 4th started in astrology and then through friends got into magick. You get the idea.

6th House: The everyday nuts-and-bolts of magick. Where you take these talents and learned skills and philosophies and use them to help run your everyday life. What you make with your hands in and for magick, the tools and objects you use in your magick, the handicrafts of magick. This house describes your garden (if any), or the herbs you use, or the style of tarot deck you prefer. These and other "props" of magick come under the rulership of the 6th house. Also any familiars, or coven siblings, or co-workers of magick. It rules Evocation, calling on the God/dess for help as an outside force. The 6th rules how the magickal working manifests upon the material plane, if at all. The 6th house also rules shamanism, which is related to, but not the same as, traditional magick. If the rulers of the 6th and 4th/8th/12th are in aspect, you may use some shamanistic techniques or props in your traditional magickal workings. Or if the 6th house is stronger than the 12th, you may work shamanistically, rather than magickally. The 6th relates more to magick used outside Circle, in the real world. The 12th relates to magick performed in Circle, in the magickal world.

8th House: How you make magick—the style or tradition you eventually settle into. Most basically how you express yourself creatively with magick. The fun of magick. The type and qualities of initiatory experiences you may (or may not) have. Again, look to the sign on the house cusp, any planets in the 8th house, the sign and house placement of the ruler of the sign on the cusp of the 8th house, and the sign and house placement of Pluto (natural ruler of the 8th house). Blending keywords can be helpful in determining interpretations. You will probably not express all the possibilities at once, but in various ways, through a tradition, a style, various divinatory systems, research specialties. This can be where you find some indication of what specialties you use (and stay with) through your magickal career. Also the topics you research and study in depth.

12th House: The spirituality and religious expression (if any) of magick. This house relates to the philosophies and mindset behind magickal expression. It also has to do with how you practice magick, like the 4th and 8th. But it also is an endpoint house, the culmination of an individual's magickal experience and expression. The 12th rules the magickal energies raised and their effect upon the magickal plane. It rules invocation, bringing the God/dess into yourself and creating change through yourself as a direct agent of the Gods on the material plane. Merging with the "Infinite" is a 12th house theme. It indicates the magickal persona you adopt in Circle, and who you are in the magickal community, in your local area and also the country and world as a whole. It becomes your "magickal ascendant," and interpreting your chart using your 12th as a "new" magickal ascendant, and renumbering the other houses accordingly, can add insight into your personality in a magickal perspective.

You could relate the 4th to the first degree magickal experience, the 8th to the second degree experience and the 12th to the third degree experience. Or the 4th to inherent talents, the 8th to acquired abilities and the 12th to how the talents and abilities are applied and utilized. There are other ways of relating these houses, but you get the idea.

The 6th house is everyday magick, while the 12th is formal ceremonial magick. The 6th is the props, and tools, and words used, and the 12th is the energy raised and thoughtforms created. The 12th is the magickal working itself and the 6th is the results of that working on the material plane.

The 4th, 8th and 12th are the potentials and interests and specialties and energies raised in magick and the 6th is where and how the individual manifests these interests and energies on the material plane. This is a broad generalization, but it is one way of looking at the way these four houses interrelate.

THE TWELVE HOUSES IN MAGICK

1st House: The Magus-self, adept or practitioner, fire, your personal style, and method of presenting yourself on a one-on-one level, how you as an individual practice magick, the mask you show to the world, your magickal persona, early life and childhood, Oestarra, east.

2nd House: Items, possessions, tools (as objects), self-esteem, music, songs and singing, what you need in sex, creature comforts, money spells, Mother, Gaia, what you value both materially and otherwise, ethics, Beltane.

3rd House: The words spoken, paper spells written on, rote memorization, short distances in magick, vehicles for travel, low mysteries, books, writing and teaching, every-day life, magickal siblings, communications in all forms.

4th House: The magickal circle, water, the altar, the home base for the working, the inward manifestation of the work-ing, weather magick, Goddess/Mother, FamTrads, your family and ethnic heritage, food magick, feasting, the grave, caves and underground places, end of the matter as mani-fested, psychological base and traits, real estate and land, Midsummer, north.

5th House: The creative force of the spell itself, love magick, Sun God, celebratory magick, children, divination, gam-bling and speculation, hobbies, creative self-expression, what ideas you bring to and add to your workings, magick as theater, Lughnasadh.

6th House: Students, disciples, magickal helpers, animal spirits, familiars, small animals, maidens, martyrs, fasting, special diets, Evocation of God/dess, tools (as active wield-ers of energy), clothing/robes, herbs, food magick, handi-crafts, Maiden, sickness and health and wellness, low magick.

7th House: The other, air, the end desired, weddings/hand-fastings, open enemies, war and peace, fine arts, diplomacy and mediation, allies and supporters, Mabon, west.

8th House: Sex magick, what you have to offer in sex, ritual magick, death and rebirth, initiation, what you owe, chthon-ian issues, banishment, elimination, spiritual development, astral travel, meditation, other people's self-esteem, other people's possessions, group resources (financial and other-wise), morality, Samhain.

9th House: Visualizations behind the words spoken, the astral plane, the religion of magick, long distance magick, higher mysteries, ethics, law, judgment, publishing and publications, understanding of how and why magick works, pilgrimages, dreams, advertising, the priesthood as a body, big rituals.

10th House: Earth, the outward manifestation of the working, what you strive to attain, God/Father, Crone, hierarchy, magickal superiors, High Priest/ess, honors and achievements, how you present yourself to large groups or the world at large, publicity and reputation, Yule, south.

11th House: Angels, magickal community, coven, "church as community," friends, aspirations, astrology, experimental stuff, wishes, other people's children, creative self-expression of others, groups and societies, Imbolc.

12th House: Magick, invocation of God/dess, spiritual merging with the other, survivors of calamity and misfortune, charity, perfumes and incense and oils, group magick, channeling, mediumship, dance, secret enemies, prison, drugs and alcohol, hospitalization and hospitals, healing, large animals, spirit guides, secret aid and supporters, secret societies, high magick.

You may find certain things mentioned as pertaining to more than one house. Well, it sort of works that way. It comes from having only a few words to deal with all the things in the world. You can get nit-picky with distinctions and fine tunings, but again, this is an overview. None of these correspondences are written in stone. The basic energies of the planets, signs, and houses are constant, but how we perceive them as manifesting in the world can vary from one person to another. You can even get extreme and make a case for all of the signs, houses, and planets having something to do with everything. But that quickly turns into mental masturbation. There are lots of books with word lists and correspondences. The lists here are compiled with a magickal slant. Some general information is also included; after all, magick deals with the real world. (It does??????? It does, take my word for it.)

These interpretations are based upon derivational house interpretations. Exactly how they were derived is a bit complicated, but seeing how they work can give a person the idea how, by using only 52 astrological words, these basic words can be expanded and refined to include everything in the world. A thing can generally be "gotten to" by using a house, a sign, and/or a planet. And a thing can be dissected and refined in its components and modes of expressions to be included in the interpretations of several houses, signs, and/or planets. Generally, the basic thing (like magick) is ruled by one house, sign, and/or planet (12th, Pisces, Neptune). But as you broaden its expression in the life, you then involve other houses, signs, and/or planets (4th, Cancer, Moon; 6th, Virgo, Mercury, and 8th, Scorpio, and Pluto). And getting more detailed and refined in expression, you then involve all the rest of the houses, signs and planets. When you include rulerships and placements and aspects between planets and by those tying together the houses they rule, both in the individual chart and naturally, you get a full life, where the areas of life and modes of expression are all intertwined. Astrology is both simple and complex. It divides everything into these 52 categories, yet by using these 52 categories and exploring how they tie areas of life (and modes of expression) together, you get things relating to all of these categories, in one way or another. (This is getting a bit deep, in more ways than one.)

THE SIGNS IN MAGICK

The twelve signs express themselves magickally in different ways. Below are thumbnail definitions of the signs and how they operate magickally.

Aries (♈): Is a leader or lone wolf. Starts projects and is full of enthusiasm, but isn't so good about finishing. Can get easily distracted by new ideas, projects, people. Is really gosh-wow-boy-oh-boy and can be wearying to more settled, mature signs. Can be the *enfant terrible* of the Circle. Has courage but can act before thinking. Patience is not one of Aries' virtues. Aries can be an energy worker, especially when there is fire involved. Aries can become a psychic warrior.

Taurus (♉): Is solid and grounded. Aesthetics, comfort, sensuality and music and song are important. Taurus can also be silent or speak very little. Taurus may have trouble connecting with the mystical unseen worlds and energies. Values and ethics are important. Also Taurus may like to collect magickal things, items, usually of value. Taurus is really interested in the "what's in it for me" aspect of magick. Taurus is impressed by results.

Gemini (♊): Is the quintessential eclectic of the zodiac. Gemini is into trivia, and reading, and communicating, and networking, and dealing with people. Gemini can be a trickster. Words and writing are tools which Gemini wields well. Gemini does not like routine. Gemini likes to mix and match techniques, borrowing from everyone. Gemini can enjoy the interplay of ideas and socializing as much as the actual magick itself. Gemini can become a telepath.

Cancer (♋): Is the psychic and medium of the zodiac. Above all, Cancer feels everything, and needs to develop a protective "shell" to be able to block out unwanted influences. Empathy and scrying are Cancer talents. Cancer is into home and family and traditions—whatever traditions Cancer can latch onto. Cancer can appear shy and reluctant, but can also blossom into a formidable leader when the Cancer feels secure about talents and abilities. Threaten Cancer's security and he or she will fight to regain it.

Leo (♌): The theatrical, elaborate, big ritual magicians. Leos love show and display. They are outgoing and charismatic, but are also into getting their own way, unless evolved and aware. Leos make effective Witch Queens. Hurt Leos' pride and they will never trust you again. Leos relate well to children. Love and romance are Leos' domain, and they can put amazing amounts of energy into love spells, for themselves and others. Leos need an audience for their magick.

Virgo (♍): Is the practical Kitchen Witch of the zodiac. Herbs and healing are Virgo's forte. Virgo is into getting things done, and being practical about it. Virgo doesn't like disorder and can go about cleaning up others' psychic messes. Virgo likes minutiae and detail and is into spells which need to be done just right to be effective. Virgo can be too hard on her- or himself, if things don't come off perfectly. Virgo plans ahead and likes to be ready for anything.

Libra (♎): Is the socialite and peacemaker. Libra is also the "devil's advocate" and likes to make sure all sides are represented, that things are balanced and fair. Libra prefers to work with a partner. Libra is a leader by example, and can also lead by committee. Libra can appear indecisive, but that's only because the Libra hasn't fully weighed and balanced all the alternatives. Libra prefers the middle way, the balanced path. Libra understands that without darkness, you cannot fully appreciate the light.

Scorpio (♏): Is into intensity. The deep profound changes which result from magick are what Scorpio is looking for. Scorpio will plumb the depths to attain the heights. Scorpio is into occult, arcane, and hidden lore, and wants to find out all about it just because someone else thought it might be too much for the populace at large. Sex is something Scorpio understands instinctively. Scorpio can be a loner or work with a partner or close-knit group. Scorpio has deep secrets which are revealed to no one, though Scorpio wants to find out about everyone else's.

Sagittarius (♐): Likes religion and big ritual. Sagittarius also likes higher knowledge, study, and the philosophy of magick. Foreign languages are absorbed instinctively. Astral travel, dream work, divination are all Sagittarian disciplines. Sagittarius can be pompous and overbearing, but means well. The sign is also often afflicted with "foot-in-mouth-disease" as Sagittarians inadvertently utter malapropisms or back-handed compliments. Sagittarius is a philosopher, enjoys study and learning, and can be a very deep thinker.

Capricorn (♑): Can be a hermit, elder or crone. Capricorn respects hierarchies and degrees and likes the more formal ceremonial types of magick. Capricorn is a hard worker and is results oriented. Capricorn can be extremely strict and hard on others, but it is no more than she or he is personally. Capricorn respects tradition and things which are old or have withstood the test of time. Wisdom and maturity are what Capricorn strives to attain.

Aquarius (♒): Is willing to try new and different things. Innovation is what Aquarius is good at, but that can also degenerate into change for change's sake. Aquarius wants to be part of a community, be it small—like a coven—or large—like a national organization. Aquarius believes in freedom and equality for all and will fight for the rights of others. Aquarius likes weird far-out new and strange things or people or ideas. Science fiction and astrology and electricity are Aquarius things.

Pisces (♓): Is a mystic and a dreamer and an idealist. Pisces can also be a psychic sponge, so needs to shield. Pisces is the ideal magician because he or she is naturally in tune with other worlds and realities, but everyday life can be something never really mastered. Pisces can get lost in the stars and is advised to work with a grounded partner, to help Pisces return to reality. Reincarnation, divination, out-of-body experiences, perfumes, incense, dance, and music are all Pisces things.

The signs have some similarity to the houses. This is one way astrology ties things together. Also some things are mentioned in connection with more than one sign. This is also normal. And things which may seem contradictory are included in signs (like music and song and also silence all under Taurus). This is because the pure energies of each sign can manifest in different and opposite ways. Hence the music and silence. Again, the expressions for each sign have tested out over the centuries. Astrologers are used to these seeming contradictions. And how well a person is expressing the energies of a sign can show in how the traits manifest—in a positive or negative way. If the astrologer percieves a person is having difficulty with a certain sign, then different ways of expressing that sign's energies are offered to give the individual a more comfortable mode of learning to live with that sign. We all have all twelve signs in us, but some signs are more prominent than others, and some people deal with the same signs in vastly different ways. It's finding the ways that are most comfortable and least disruptive to the world at large which is the challenge we each face.

PLANETS IN MAGICK

The planets that relate most strongly to magick are those which rule the magickal houses, with the addition of Uranus. These planets are the Moon, Mercury, Pluto and Neptune. Having these planets in magickal houses or signs, or highly prominent in your chart (like on or near the ascendant or midheaven or involved in a lot of aspects) can indicate magickal talent. Or having the Sun, Moon, ascendant or ascendant-ruler in one of the magickal signs or houses are also good indicators. Having three or more planets (any three not just magickal ones) in a magickal sign or house can also indicate aptitude. What you are looking for is some weighting of the chart toward the magickal signs, houses, or planets. There are other weightings which are more subtle and less readily apparent, but generally the techniques mentioned above are sufficient. And if, dear reader, you seem to have none of these indicators in your chart, don't despair. You can do magick, also; you may just have to work at it a bit harder. Or you may practice a brand of magick which is different or non-traditional. Whatever works.

In Part Three, the attributes of each planet are explored in depth. For now, just know that the Moon, Mercury, Uranus, Neptune and Pluto are the main magickal planets. All the planets have some influence upon magick, and have specific modes of operation, but some are inherently more "magickal" than others.

INTERPRETATION IN BRIEF

When I look for magickal/psychic potential and/or interests in a chart, I first look to see what the Sun, Moon, and ascendant signs are. Then I look at the houses that the Sun, Moon, and ascendant ruler are in. I then look for planets on, in, or near the ascendant or midheaven. I look at the planets which aspect the Sun, Moon, and ascendant-ruler, especially by conjunctions. Then I look at planets in the 4th, 6th, 8th and 12th. Are there any planetary patterns which focus upon the 4th, 6th, 8th or 12th? Are there any groups of planets in the 4th, 6th, 8th, 12th, or Cancer, Virgo, Scorpio, or Pisces? Where are the rulers of the signs on the 4th, 6th, 8th, and 12th? Are they well placed by sign? Are they well aspected? What about the Moon, Mercury, Pluto, Neptune and Uranus? Where are they? Are they well placed by sign?

Are they related by aspect or mutual reception? Where is Chiron? How is it placed by sign and house? What are its aspects? I formulate in my mind a basic psychic potential from all of this.

Then I talk to the client. Is this person interested in psychic things? Does the client have the opportunity or interest for pursuing psychic studies? Is this person operating on a spiritual level, or is he or she totally uninterested in things which are intangible, spiritual or philosophical? Does the client have a sense of wonder, the ability to suspend disbelief, a sense of humor, an active imagination? Has this person ever had a psychic experience? Is the client at a place in life where she or he feels comfortable with pursuing psychic interests? Is this person among people who are tolerant or at least indifferent to psychic studies? Does the client have the time and resources to pursue such studies? I generally do not ask these questions directly, but through the dialogue which is the reading, I am able to get answers to these questions and if it seems generally favorable, I will then pursue the subject more directly. If the client shows interest, I will tell him or her what the chart shows in the ways of talents and interests and possible aptitudes and offer suggestions for areas of study, and places to go to find books and/or teachers. Then it is up to the individual.

A chart may show great potential, but if the individual is uninterested or discouraged from such studies for various reasons, then I will let the subject drop. If I know the client is a practicing magician, I will then just jump into the subject at the start. I prefer to be more general and circumspect about such topics. People nowadays are more interested and open about magick and other psychic studies, but there are still those who are strongly against such things for many and various reasons.

In high school I had a chemistry teacher who threatened to flunk me, despite an "A" average, unless I immediately gave up astrology because it was totally unscientific and unfounded, and only ignorant and deluded people bothered with such "trash." I was too intelligent and educated to follow such mumbo-jumbo. The teacher was a Taurus, so I knew there was no reasoning with this otherwise interesting and charming person. So I just smiled, said, "you're right," and never mentioned the subject again in that person's hearing and quietly kept on studying and taking classes on my own. Sometimes it's just better to let the subject drop rather than getting into an argument that has no winner and can create many unpleasant animosities.

The third part of the book is devoted to interpretations of the houses, signs, and planets, and how they relate to magick. This section is only an overview of the specific elements in the chart that are directly related to magick. Other research is ongoing, and there are additional schools of thought which take into account the "big four" and the minor asteroids, esoteric and Uranian studies and other things which are beyond the scope of this book. The bibliography lists a number of interesting books which can be read for additional material on some of these subjects.

PART TWO

MAGICKAL
TIMING TOOLS

HOW TIMING WORKS

This section is designed to give you the knowledge and tools to use astrology to add effectiveness to magickal rituals and workings. You do not need to know math or how to cast a chart—though this knowledge would add to the effectiveness. The tools you need are either an astrological almanac or calendar—one which shows daily aspects and times, like Jim Maynard's *Celestial Guide* or Llewellyn's *Astrologers Daily Almanac* or Dell *Horoscope* magazine, or any other publication that lists Moon signs, aspects, and times, and the time the Moon moves into signs and times of the Void-of-Course Moon. A copy of your natal chart is also useful, but not required. These and a basic knowledge of the Moon's effect in signs and houses and you are ready to add effectiveness to your magick.

Some Astrological calendars also have this information on them (the wall-size calendars) but be careful when buying them. Do not assume that just because it appears to be astrological that it will have the information you need. Some calendars list aspects but with no times, some list sign changes and times but not void-of-course times, some list only Moon aspects and ignore other planetary aspects. There are also some calendars which are more accurately proofed than others. In choosing these tools, the pretty pictures for each month are definitely secondary, if not optional.

The Moon is the main timer and activator in horary and electional astrology. It is the fastest moving "planet" and aspects all other planets.

Other planets receive aspects from some planets and make aspects to others. As I said earlier, technically, the

Moon is not a planet—it is one of the "lights," the Sun being the other. But in general astrological nomenclature both are lumped under the group term "planets."

The planets make and receive aspects in a definite hierarchy and order. It goes: Moon, Mercury, Venus, Sun, Mars, Jupiter, Saturn, Uranus, Neptune, Pluto. These are in order of their average daily speed. The faster planets always aspect the slower ones. Currently Pluto is orbiting inside the orbit of Neptune, so technically Pluto aspects Neptune. Again this is one of those things which works both ways. You can try it both ways, and each will work. This aspect hierarchy is fixed, no matter what the actual daily speed is of the planet in question, which can vary quite a bit due to retrograde motion. We'll get to that later.

As the Moon moves through the signs and aspects planets, it partakes of the effects of the sign it is moving through, and this is colored further by the effects of the planets it aspects and the nature of the aspects involved. The Moon defines the astrological "weather," which is constantly changing as the Moon moves from sign to sign and aspect to aspect.

This system advocates that you tailor your magick to match the prevailing astrological weather. Use the Moon and other planets and work with them—rather than doing whatever whenever. It's like planning an outdoor barbecue—you'd rather have a bright sunny warm day than try cooking over the grill in a blizzard at midnight. Both times you get cooked food, but one climate is more hospitable, and the food will come out better.

In horary and electional astrology, aspects are in effect only through exactitude. Once an aspect becomes exact—perfect—its influence is greatest. Afterwards it is no longer in force. It is like waiting for a bus; you are at the stop and can see the bus coming. It gets there and you can either take it or not. Once the bus has passed, it is gone—the bus will not reverse and you can't catch up with it—you have to wait for the next bus. Planning your activity to start just before an aspect becomes perfect is best—you have extra time to take care of unexpected glitches, and a delay will not put you past the time of the exact aspect. After the aspect has passed it is no longer an influence—the next aspect comes into influence. If you started your activity, it has the influence of that aspect stamped into it. It is part of the birthchart of the activity. But if you start after the aspect has passed, you missed it. You have to wait for the next time. THIS IS A HARD AND FAST RULE! Do not ignore it! Otherwise you lose the effectiveness of timing Moon aspects.

If you remember nothing else, this is what you should absorb. In the craft, the Sabbats and Esbats are celebrated generally AFTER the astrological event has occurred. This is exactly the opposite of how astrologers would do it. Astrologers, especially if they are familiar with horary and electional astrology, when they want the influence of an aspect (like a new Moon) start the thing immediately before or when the aspect becomes exact, NEVER after the fact. This will require a bit of a head change for longtime Wiccans and other magickal practitioners, but it can be well worth it. And, in the end, if all of this doesn't work out for you, you can still go back to your old ways and (hopefully) be none the worse for wear.

When you start a thing is your timing point—however you define the start. You can, for example, cast a circle, cleanse the circle, summon the quarters, and THEN start the main working—using that as your time. Or you can time the start from the start of the whole thing—be it from lighting the candles to describing the circle to calling the quarters. But once you make a decision on what is the start for a particular activity, stick with it. You can experiment from working to working, seeing which start points work best for you. And what works best for you may not work well for the next person. This is a system which allows you to individualize your magick. Play with it! Let your individuality shine. Experimentation is highly encouraged. Personally, I time from the lighting of the candles. I know of one ritual which timed from the start of the main working, and that worked also.

This system starts with very basic timing techniques and gets progressively more precise. You can choose the level of complexity you feel comfortable with. Generally, a good rule of thumb is how important is this activity? If it's a simple Esbat, use the simpler methods. If it's a Handfasting you expect to last for years, or a house blessing of your permanent home, or the naming of a baby, then get fancy and complex. And if you are so inclined, you might want to get a professional electional astrologer to cast a full chart so as to maximize the influences. Ahem. End of commercial. Actually, I have to insert a disclaimer here, for this system is not meant to replace a professional electional astrologer. It is for your individual use, in the privacy of your home or wherever you practice magick. If you really want to get elaborate, you are always welcome to take up the study of astrology yourself. Here is the list of most basic to most complex timings:

> Waxing/Waning Moon;
>
> Avoiding Void-of-Course Moon;
>
> Avoiding Retrograde Mercury;
>
> Moon in Signs;
>
> Planetary Hours;
>
> Moon in Houses of your own chart;
>
>> Secret Timing Tools;
>
> Final Moon aspect;
>
> Next Moon aspect (with final Moon aspect);
>
>> Rulerships;
>
>> Mutual Reception;

Aspects between other planets;

(using Moon aspects to fine-tune);

Ascendant/Midheaven degrees;

Moon house placement in the transiting chart;

Full electional chart.

The more of these factors you can coordinate, the more effective results you can get. You can also go insane trying for perfection. When in doubt, remember the KISS rule— Keep It Simple, Stupid! After all, you got along before you learned this, so now you know your magick will NOT fall apart if you ignore it. I guarantee it! You should be no worse off than before. All this timing will NOT make up for sloppy spellcraft, but it will increase the effectiveness of a good working, and it may help fine-tune results.

Remember, once the aspect has passed, you've missed the bus and need to wait for the next one. It's best to get to the stop (or start your working) a little early, so as not to miss the bus.

READING AN ASTROLOGICAL ALMANAC

○ Full Moon 10:59 A.M.   [Full MOON 10:59 A.M.]

☽ v/c 6:14 A.M.   [MO v/c 6:14 A.M.]

☽ → ♊ 8:24 A.M.   [MO > GE 8:24 A.M.]

☿ ☍ ♇ 12:01 A.M.   [ME opposite PL 12:01 A.M.]

☿ ☍ ♀ 2:12 A.M.   [ME opposite VE 2:12 A.M.]

☿ → ♊ 3:42 A.M.   [ME enters GE 3:42 A.M.]

☽ ☍ ♀ 6:14 A.M.   [MO opposite VE 6:14 A.M.]

♀ ☌ ♇ 7:58 A.M.   [VE conjunct PL 7:58 A.M.]

☽ ☌ ☿ 8:26 A.M.   [MO conjunct ME 8:26 A.M.]

☽ ☍ ☉ 10:59 A.M.   [MO opposite SU 10:59 A.M.]

☽ ✶ ♃ 11:45 A.M.   [MO sextile JU 11:45 A.M.]

☽ ☌ ♂ 4:47 P.M.   [MO conjunct MA 4:47 P.M.]

♄ SℝR 7:03 P.M.   [SA S Rx 7:03 P.M.]
♅ SD 8:02 P.M.   [UR S D 8:02 P.M.]
☉ △ ♃ 11:27 P.M.   [SU trine JU 11:27 P.M.]
☽ □ ♆ 11:53 P.M.   [MO square NE 11:53 P.M.]

This is a made-up page from an astrological almanac. Few days have as much activity as this one does, but the things included are meant to serve as examples. First, usually at the top of the day block, is the Moon information. MO v/c 6:14 A.M. means the Moon goes void of course at 6:14 A.M. Later in the column, you can see that also at 6:14 A.M. the Moon opposes Venus (MO opposite VE). You will ALWAYS have some Moon aspect at the same time the Moon goes void of course. Remember, the last aspect the Moon makes before going void is what defines the void condition. If no Moon aspect is listed at the same time as the Moon going Void of course, then a mistake has been made. The next thing listed is MO→GE 8:24 A.M. This shows the Moon moved into Gemini at 8:24 A.M. So the Moon was void from 6:14 A.M. to 8:24 A.M. Sometimes the Moon will go void one day and not move into the next sign until the next day (or even the day after.) That means that the Moon is void for all that time, a day or two. Even though the day changes , the Moon is still void until it moves into the next sign, no matter when that happens. The Moon can be void for as short as a minute, and as long as two-and-a-half days. Also listed at the top is Full Moon 10:59 A.M. You see that in the aspect column is listed MO ☍ SU 10:59 A.M., which is the aspect which determines the exact time of the Full Moon. Again, if you have a New, Quarter or Full Moon, and no corresponding Moon-Sun aspect in the aspect column (conjunct, square, or opposition), then a mistake has been made. This may sound like nit-picky stuff, but these little things show how well-proofed your almanac is. The same applies to things like a Gemini eclipse in late February. Since the Sun is in Pisces, a solar eclipse would be in Pisces and a lunar eclipse would be in Virgo. An eclipse in Gemini in late February is astronomically impossible. If you cannot see inside the calendar or almanac before buying it, do not assume it will be right for your needs.

The next column shows the aspects and other planetary activity for the day, in chronological order. Our sample shows an unusually busy day. Occasionally you see a day listed with the phrase "no exact aspects." This means that no aspects were made that day. The Moon is still in some sign, but it cannot go void that day, because you need a Moon aspect to go void. The Moon can be void or not on a day with no exact aspects. Going back to our hypothetical example, the first aspect listed is ME ☍ PL 12:01 A.M. Mercury opposed Pluto at 12:01 A.M. Then ME ☍ VE 2:12 A.M., Mercury opposed Venus at 2:12 A.M. These planetary aspects which do not include the Moon are included, but they have no bearing upon the Moon's condition. The next thing which happens is that ME→GE 3:42 A.M.; Mercury goes into Gemini at 3:42 A.M. Then MO ☍ VE 6:14 A.M.; Moon opposed Venus at 6:14 A.M. This is the last aspect the Moon makes before going void. The next aspect listed is VE ☌ PL 7:58 A.M.; Venus conjuncted Pluto at 7:58 A.M. There are a couple of things indicated here. First Venus was ahead of Pluto in degrees (Mercury opposed Pluto first, then Venus, then moved into Gemini.) Yet now Venus is conjuncting Pluto. Venus would have to move backward to do that, and indeed it has. Venus is retrograde in this example. The almanac will list the day and time Venus went retrograde, but you have to remember it is moving backward; there is no daily reminder of direct or retrograde motion. If there is an ephemeris at the top of the page, it will show an ℞ or R beside Venus when it went retrograde (or the beginning of the month if it was already retrograde at the start of the month.) So you have another reference for retrograde. If a planet has ℞ beside it at the beginning of the month and a D beside it later in the month, it means it was retrograde at the start of the month, and went direct the day that the D is beside it. The almanac should then have a notation of the planet going direct at a certain time on the day indicated. This Venus conjunct Pluto occurs during the time the Moon is void. It has NO EFFECT upon the condition of the Moon being void or not. This aspect doesn't include the Moon. This is an important concept. Some people seem to think that if there is another aspect while the Moon is void of course, it somehow negates the void condition. THIS IS NOT SO. *Only Moon aspects and sign placements affect the Moon's void of course condition.*

The next aspect listed is MO ♂ ME 8:26 A.M.; Moon conjunct Mercury at 8:26 A.M. Notice that the Moon moving into Gemini is NOT listed in the aspect column. All other planetary ingresses (planets moving into a new sign), will be listed in the aspects column, but NOT Moon ingresses. Then comes MO ♂ SU 10:59 A.M.; Moon opposite Sun at 10:59 A.M., the Full Moon. Next is MO ⚹ JU 11:45 A.M.; Moon sextile Jupiter 11:45 A.M. Then MO ● MA 4:47 P.M.; Moon conjunct (with the hole darkened) Mars 4:47 P.M. The darkened hole is NOT a typo, it indicates a unique planetary condition. That is a special type of a conjunction called an *occultation*. It means that the Moon is not only conjunct in degree, but it actually passes over the planet in question. If it were the Sun, there would be a solar eclipse. But the Moon can occult the other planets as well. It is technically CONJUNCT PARALLEL (same declination as well as degree), and acts as a "super conjunction." Occultations are rare, but they are very powerful.

The next thing listed in the aspects column is not an aspect at all, but a station. SA S℞ 7:03 P.M.; Saturn turns stationary retrograde at 7:03 P.M. This is the time when Saturn, after slowing down for some time, actually appears to stop and reverse motion in the sky. In actuality, the motion is so slow, it is not seen, but this is the mathematical point when it occurs. Before this, Saturn was direct in motion. Now Saturn is retrograde. The Saturn energies are going to be experienced in a retrograde fashion—inwardly and subjectively—rather than outwardly and objectively. With the outer planets (Uranus, Neptune, and especially Pluto), the times for stations may differ from almanac to almanac. This is normal. It is a function of which set of mathematical equations the author of the almanac is using. The same for outer planet aspects, those between the three outer planets, Uranus, Neptune, and Pluto. Times listed for the Uranus-Neptune conjunctions in 1993 varied by as much as twelve hours between almanacs. This is also no big deal. If you are using those infrequent outer planet aspects for workings, timing for the day of exactitude should be good enough.

The next thing listed is UR SD 8:02 P.M.; Uranus stationary direct at 8:02 P.M. Uranus came to the point in the sky when it appeared to slow down from moving backward, and then stopped and started moving forward again. This is another mathematical point, and may vary from almanac to almanac. If you look up in the ephemeris, there should be an "R" next to Saturn and a "D" next to Uranus on this day. The next thing listed is SU △ JU 11:27 P.M.; Sun trine Jupiter at 11:27 P.M. Again, aspects not involving the Moon do not affect the Moon's condition of void of course or not. The last aspect is MO □ NE 11:53 P.M.; Moon square Neptune at 11:53 P.M.

That is all the aspects for this day, and what a busy day it is! Hopefully, this will give you some idea how to read your almanac or calendar, so you can take advantage of the aspects and time your activities accordingly. Two possibilities for this day are to use the Venus conjunct Pluto for a binding spell to revitalize a sexual relationship (though not a wedding or handfasting, as Venus in Scorpio is a bad placement for Venus in a wedding/handfasting chart). Or you could do a working to help you with long-term investments. You would time it so the start of your ceremony was before 7:58 A.M. The other possibility would be to dedicate a temple or God statue using the Sun trine Jupiter aspect, starting that ceremony before 11:27 P.M. You could also try for a prosperity spell with Sun trine Jupiter as well.

Here is another way to list aspects for the same day:

☿ ☍ ♀ 28♉-♏ [ME opp PL 28 TA SC 12:01 A.M.] Angry words will be regretted, so keep your mouth shut.

☿ ☍ ♀ 28♉-♏ [ME opp VE 28 TA SC 2:12 A.M.] Put some torch songs on the CD and relax.

☿ → ♊ [ME enters GE 3:42 A.M.]

♄ ∥ ♆ [SA par NE 4:37 A.M.] You can't fool all of the people all of the time.

☽ ☍ ♀ [MO opp VE 6:14 A.M.] Being lazy seems fine about now, hang out and be a couch potato.

☽ ⚼ ♅ [MO conpar UR 7:27 A.M.] Crazy ideas may seem normal, think before you act.

♀ ☌ ♀ 28 ♏ [VE con PL 28 SC 7:58 A.M.] Oodles of sleazy sex abound, wear that see-through nightie.

☽ ∠ ♅ [MO ssq UR 8:10 A.M.] Weird people may come out of the woodwork.

☽ → ♊ [MO enters GE 8:24 A.M.]

☽ ☌ ☿ [MO con ME 8:26 A.M.] Your mind is at 45 RPM and your mouth at 78 RPM.

☽ ☍ ☉ [MO opp SU 10:59 A.M.] Short or long trips is the dilemma all must face.

☽ ✳ ♃ [MO sxt JU 11:45 A.M.] Happy, happy, joy, joy is the prevailing mood.

☽ ∥ ♂ [MO par MA 4:10 P.M.] You may feel like you have ants in your pants.

☽ ☌ ♂ [MO con MA 4:47 P.M.] Emotions are at a fever pitch.

☽ ⬛ ♄	[MO sqq SA 5:03 P.M.] Obstacles cause delays.
♄ ℞	[SA ℞ @ 7:03 P.M.]
♅ D	[UR D @ 8:02 P.M.]
☉ △ ♃ 1 ♐ -♈	[SU tri JU 1 SA AR 11:27 P.M.] Go for it is the watchword.
☽ ☐ ♆	[MO squ NE 11:53 P.M.] Watch out for pickpockets and con-artists.
☽ ∥ ♃	[MO par JU 11:59 P.M.] Optimism may make you overconfident.

This aspect list is different from an almanac type of listing, because there are non-classical aspects listed. Remember, the void Moon is figured from the last classical aspect (conjunction, sextile, square, trine, opposition). The Moon has a contraparallel and a semi-square after the opposition to Venus, but they do not count in determining the void Moon. Also the time the Moon is void is not listed. That may be in a separate list, elsewhere. But you can determine the time the Moon is void by going backwards from when the Moon enters Gemini, and finding when the previous classical aspect the Moon made was. That is the time the Moon goes Void of course. It takes a bit of working out and is not as automatic. But this type of listing has the advantage of showing all the other non-classical aspects which can also be used in workings. Saturn parallel Neptune is a good aspect for making the intangible concrete. Perhaps you could charge a magickal wand with ethereal energies. Start your working before 4:37 A.M. Parallels act like conjunctions and contraparallels act like oppositions. Using the minor aspects allows you access to outer planet energies which occur infrequently in classical aspects. These minor aspects aren't that frequent either, but there are more of them, so your chances are increased for finding some link between the slower planets. The little phrases of description are fun, but remember that each planet, sign, and aspect has many meanings, so do not limit yourself to only the descriptions listed.

WAXING/WANING MOON

The Moon is waxing when it is between new and full, increasing in light. The Moon is waning when it is between full and new, decreasing in light. At full it is considered "most waxed"—the influences of a waxing Moon are most potent. At new it is "most waned"—the influences of a waning Moon are most potent. After new is exact, it is waxing; after full is exact, it is waning. See figure 4.

This may seem simplistic, but these exact nuances are important. With this type of astrology, you are thinking in new and different ways, with very precise rules. Best to start doing it correctly from the beginning.

Waxing Moon: good for starting things, new things (experiences, ideas, people, places, tangible items, etc.), things which need to increase or grow, planting, planting above-the-ground crops, leaving on a trip, things which will be brought out into the open, bringing together, building, binding, gathering, summoning, action, birth and growth, vitality is high.

Waning Moon: good for ending ventures, things which should decrease, wither or die, dieting, harvesting, planting below-the-ground crops (root crops), things which should remain secret, banishing, losing, sending away, returning home from a trip, reaction, loss, letting go, give-away, death and decay, vitality is lessened.

That's the first technique. Pretty simple, isn't it. Really this stuff isn't all that awful as you had imagined. And I am being very gentle.

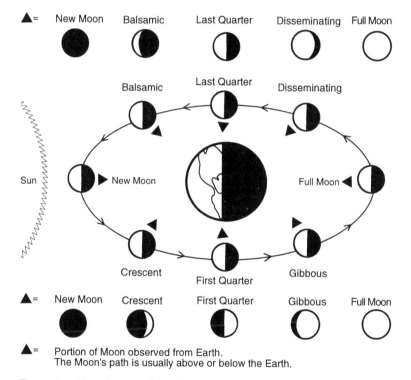

▲= Portion of Moon observed from Earth.
The Moon's path is usually above or below the Earth.

Figure 4.   The phases of the Moon. A basic knowledge of the Moon's effect in signs and houses will make your magick more effective. (Adapted from *A Spiritual Approach to Astrology* by Myrna Lufthus.)

AVOIDING A VOID-OF-COURSE MOON

As the Moon moves through each sign, it aspects the other planets. Eventually, it comes to a point when it has made its last aspect in that sign. By aspects I mean the basic classic aspects: conjunction, sextile, square, trine, and opposition. Once it has made that last aspect, it still has a portion of the sign to traverse, yet no aspects are coming up while it traverses that sign. That time is when the Moon is said to be void-of-course. It has done its business, so to speak, and is just "marking time" until it enters the next sign and begins the next sign's work. This period of being void-of-course (or "void" for short) can be as short as a couple minutes to as long as a couple of days, depending on where the other planets are in the zodiac. With planets in late degrees, the voids will be short. With planets all in early degrees, the voids will be long. The almanacs will give a time and have v/c next to that time. This is when the Moon goes void-of-course. When the Moon enters the next sign, it is when it is back to work, so to speak.

Some astrologers use more than the traditional aspects to figure voids, counting parallels, contra-parallels, semi-sextiles, inconjuncts and even semi-squares and sesqui-quadrates. Again, you may experiment, if you like. The most conservative line, which will be reflected in all the almanacs, is to use the traditional aspects.

While the Moon is void, other planets may be aspecting each other. The condition of void-of-course is most properly applied only to the Moon. And as the Moon is the timer in electional astrology, it is the Moon's aspects which count, and only the Moon's in using void-of-course timing.

There are people who count other voids. They use Sun voids and look to the planet which is void in a natal chart and other strange stuff. I have pointed these things out, in a spirit of completism. Yes, this stuff is out there, but if you sit and figure it all out every day, and try to live your life accordingly, you will spend all your time working this stuff out, and have no time left to do your daily tasks. There comes a point (even with astrologers) when enough is enough, and you just have to let it go and cast your fate to the vagaries of whatever comes along. These techniques work with the real world too (oops, another big astrological secret divulged!), but you can also go crazy trying to live according to this stuff. Save it for the important things—job interviews, mailing manuscripts, proposing marriage, closing on a house. McDonald's serves hamburgers most anytime, even when the Moon is void. Don't sweat the small stuff.

Void-of-course Moon: best for subjective, spiritual, nonmaterial concerns, prayer, yoga, play, parties, psychotherapy, sleep, meditation. Decision-making turns out to be nonrealistic. Creativity takes unplanned directions, detours, improvisations. False starts and errors abound. Judgment is more fallible. Routine and habit proceed smoothly, but may need adjustment later (when the Moon is no longer void). ESP is more active (though not necessarily more accurate). Voids are good for mind expanding stuff—like getting drunk or high, comedy writing. It is like a mini-weekend every few days or so, when the cosmos kicks back and takes a bit of a rest. If you ask a horary question during a void Moon, it cannot be answered except with, "don't worry, everything will turn out all right," which can drive an anxious client bonkers. But that same "don't worry, be happy" atmosphere is what the thing is all about. If you leave on a trip (some say arrive at your destination), on a void Moon, be prepared to take what happens—plans will be altered, itineraries go out the window, new and strange experiences will manifest. Fun for a vacation, bad for a business trip. Business moves fail to generate profits or meet with unexpected difficulties. Objects bought either never get used or are "not right" in some way, or you don't find what you were looking for in the first place. Delay and frustration run higher than normal. Neurotic tendencies and bad habits are more open to change. Historic events have wild unpredictable impact on evolution—or no impact at all. If you have to work on a void Moon, stick to routine and don't try strange new stuff. Don't sign contracts or make deals on a void Moon, they will either have to be changed later, or will turn out to be null and void (no pun intended—this may be where the term originated).

Generally, if you want a working to have a tangible effect, do not start it when the Moon is void. If you want meditation, or mind expansion, or a bit of play/rest/relaxation, then the void Moon is the time for you. Be careful, you have more of a tendency to get "lost in the stars" during a void Moon. Things are not as grounded and centered. Space cadets are more spacey, and the old solid fuddy-duddies have even been known to unbend and let their hair down. If your working is a celebration or simple Esbat with no tangible end other than pure worship, then a void Moon may work to your advantage. Experiment and use your judgment.

This brings me to an interesting personal observation about void Moons. During the Reagan years I watched his many press conferences. He went on TV often, sometimes two to three times in a month. I would hear he had called a press conference for 8 P.M. I would be in front of the TV at 8, but more often than not, President Reagan would not come on until 8:07 or 8:22. The news anchors would babble on and on about what the President would talk about, or the topic in question, or just babble and wait for him to show up.

Invariably, when there was a delay, President Reagan would be planning on talking about something controversial or unpleasant to his administration. And I would look in my little almanac which I carry in my purse, and sure enough, the Moon had gone void 3 or 4 minutes before he finally would appear. President Reagan was using the Void-of-Course Moon to avoid longterm effects of his "revelations" during those press conferences. He would say the most amazing things, and there would be spirited questions, but after a day or so, nobody remembered or cared about what was (or more often, was not) said at the press conference.

To an astrologer, the conclusion was obvious. OF COURSE President Reagan used astrology. That was his "teflon." He made sure that the unpleasant revelations were made on void Moons, and the whitewash PR-type announcements were made on non-void Moons, usually with a beneficial final aspect. Whether this was an unethical use of astrology probably depends upon your personal feelings about President Reagan. My feelings are that it was not unethical to use astrology in this manner, but to lie about it and cover-up what one is doing, thereby denying the people the full import of what is being done IS manipulative and self-serving. It also points up how insecure the Reagan Administration must have been to go to such lengths to keep the American public from learning fully about certain topics.

The trouble is, that where you can hide what happened, unless the event itself occurred on a void Moon, the truth will eventually come out. It will be interesting to see just how much comes out now that the Republicans no longer control the White House. Even when Nancy Reagan admitted on network TV during the 1988 Republican National Convention that she DID use astrology, it was during a void Moon. It figures.

RETROGRADE MERCURY

Except for the Sun and Moon, every other planet exhibits retrograde motion periodically. This retrograde motion means the planet appears to stop and move backward against the zodiac for a time, then it stops and begins to move forward again. It is symbolized by an R or R_x in an ephemeris and is placed by the planet affected. (See figure 1. Retrograde motion, p. 19.)

Now this does not mean that the planet actually moves backward, it just appears to do so. To explain this you need to understand that while the cosmos appears to move around Earth, it is Earth, itself, which is actually moving. The planets all move around the Sun (and the Moon also moves around the Earth). But as we are on Earth, we perceive it as the planets and Sun and Moon moving around Earth. When planets seem to move backward—retrograde—its like you are in a car, driving down the freeway. You are moving, and so are the other cars, some slower and some faster. If you move up to, and then overtake another car, it seems to be moving backward relative to your motion forward. If another car overtakes you, then you would seem to be moving backward to people in that car. Each of the cars may have a constant speed, but because some are slower and some faster, they seem to be moving forward or backward relative to each other.

Mercury retrogrades the most often, for the shortest period of time, Venus the least often, and Pluto for the longest period of time.

Because Mercury is the planet of communication and everyday occurrences, its retrogrades cause the most problem in the everyday world. Mercury retrogrades about three times a year for about three weeks at a time. It is fun to track the periods of Mercury's retrogrades and see how the world becomes a bit more disorganized and confused. You get bigger traffic jams, more political gaffes, more weird TV and radio transmission problems. Really. But then I have a perverse sense of fun. When any planet is retrograde, its energies are turned inward. People experience the matters of that planet subjectively, and from within, rather than objectively and from without. This applies to all the planets which do go retrograde, both as transits in the sky and as they are in a natal chart.

Mercury Retrograde: is a period of communication upsets. Communication—in all forms—is more often delayed, garbled, misunderstood, misdirected, lost in the ether, blown out of proportion, ignored, minimized, and generally screwed up. Travel is delayed, re-routed, over-booked, detoured, cancelled and generally screwed up. Items bought (especially appliances) are either defective, don't perform as promised, or are not right, for one reason or another. You should not sign contracts—they will have to be altered or will not be honored. You can stall and put off and miss deadlines, because if you do deliver, the work will have to be revised or may be rejected anyway. Retrograde Mercury is good for cleaning up old stuff, from cleaning closets and desks to finishing matters which have been left hanging, to cleaning out your life. It is a time of reflection, introspection, looking back, working out old business, looking up old friends you haven't seen in ages, getting to those "rainy day" projects you have been putting off, dwelling on the past, nursing old grudges, nostalgia, re-living the "good old days," finishing old abandoned projects, getting a second chance. It is also good for dealing with "other worldly" matters. Retrograde Mercury times can resurrect dead issues and put a new light on them. Everyday, routine occurrences can be seen in a new light. It is a bad time for starting new ventures; they will either never come to fruition, have to be re-started after much work, or never be effective. Best to keep things light, do not act anymore than you have to. Reaction is ok. Judgment is faulty. Partying is good. If you want tangible results from a working, wait until Mercury turns direct. If you are doing a follow-up working, it's a good time. Regression would be interesting, and results would probably be easier. Any psychic activity linked with looking into the past would be helped—psychometry, psychic archaeology. And general historical research would also be favorable. Doing stuff over again is good for retrograde Mercury, especially stuff that may not have turned out right the first time (like re-taking tests, or re-painting the bedroom, or re-banishing that troublesome spirit in your house who likes to hide your keys all the time).

If a lot of this sounds like Void-of-course Moon, it is because the two times have similar effects. Retrograde Mercury is like cosmic clean-up time, and Void-of-course Moon is like cosmic relaxation time. Both are subjective and introspective, reactive, and deal with other-worldly matters. Both are a break from routine and a time to kick back and do different and interesting things. Both are not good times to start stuff, take actions which are intended to have a lasting effect, make purchases or decisions, or initiate action.

MOON IN THE SIGNS

Each month the Moon moves through all twelve signs. It spends about two and one-half days in each sign, more or less depending upon how fast the Moon is moving. The Moon's daily motion varies from about 11 to 15 degrees. So it can be in a sign as long as three days and as short as two days. As the Moon moves through each sign, it becomes colored by the influence of each sign. It so happens that certain signs are good for some things and not good for others. This is a very old application of astrology. Some things will apply to two or more signs, or to two signs in different ways. The more specific a thing, the more narrow the focus in that sign. Again, these lists are not written in stone, nor are they exhaustive, by any means. They are meant to give you an idea of the issues and topics which pertain to each sign. Then if you need something which is not listed, you might be able to figure out the astrological correspondence by finding similarities. Try it. Go ahead. That's how you learn.

Moon in Aries: Beginnings, starting new ventures, pioneering, war, conflict, energy, ego, self, stuff for me and mine, weapons, guns, knives, sharp things, things which cut, surgery, razzle-dazzle, impatience, sarcasm, quick results, making trouble, rescuing people in trouble, heroism, naivete, restlessness, me-first attitude, courage, sticking up for yourself.

With Aries Moon you succeed by using your own initiative, taking the initiative. Doing it "my way." Be wary of impatience, overconfidence, egotism.

Moon in Taurus: Anything to do with money, possessions, values, sensualism, dance, music, silence, Gaia, Earth Mother stuff, planting food crops, fertility and earth matters, wealth, security, greed, careful and conservative things, soothing, solid, an immovable object, cuddling, discovering/explaining what you need in sex, unshockable, reliable, hard work, slow and steady progress, Mother, jewelry as wealth and possessions, values and ethics.

With Taurus Moon you succeed by being patient, being mellow, being an immovable object. You can build something solid and lasting. Be wary of blind stubbornness, bull-in-the-china-shop rages.

Moon in Gemini: Things of a dual nature, buying and selling, words, writing, communications, cars, telephones, transportation, jack-of-all-trades—master of none, dual results, sleight-of-hand, thievery, basic education, low mysteries, teaching, storytelling, networking, short trips, field trips, siblings, relatives in general, neighborhood and neighbors, rote learning, play it light, reading, radio, never stop learning, movement, trivia, flexible values, gossip and innuendo, mimicry, imitation, computers.

With Gemini Moon you succeed by networking, talking to lots of people, being objective. You can do two things at once. It can signify something which needs to be corrected. Be wary of vacillation, spreading yourself too thin. You can try to do several unrelated things in one ritual.

Moon in Cancer: Anything to do with home, food, security, real estate, psychic stuff, divination, myths and archetypes, mother, Mother, nurturer, looking into the past, traditions, the family in general, cooking and eating, planting, fishing, home and hearth, altar consecration, restaurants, good for listening to others, helping others with problems, sentiment, keeping secrets, doing things at home or for the home, roots, integrity, graves, underground places, inherited traits, weather and climate, the altar as a base for workings, gentle self-effacing humor, psychic, land and real estate,

With Cancer Moon you succeed by appealing to sentiment, emotions, mom and apple pie. Recall the past and childhood. You should feel more secure in your home base. Be wary of over-emotionalism, wallowing in old hurts and slights. This is the strongest Moon. You have the right to be there, to do the thing.

Moon in Leo: Creativity and self-expression, play, fine arts, children, for naming a child, theater, being a host/ess, parties, celebrations, love and romance, hobbies, games, lovers, gambling and speculation, showing off, warm-hearted, pride, cheering up, loyalty from others both giving and getting, chivalry, clowning around, amusements, doing it with style, risk taking, investing and investments, stocks and bonds.

With Leo Moon, you succeed by exaggeration, delegation of authority. You can gain authority from another. If you fail, it is because you overstepped your authority. Be wary of becoming dictatorial. You can be child-like, but beware of being childish.

Moon in Virgo: Health and sickness and wellness, food and nutrition, herbs, vitamins, plastic arts and crafts, how weather affects health, armed forces, Maiden, pottery, craftspersons, hunting, tools, pets, small animals, familiars, ecology, recycling, clothes, work, workplace, co-workers, planting herbs, computers, cleaning, cleansing, exercise and fitness, healing, detail work, critical and nitpicky people, work ethic, guilt, need to help others, obligations, inventiveness, community needs, magick, evocation, coven workings, low magick.

With Virgo Moon you succeed by doing it all yourself, being nit-picky. Pay close attention to details and the big stuff will work itself out. Use the bureaucratic hierarchy. Expect and demand perfection. Watch out for criticism and being a martyr. Doing a task for someone else can be effective.

Moon in Libra: Marriage and partnerships, planting ornamental plants, war and / or peace, diplomacy, negotiation, jewelry and ornamentation, justice, balance, beauty and harmony, debate and discussion, politeness, etiquette and manners, open enemies, socializing and socialization, meeting people, get social, laziness, mooching, tyranny of the weak, romanticism, yes person, use people nicely, get pretty, mentors, contracts, legal matters, the other guy, workings with two people, or your significant other.

With Libra Moon you should work with a partner to get success. Defer to the other guy, explore both sides of issues. Good manners will help you go far. Be wary of identifying too closely with the other guy.

Moon in Scorpio: Death and dying, sex, psychic talents, merging with another, emotional truths, hidden talents, taxes, insurance, ritual magick, taboos, surgery, transformative experiences, rebirth, obsession, intensity, research, solitude, solo workings, workings with two people, noble motivations, sneaky tactics, extremes, mastery of the self, willpower, courage, keeping secrets, dealing with crises, paranoia, bluntness, the occult in general, black magick, magick, secret societies, accepting yourself—warts and all, integrity, soul mates, dirty jokes, initiations, uncovering secrets.

With Scorpio Moon you succeed by being sneaky and underhanded, getting an inside lead, "knowing someone," keeping secrets. Be wary of things which are not on the up-and-up. Be intense and use your willpower. Tell it like it is.

Moon in Sagittarius: Religion and philosophy, law and judges, ethics and principles, parties and fun, long journeys, dreams and dreamwork, high mysteries, ceremonial magick, higher learning and teaching, sports, good deeds, goodwill, fame, generosity, go to court, wild abandon possible, eternal optimism, resilience, rationalization, future-oriented, movement, funny stuff, mind expansion, gurus, spiritual occurrences, ability to perceive right and wrong, faith, television, import/export, languages, legal matters, pratfall humor, divination, churches, publishers and publishing.

With Sagittarius Moon you succeed by being an expert, or going to an expert. You can do two things at once. Be wary of faux pas, your big mouth. If you do it big, you add to your chances of succeeding. Don't be naive or Pollyannaish. This is the Big Ritual moon.

Moon in Capricorn: Profession, honors and recognition, inherited traits, responsibility, public eye, promotion, hermit, solitude, social standing, degrees and advancement, Father, the boss, establishment, mountains, rocks and stones, hard work, social climbing, no-nonsense, depressive, time and clocks, ruthlessness, use people not nicely, the ends justify the means, things you want worse than anyone else, conscience, profound, wisdom, Crone, paranoid, dry wry humor, long term results, respect.

With Capricorn Moon you succeed by delegating authority, using authority (yours and others'). Use "insider trading," use fewer than normal channels (go over people's heads). "Knowing someone" can be an asset. Be careful you do not get too power mad, be manipulative, or step on too many toes. This is the ruthless Moon. Being "on time" helps.

Moon in Aquarius: Friends and peers, surprises, luck, circumstances beyond your control, groups and clubs, the future, politics and causes, social awareness, astrology, anarchy, advice and advisors, social upheaval, bettering the human condition, legislative bodies, electricity, energy and energy work, meet new people, workings with a coven, covens, honesty, nonemotional and objective, trustworthiness, fair, reasonable, straightforward, gadgets, computers, television, aspirations, freedom, bigotry, genius, idealism, peer group pressure, ideals.

With Aquarius Moon you succeed by working for the common good—not just your self-interest. Try off-the-wall approaches, be really weird and radical. Don't get anarchistic or destructive just to create change. Don't go so off-the-wall that you lose sight of your original purpose. Write down those wacky ideas which come from out-of-the-blue. They may not be so wacky, after all.

Moon in Pisces: Karma and reincarnation, secret enemies, escapism, banality, psychic healing, fishing, planting, solitude, magick, possession, spies, secret societies, secrets, hidden or lost things, merging with God/dess, alcohol, the past, the still small voice, dance, invocation, large institutions, oils and perfumes, poison, drugs, potions and elixirs, prison and confinement, spirituality, charity, humanitarian concerns, large animals, insanity, faith, music, keeping secrets, deep very psychic stuff, vulnerability, facing fears and conquering them, facing the past and overcoming it, divine madness, endings, aloneness, high magick.

With Pisces Moon you succeed by making "them" feel sorry for you. You can do two things at once. Use magick. Ply them with alcohol. Be wary of swindlers, get-rich-quick schemes. If it seems to good to be true, it probably is. Don't lose yourself in the cosmos, try to retain some grounding. Let the Love of the Universe fill your being.

PLANETARY HOURS

Planetary Hours is an old system developed by the Chaldeans, those original astrologers. They have little astrological basis which can be codified and defined. They do not necessarily correspond to the modern astrological logic. But they work and have worked over the millennia. They are, in some ways, the most easily accessible astrological timing method. But with standard time zones and people living in all sorts of places on the globe, they are not as easy to figure as they once were. They use planetary correspondences for things, actions, moods, etc., and a person can tailor actions to match the prevailing mood of the hour, or wait for a propitious hour to do something, and increase the chances for success. It does not correspond at all to the planets in the sky or Void Moon or any of the rest of this stuff. But when used in combination with these other techniques, the chances for success are increased.

This is a Kabbalistic method for determining good and bad times for things. The day is divided into two parts, starting with sunrise and sunset. So the two parts are day and night. Each part is then divided into twelfths. So the day has twenty-four divisions. The twelfths of the day parts are all equal, and the twelfths of the night parts are all equal, but the day and night parts are not equal, except at the equinoxes. Further, as the times of sunrise and sunset vary with the seasons, as well as the length of day and night, there is no standard from day-to-day of planetary hours. However, the planetary hours do not vary much from year to year, so the planetary hours for Samhain 1993 will be the same as Samhain 1991, or 1891 for the same place. As sunrise and sunset also vary from place to place depending on how far from the equator you are, again the planetary hours will be different for Samhain in Chicago and Samhain in New Orleans. It is a day-of-the-year and distance-from-the-equator oriented system.

If all that is too strange and difficult to understand, I have created a sample of a planetary hours table to help you learn how to use them. (See Table 3 on p. 90.) All you need to know is your latitude (how far north or south you are from the equator) and the local mean time variation (ask your local astrologer).

The influence of the hours are determined by a specific plan. There is a planetary order—Saturn (♄), Jupiter (♃), Mars (♂), Sun (☉), Venus (♀), Mercury (☿), Moon (☽)—(in descending order of the length of time it takes to go through the zodiac). The hours start at dawn, and the first hour after dawn is ruled by the planet of the day.

Sunday = Sun;

Monday = Moon;

Tuesday = Mars;

Wednesday = Mercury;

Thursday = Jupiter;

Friday = Venus;

Saturday = Saturn.

No matter which day of the week you start with, if you start with the planet of the day and keep to the order, you will end up with the hours in order and the first hour of each day corresponding to the planet of the day. It's kabbalistic magick.

You can calculate the planetary hours yourself, if you have access to sunrise and sunset times for your locality. Llewellyn publishes planetary hour tables in their *Moon Sign Book,* and planetary hours tables are available from various publishers. One thing to remember: the planetary hours tables are published for local mean time, which can vary up to 35 minutes in some localities from clock time. And then you have to correct for daylight saving time also,

Table 3. Planetary Hours Table for Nov. 1–7 or May 1–7.

November 1–7 in any year North Latitude

Sunrise to Sunset—Local Mean Time

Lat 27	Lat 31	Lat 35	Lat 39	Su	M	Tu	W	Th	F	Sa	Lat 43	Lat 47	Lat 51
06:10	06:14	06:20	06:27	☉	☽	♂	☿	♃	♀	♄	06:34	06:42	06:51
07:06	07:09	07:14	07:20	♀	♄	☉	☽	♂	☿	♃	07:26	07:32	07:40
08:01	08:04	08:08	08:13	☿	♃	♀	♄	☉	☽	♂	08:17	08:23	08:28
08:57	08:59	09:02	09:05	☽	♂	☿	♃	♀	♄	☉	09:09	09:13	09:17
09:53	09:54	09:56	09:58	♄	☉	☽	♂	☿	♃	♀	10:00	10:03	10:06
10:48	10:49	10:50	10:51	♃	♀	♄	☉	☽	♂	☿	10:52	10:53	10:54
11:44	11:44	11:44	11:44	♂	☿	♃	♀	♄	☉	☽	11:44	11:44	11:44
12:40	12:38	12:37	12:36	☉	☽	♂	☿	♃	♀	♄	12:35	12:34	12:32
01:35	01:33	01:31	01:29	♀	♄	☉	☽	♂	☿	♃	01:27	01:24	01:20
02:31	02:28	02:25	02:22	☿	♃	♀	♄	☉	☽	♂	02:18	02:14	02:09
03:27	03:23	03:19	03:15	☽	♂	☿	♃	♀	♄	☉	03:10	03:05	02:58
04:22	04:18	04:13	04:07	♄	☉	☽	♂	☿	♃	♀	04:01	03:55	03:46

Sunset to Sunrise—Local Mean Time

Lat 27	Lat 31	Lat 35	Lat 39	Su	M	Tu	W	Th	F	Sa	Lat 43	Lat 47	Lat 51
05:18	05:13	05:07	05:00	♃	♀	♄	☉	☽	♂	☿	04:53	04:45	04:35
06:22	06:18	06:13	06:07	♂	☿	♃	♀	♄	☉	☽	06:02	05:55	05:47
07:27	07:23	07:19	07:15	☉	☽	♂	☿	♃	♀	♄	07:10	07:05	06:58
08:31	08:29	08:26	08:22	♀	♄	☉	☽	♂	☿	♃	08:19	08:15	08:10
09:35	09:34	09:32	09:29	☿	♃	♀	♄	☉	☽	♂	09:27	09:24	09:21
10:40	10:39	10:38	10:37	☽	♂	☿	♃	♀	♄	☉	10:36	10:34	10:33
11:44	11:44	11:44	11:44	♄	☉	☽	♂	☿	♃	♀	11:44	11:44	11:44
12:48	12:49	12:50	12:51	♃	♀	♄	☉	☽	♂	☿	12:53	12:54	12:56
01:53	01:54	01:56	01:59	♂	☿	♃	♀	♄	☉	☽	02:01	02:04	02:07
02:57	03:00	03:03	03:06	☉	☽	♂	☿	♃	♀	♄	03:10	03:14	03:19
04:01	04:05	04:09	04:13	♀	♄	☉	☽	♂	☿	♃	04:18	04:23	04:30
05:06	05:10	05:15	05:21	☿	♃	♀	♄	☉	☽	♂	05:27	05:33	05:42

May 1–7 in any year South Latitude

if it's in force. Your local astrologer can give you the local mean time correction for your locality, or the local library also has access to that information, though you would have to look under astronomy for this. And your local weather-man will also have access to that information. That's why planetary hours are more advanced than other methods; it's not automatic.

Each day has four hours with the planet of the day and the planet of the hour the same. They are dawn (sunrise), early afternoon, mid-evening, late night before dawn. These are general hours. But if you know these "double whammy hours" are available, you can take advantage of them. Plan-etary hours is a good technique for people who decide to do a working that day, and aren't willing to wait for elaborate planning. Each planet has three or four hours per day, and it should be relatively painless to wait for the hour which corresponds to the planet ruling the desired outcome. Of course, the more timing techniques you can coordinate, the more effective you can be with your workings.

Table 3 is a sample page from a planetary hours table. At the top and bottom is a range of days. These are the days that these times are in effect. Because there is a week (or so) of duration, the times may be off by a minute or so for a certain day. Some people prefer to calculate exactly for every day, but for the average person, these tables should be sufficient. There is also another issue involved; that is, when do you count exact sunrise and sunset? Most meteorological calendars time from first light for sunrise and last light for sunset. This is the actual light of the Sun as it appears/disappears on the horizon. If you've ever actually watched a sunrise/sunset, you know it can take about five minutes for the full sunrise/sunset. That is, it takes about five minutes for the full disk of the sun to appear to contact and then be fully above or below the horizon. When in that time is it exactly sunrise or sunset? Some time from the astrological phenomenon of the Sun being exactly on the Ascendant/Descendant. I have wondered about those times when the Sun is neither fully up or down, those two, five minute periods each day. Could it be those times are different and unique, being neither day nor night? You can time it as you wish, but such precision may end up being more work than it is worth. Allow a minute or two either way (or even five if you like) and you are still using planetary hours in an effective way.

The table has dates at both the top and bottom (there are 48 in all). You have to know whether you are in the northern latitudes or southern latitudes, meaning the northern or southern hemisphere. It is not recorded what you do if you are exactly on the equator. (Maybe an astrologer in Quito, Ecuador, will let the rest of us know what is done there.) You also have to know the local mean time variation for your locality. This can be obtained from an astrologer, an astronomer, a meteorologist, or your local TV weather person. There are ways to calculate it, but I said "no math" so it will be left out. The local mean time variation is the amount of time difference between clock time, and true local time. Standardized time zones have Noon in New York, Miami, Indianapolis, Knoxville, Atlanta, Toronto, Montreal, and every other city in the Eastern Time Zone at precisely the same instant. However, the Sun is not directly overhead (which is True Local Noon) in all of them at that precise instant. Therefore you need to know how much ahead or behind the clock is from that astronomical event. You also need to know if you are on Daylight Savings Time. If you are, subtract an hour from the clock time, in addition to all the other calculations.

To determine the planetary hours for Sunday, in a city at about 43 degrees latitude North, you first find the local mean time variation. For York Beach, Maine, this is +17:34. You add 17 minutes and 34 seconds to the clock time to get true local time. If you were in Easton, Michigan, the local mean time variation is –19:32. You subtract 19 minutes and 32 seconds from clock time to get true local time. Once you have the true local time, you find that time in the table under latitude 43, and read across to see what the planetary hour is. If it is noon, in York Beach the true local time is 12:17:34 P.M. On a Sunday, from November 1 to 7, that is the hour of Mars. In Easton, at Noon the true local time is 11:40:28 A.M., and on a Sunday from November 1 to 7, that is the hour of Jupiter. The time on the clocks is the same, but the true local times (and planetary hours) are different. Generally you round to the nearest minute, since few of us have clocks accurate to the precise second of the international time standard. That is another reason you might allow five minutes leeway in the changes of the planetary hours. If you are at an even latitude, you could split the difference between the times of the odd latitudes, but you could also just round off, and use the five minute leeway.

Let's try another example. You are in Miami, Florida. Miami is at 25 N 46 with a LMT variation of –20:47. So at 10:45 P.M., on the clock, the true local time is 10:24 P.M. (I rounded –20:47 to –21 minutes, and subtracted 21 minutes from 10:45 P.M.). It is Wednesday, November 4th. Looking across, the planetary hour in Miami at 10:24 P.M., true local time is Saturn. The Jupiter hour begins at 10:40 P.M. true local time. We used 27 degrees North, because the tables do not go farther South (or North) than 27 degrees. If you want exact precision, collect sunrise/sunset times for your locality from your local paper every day for a year, and calculate the planetary hours yourself. But that requires math, which is why there is a sample table here.

One caution: with planetary hours, the day of the week doesn't change until sunrise. So 3 A.M. Monday is still considered Sunday night for planetary hours purposes. Look on the Sunday column for the hour, not the Monday column. This is the most common mistake made. But you can be careful, and it isn't all that complicated.

So to summarize, you need to know your approximate latitude North or South, your local mean time variation rounded to the nearest minute, the day of the week, and day of the month, and whether you are on Daylight Savings Time. (If you are, subtract an hour before starting the whole process.) With these things, and the planetary hours tables, you can find the planetary hours for any day and time. It seems cumbersome, but with practice it becomes automatic, and fairly easy.

To use the tables, decide what your desired activity is, and then look under the planetary rulerships and determine which planet governs the activity in question. Then pick a planetary hour governed by that planet to start your activity. Being more specific about desired outcomes in determining the planet in question helps. And remember, that in this system, the day of the week does not change until dawn, about 6 A.M. depending on the time of the year. So 2 A.M. Sunday is still Saturday, kaballastically speaking. Think of the *T.V. Guide* listings, they also operate (roughly) on a planetary hours day, beginning each day at 6 A.M. and listings for programs before 6 A.M. are under the previous day's listings. This is critical, because if you are looking at the wrong day, you are getting the wrong planetary hour ruler and can really screw things up if you need a certain influence, and possibly even sabotage your efforts. I hate to harp on this stuff, but it is important and you want to do it right, or else why bother in the first place?

Dell *Horoscope Magazine* publishes Planetary Hours Tables monthly for various latitudes. It's another reason that *Horoscope* is a good astrological tool.

Sun—Ruler of Leo: Metal—gold; colors—golds, yellows, and oranges; rules Sunday. Rules leaders, persons in authority, vitality, life, men, the God, self-expression, executives, heart, confidence, the will, ambition, individuality, employment, promotion, rulers in general, the center of things, authority, the body as a whole. Attributes are forceful, life-giving, rhythmic, strong, structural, diurnal, active, open, generous, fiery.

Moon—Ruler of Cancer: Metal—silver; colors—pearl, green, and iridescent hues; rules Monday. Rules the public in general, food and drink, water and liquids, domestic affairs, home, family, country, short journeys, Mother, temporary plans, women, emotion, unconscious, the past, mother, Goddess, memory, soul. Attributes are changeable, dissolving, fertilizing, fruitful, periodic, sensitive, visionary, wandering, imaginative, impressionable, instinctive, nocturnal, passive.

Mercury—Ruler of Gemini and Virgo: Metal—mercury (quicksilver); colors—blue and grey; rules Wednesday. Rules communication, writing, words, The Magus, education, neighbors, relatives, merchants, businesspeople, messengers, mind, mentality, magick, books, travel, thieves, manual dexterity, consciousness, speech, coordinating, dualities, radio and television, lying, nervous, reasoning, low magick, lower mysteries. Attributes are wit, worrisome, dual, impulsive, quick, irrational, intelligent, nervous, rational, reasoning, restless, moving.

Venus—Ruler of Taurus and Libra: Metal—copper; colors—bright blue and pastels; rules Friday. Rules love and romance, art, music, social matters, marriage, beauty, jewelry and ornament, refinement, sensuality, women, peace, maiden, compromise, negotiation, indolence, pleasure, creature comforts. Attributes are lazy, indulgent, amorous, artistic, cheerful, dissolute, erotic, fertile, graceful, immoral, musical, relaxing, soothing, soft.

Mars—Ruler of Aries and Scorpio: Metal—iron and steel; colors—red, dark red, and magenta; rules Tuesday. Rules physical exertion, ego, self-assertion, energy, action, sex, men, war, conflict, anger, weapons, soldiers, courage, danger and excitement, pain, burning, poisons, wounds, violence, police. Attributes are amorous, aphrodisiac, burning, combative, cruel, dangerous, exciting, explosive, fearless, forceful, rough, sharp, violent, wounding.

Jupiter—Ruler of Sagittarius and Pisces: Metal—tin; colors— purple and indigo; rules Thursday. Rules, law, judges, physicians, religion, philosophy, expansion, philanthropy, gain and increase, ritual, gurus, freedom, fun and laughter, joy, confidence, optimism, generosity, sports, higher education, high magick, higher mysteries, favors, buying, lending, start of new undertakings, mercy, dharma. Attributes are pompous, jovial, happy, benevolent, buoyant, confident, corpulent, enriching, generous, just, optimistic, reverent, naive, abundant.

Saturn—Ruler of Capricorn and Aquarius: Metal—lead; colors—brown, dark green, dark blue and black; rules Saturday. Rules limitations, time and clocks, the reaper, severity, contraction, business, father, karma, hermits, Crone, Father, control, mountains, pessimism, melancholy, things which require patience and endurance, longterm gains and goals, masons, decrease, spirituality, the teacher, rocks and stones, duty and responsibility, work. Attributes are controlling, limiting, pessimistic, abortive, barren, enduring, frugal, paralyzing, selfish, serious, skeptical, tactful, punctual, ascetic.

These are the planets traditionally used with planetary hours. The meanings are the same for other uses, like aspects and such. As I am listing the meanings and rulerships for planets here, I will also add the last three "modern" planets, to keep them all in one area. (The colors representing the modern planets are not generally agreed upon, so they are not included here.)

Uranus—Ruler of Aquarius: Metal—Uranium and rainbow-hued metals; rules electricity, metaphysics, occultism, revolution, upheaval, divine inspiration, television, genius, mental insanity, the unusual, the future, astrology, freedom, democracy, chaos. Attributes are original, erratic, unusual, eccentric, irreverent, abortive, chaotic, independent, nonconformist, anarchistic.

Neptune—Ruler of Pisces: Metal—Neptunium and the Noble Gases. Rules fog, illusion, deception, emotional insanity, visions and voices, magick, psychism, spirits, merging with God/dess, spiritualism, martyrdom, empathy, earthquakes, oils, poisons, perfumes, secrets, addiction, alcohol and drugs, oceans, idealism, saints, con-men, large institutions, dreams and imagination. Attributes are subtle, abstract, psychic, magical and magickal, musical, impressionable, willing to see only the good, imprisoned, confined, unfortunate, hospitalized, handicapped, spiritual, idealistic, charismatic, sensitive.

Pluto—Ruler of Scorpio: Metal—Plutonium and Radioactive elements. Rules volcanism and plate tectonics, resurrection, death and rebirth, obsession, archetypes, research, upheavals and radical transformative changes, rape, metamorphosis, mobs and riots, the Mafia, chaos, alchemy, ESP, black magick, force and willpower, phoenix, depths and heights, sex, merging with a partner. Attributes are violent, regenerative, reincarnating, chaotic, forceful, excessively violent, reforming, rebuilding, redeeming, initiatory, stripping down to basics, explosive, subtle, deep, unknowable, demanding to know, nuclear, dictatorial, Svengali-like, intimidating.

There are ways you can use the modern planets—Uranus, Neptune, and Pluto—with planetary hours. There are several techniques. Experiment and see which works best for you.

1) Uranus is the higher octave of Mercury; Neptune is the higher octave of Venus; Pluto is the higher octave of Mars. Higher octave means it is like a more powerful souped-up version of the classical planet. They do have issues in common. For each of the modern planets, use the hours of its lower octave, keeping in mind you are trying for the influence of the modern planet. For Uranus use Mercury. For Neptune use Venus. For Pluto use Mars.

2) When the modern planets were discovered, they were assigned rulerships of certain signs, which already had classical rulers. When one planet rules two signs, it is said to have a "day house" and a "night house," meaning in a day chart that the day rulership is more powerful; and in a night chart, the night rulership is more powerful. Uranus took over the rulership of Saturn's day house, Aquarius. Neptune took over the rulership of Jupiter's night house, Pisces. Pluto took over the rulership of Mars' night house, Scorpio. So for planetary hours, use Saturn's day hours for Uranus; use Jupiter's night hours for Neptune; use Mars' night hours for Pluto.

3) When the modern planets were discovered, they were given rulership over the second sign belonging to three of the classical planets. So use the second (and fourth if four in a day) hours of those planets for the modern planets. For Uranus use the second and fourth Saturn hours. For Neptune use the second and fourth Jupiter hours. For Pluto use the second and fourth Mars hours.

Personally, I prefer the first technique. Use your own choice. Have fun trying to see which works best for you.

Where you start in a day and how you figure planetary hours is a subject with many and varied answers. The traditional method has been outlined above. There are other methods. There are proponents of each of the various methods, and each seems to work. The key is consistency. Pick a method and stick with it. Don't shop methods depending on what hour you need—for they will vary from system to system. If you want to experiment with another system for a while, then by all means, do so. But if you need a certain planetary hour to enhance a working and your usual system isn't cooperating, but another will provide the rulership needed, don't do it. That's cheating. The God/dess will know.

All systems of determining planetary hours use the same order of planets: Saturn, Jupiter, Mars, Sun, Venus,

Mercury, Moon. All that differs is the starting point and/or the length and calculation of the hours.

Alternate Methods for Determining Planetary Hours

1) Start at 6 A.M. (average sunrise) and have 24 equal hours to the next day starting at 6 A.M. Just use the clock. Each hour starts a new planetary hour and rulership. There is no figuring needed. You can adjust for Daylight Savings Time or not, as you choose.

2) Start at midnight, use 24 equal hours to the next day at midnight. This is another technique which requires no figuring. It is a concession to the civil day which is figured from midnight to midnight.

3) Start at noon and use 24 equal hours to the next day at noon. Still no figuring. High noon is considered to be the strongest part of the day.

4) Start at LOCAL midnight, and use 24 equal hours. This requires an adjustment for local mean time, and you have to pay attention to daylight saving. Only one calculation is needed, then you have it for your location forever (and you still have to allow for daylight saving time if applicable).

5) Start at LOCAL noon and use 24 equal hours. Same local mean time adjustment needed and attention to daylight saving time.

These various techniques all have various justifications. The ancients could easily tell local noon (which was just NOON until we imposed time zones on our world) by seeing when the shadow cast by the Sun was shortest. Midnight was another matter. The middle of the night is a measurement which must be calculated, or conversely, you must know what degree the Sun is in, what the degree opposite that is, and where that degree is in the ecliptic and then observe when that degree is on the midheaven. Whew, that's a lot of work. Sunrise/sunset are easily discernible.

Nowadays, many of us are urban magicians or urban shamans. We live in cities of asphalt, concrete, steel, and glass. All manmade terraformed things. We are divorced from nature and natural cycles except for the most obvious. Even our yards are cultivated; city ordinances mandate how we must keep our yards and gardens, what trees we may plant and so on. Zoning laws regulate land use. We are divorced from nature. Yet the craft is a nature-oriented religion. How do we reconcile living in cities and worshipping nature? We can go wholly technological—and use a time-zone midnight 24 equal hour planetary hours tables, or we can be as honoring of nature as we can—using the old local sunrise/sunset method with two sets of 12 equal hours, figured for each day and our special location. It's up to you.

THE MOON IN HOUSES

The next way to help with planning when to do workings, is to coordinate with the transiting Moon going through the appropriate house in your personal astrological chart. This naturally requires that you have a copy of your chart, and can understand which houses are which, and make approximate calculations when the Moon will be in which house. As a rule of thumb, the Moon moves about one degree every two hours. If you can look in your almanac and see when the Moon aspects a planet, you know what degree it is from the planet it is aspecting (if it is trine Mercury at 14° Leo, then the Moon is at 14° Aries or 14° Sagittarius). Then add or subtract hours to get the approximate degree. Allow for some leeway here, as this is not exact if the Moon is especially fast or slow. If you can calculate more precisely, all the better. Then find which house governs the desired end, and wait until the days of the month when the Moon is transiting that house. If you can also coordinate the sign the Moon is in, all the better. At least try to have something which pertains to the sign, as it adds more factors.

Because this book is written for non-astrologers, signs and houses will be used more or less interchangeably. They are not really the same, but there are many correspondences, and the two are close enough that this method will work well enough for the level of complexity and accuracy in this work.

Reading the Moon in Houses

1st House—read Moon in Aries;

2nd House—read Moon in Taurus;

3rd House—read Moon in Gemini;

4th House—read Moon in Cancer;

5th House—read Moon in Leo;

6th House—read Moon in Virgo;

7th House—read Moon in Libra;

8th House—read Moon in Scorpio;

9th House—read Moon in Sagittarius;

10th House—read Moon in Capricorn;

11th House—read Moon in Aquarius;

12th House—read Moon in Pisces.

SECRET TIMING TOOLS

You can plan workings when things are "in your favor" cosmically, so to speak. If you have your chart, you know what signs your Sun, Moon and ascendant are in. When the transiting Moon is moving through the same sign as your

Sun, Moon, or ascendant, things tend to go more your way. You are getting a dose of extra energy by having the Moon's extra transiting energy added to that of your own Sun, Moon, or ascendant. If the Moon is moving through the sign opposite your Sun, Moon, or ascendant, it is time to defer to the other guy. You are not as effective and the energy is with the other guy for those days. You have very low sales resistance. So don't plan something which requires that you be assertive and have lots of energy during those days. If your Sun, Moon, or ascendant are in opposite signs in your natal chart, then you will have energy and non-energy times simultaneously. But that also means you are constantly dealing with self vs. other issues in your life, so hopefully you will have developed a coping mechanism by now. If you haven't, this simple method won't be any more than a bandaid anyhow.

Using the Moon in the same sign which is on the cusp of the house which rules a thing you are working with, or a goal you are striving for, is another helpful secret timing tool. Like using the Moon in the sign on your 4th house cusp when looking for a place to live, or the Moon in the sign on the cusp of your 6th house (job and work), or 10th house (career), when job hunting, or when the Moon is in the sign on your 5th house cusp when doing workings for romance and love. This adds a fourth timing element to both fine-tune and also offer more opportunities for enhancing effectiveness.

These Moon sign correspondences are apart from those of your Sun, Moon, or ascendant. You are getting more detailed in your fine-tuning, by zoning in on the end desired. You can also get more possible days for action by using house correspondences. If you are looking to get a loan, and the Moon is in the sign of your ascendant on a weekend (when most banks are not open), it will be in the sign on your 2nd house for the next couple of days, which will be weekdays. And as the 2nd house rules money, you are then able to use this Moon timing for the loan. With the

Sun, Moon, and ascendant signs, you are generally more effective, it works for most everything you do. With the signs on the specific house cusps, you are empowered in the areas ruled by that specific house only. It adds another way of getting at a desired end.

Aries is opposite Libra;

Taurus is opposite Scorpio;

Gemini is opposite Sagittarius;

Cancer is opposite Capricorn;

Leo is opposite Aquarius;

Virgo is opposite Pisces;

and vice versa.

Yet another tidbit thrown in to enjoy. This also works in the real world, and is uncannily effective. Almost down to the minute, you can see people responding to you well or not so well as the Moon's energy is in your favor or not. It's these little things which really prove the validity of astrology, scientists and statistical analysis notwithstanding.

LAST ASPECT AND NEXT ASPECT

As the Moon traverses each sign, it partakes of the "flavor" of each sign. But added to this is the influence of the aspects it makes to the various planets in the sky—transiting aspects. As the Moon moves through each sign, it also aspects planets and points in your personal chart—or anyone's chart—which adds a personal dimension to the transiting aspects, and, some say, accounts for the day-to-day occurrences of life. These last aspects and next aspects can apply to your natal chart, but to figure when the transiting Moon exactly aspects things in your natal chart requires math that's beyond the minimal basics used here. You can more easily see when the other planets are aspecting things in your natal chart because they move more slowly. Again, use the applying aspects only, don't miss the bus.

LAST ASPECT

The last aspect is just that, the last aspect the Moon makes before going void-of-course. Traditional astrology only counts the conjunction, sextile, square, trine, and opposition, as the aspects to be used. Some add the parallel and contra-parallel. I have found the semi-sextile and inconjunct to also be valid. Some also use the semi-square and sesqui-quadrate. To be safest, start with the traditional aspects only and branch out later as you experiment. The *Celestial Guide* and *Astrologers Daily Guide* only list traditional aspects. Dell *Horoscope* shows all aspects, but lists voids from the traditional aspects.

The last aspect colors the Moon's influence as it transits that sign. If the last aspect is easy, (sextile or trine), it is a pleasant feeling. If the last aspect is difficult (square or opposition), it can be more active and tense. With the conjunction there is a union of different energies, how easy or difficult depends upon the planet involved.

If you want a happy ending, plan your working with a trine as last aspect; a separation, use the opposition; to stir things up and incite to action, use the square; create opportunities or enhance communication, sextile; bring things or people together, conjunction. Using the nature of the aspect alone, irregardless of the planet involved, is most basic. The closer you time your working's start to the exactitude of the last aspect, the sooner the results will manifest. If you want to have a longer term effect or take a longer time to manifest, start with the last aspect farther off. Any intervening aspects will show the bumps in the road to the final end. Difficult aspects with an easy aspect last shows there may be a tough time getting going, but it will turn out well in the end. Easy aspects with a difficult last aspect means things will go well, but fall apart in the end.

You can coordinate the last aspect with the planet in question ruling the thing you are after. Then wait until the final aspect is favorable with the planet you need and time from there. This may be more difficult than it at first seems, especially if you are using a slower planet with still slower planets in later degrees. You could wait, literally, years.

NEXT ASPECT

All this leads to the "next aspect" method of timing. It is used for more finely-tuning results. You choose the aspect and planet you want as the influence and coordinate it with the last aspect of the Moon (so you don't sabotage your efforts). You then time your start to that next aspect. The working partakes of the influence of that next aspect of the Moon and also the last aspect of the Moon. It also has the influence of any other intervening aspects, but you are planning on that last aspect as cementing the working and stamping its influence on the whole. With next aspect timing, you must coordinate with the planet ruling the matter at hand. The planet aspected by the Moon at the last aspect is not crucial, but if you can use a planet which has a relevance to the matter, the more effective you can be.

This helps alleviate the problem of having to wait years (or weeks, or whatever) for the correct planet to be involved in the proper final aspect with the Moon. You just pick the planet and aspect, and then make sure the final aspect is also compatible with the desired outcome.

The Moon makes each aspect to each planet every month, mostly. Mercury and Venus move faster than the Sun, so you may have to wait longer for a particular Mercury or Venus aspect. Generally, the most you should have to wait for a particular aspect is a month to six weeks. But you also have to get an appropriate final aspect. With the sextile, square, and trine, you get two to each planet, so it becomes easier. With the conjunction and opposition, there is only one per revolution, so the timing can be more difficult. Again, if the thing is important, it is worth waiting for. If waiting a month to six weeks in a non-emergency situation is excessive for you, then it probably wasn't that important in the first place. I prefer to have a several month window to work with in determining timings. The wider the window, the easier it is to get an ideal (or near ideal) time for a working. If you have a whole year to work with, it becomes easier. A decade can be even better. You get the idea.

With the "next aspect" method, you use the planet of the thing you are after, the aspect of how you want it, and try to match a compatible Moon sign and a favorable final aspect, and then plan your working accordingly. You may have to wait for a planet to change signs, or go direct (not retrograde) or a month or two to get a favorable aspect with a good final aspect from the Moon. How many factors you can coordinate is dependent upon your patience, and how badly you want the influences to assist. Having the next aspect and final aspect coordinated are more important than having a favorable Moon sign. The Moon sign (and/or house) being compatible are "the icing on the cake" as the electional astrologers say.

ASPECTS

Here are the effects of the aspects and influences of the planets.

☌ (||) *Conjunction (and Parallel):* Blending, uniting, brings together, binding, forced union, beginnings, focus, intensity, unity, working together toward a common goal, most intense aspect.

✳ *Sextile*: Opportunity, productivity, brings together and provides opportunity for cooperation and harmony (though does not guarantee), aspect of creativity, communication, a people aspect, working on complementary projects.

□ *Square*: Friction, competition, obstacles which can be overcome with effort, stirs things up, gets things going, incites to action, challenge, stubbornness, neither side wants to compromise, working at cross-purposes.

△ *Trine*: Harmony, benevolence, ease of accomplishment, takes stuff for granted, can be lazy, indulgent, easy results, gifts, inherent talents, working in harmony.

☍ (∦) *Opposition (and Contra-Parallel)*: Awareness, polarization, separation, one or the other, or good for cutting away, separation, getting rid of, for confronting "the other"—partners, open enemies, rivals—can be revealing, may not be pleasant but can bring an end to things, fulfillment or failure, illumination, working in opposite directions.

Other Aspects

⊥ or ⊼ *Inconjunct (also called Quincunx)*: Adjustment, accommodation, inconvenient benefic, brings results but may be more trouble than it's worth, may make more work than you're willing to do, compromise required, each must be willing to bend.

⊻ *Semi-Sextile*: Mildly fortunate, natural progression, brings results but may not be what you expected, brings things out into the open for good or ill, growth.

∠ ⊡ *Semi-Square and Sesquiquadrate*: Friction, mental stirring up, arguments, agitation, may bring inspiration or visions but not necessarily comfortable or welcome, incitement to action, creativity, emotional zeal accompanies effects, not as strong as the square.

RULERSHIPS

This brings us to rulerships. This is another fine-tuning technique you can coordinate with the next and last aspect methods. All planets are more effective in certain signs and less effective in others. There are also a few key phrases which correspond to rulership, etc., in general. They can be helpful, if they apply to your situation.

Planets in their rulership have the right; the right to be there, the right to take action, etc. They are operating most strongly and purely, for good or ill.

Planets in their exaltation rise to a higher position. They are in a sign which greatly enhances their energies, and can operate most effectively.

Planets in their detriment are doing what they shouldn't be doing, or going where they aren't wanted, or shouldn't be. They are in the sign opposite their rulership and their energies are most inhibited.

Planets in their fall are in the sign opposite their exaltation, and have something to apologize for. They are in a sign which puts up more blocks and obstacles than normal. They are at their weakest, their most disadvantaged.

These are general statements. You may need to use a Capricorn Moon for a certain effect. Ok, use it, but know that the Moon is not happy in this sign and will not be as effective as if it were in Taurus (for example). If a planet is in a sign which is not its rulership, exaltation, detriment, or fall, it is not noneffective, it is just neutral—neither helped by sign, nor hindered. Some astrologers assign different signs of detriment or fall to the outer planets. Use those, if they make you happier. These are the most commonly accepted assignments. The rulerships are pretty well agreed

Table 4. Rulership, Detriment, Exaltation, Fall.*

Planet	Rulership +	Detriment –	Exaltation +	Fall –
Sun ☉	Leo	Aquarius	Aries	Libra
Moon ☽	Cancer	Capricorn	Taurus	Scorpio
Mercury ☿	Gemini Virgo	Sagittarius Pisces	Aquarius (Virgo)	Leo (Pisces)
Venus ♀	Taurus Libra	Scorpio Aries	Pisces	Virgo
Mars ♂	Aries (Scorpio)	Libra (Taurus)	Capricorn	Cancer
Jupiter ♃	Sagittarius (Pisces)	Gemini (Virgo)	Cancer	Capricorn
Saturn ♄	Capricorn (Aquarius)	Cancer (Leo)	Libra	Aries
Uranus ♅	Aquarius	Leo	Scorpio	Taurus
Neptune ♆	Pisces	Virgo	Cancer	Capricorn
Pluto ♇	Scorpio	Taurus	Aquarius	Leo

*Signs in parentheses are the "old rulerships" in effect before the discovery of the outer planets. They still work, especially in horary and electional astrology.

upon. Occasionally you find a book written in the 30s which assigns Pluto's rulership to Aries, but that's old hat. See Table 4 on page 109.

Again, if you can coordinate a planet in rulership or exaltation to aid its influence, all the better. Try to avoid the detriment or fall, unless you want that planet (and what it symbolizes) operating at a disadvantage. More fine-tuning, and crazy-making. At the end, remember the KISS rule (Keep It Simple, Stupid!). And plan to be at the stop early enough so you don't miss the bus!

Mutual Reception

Mutual reception is another concept used in horary and electional astrology. It can provide another means of getting at certain energies in a chart. Mutual reception happens when two planets are in each others' signs of rulership—like Mars in Cancer and Moon in Aries. This sets up a sort of feedback loop. Mars is in Cancer, so the Moon has influence over Mars, as Moon rules Cancer in the mundane wheel. With the Moon in Aries, Mars has influence over the Moon, as Mars rules Aries. With both these planets in each others' signs, each has influence over the other, and referring to one gets you the other, which refers you back to the original, which then refers you to the other, etc., etc., ad nauseum. It then becomes an endless loop. The two planets, being in each others' signs are considered to support each other. This can erase debilities (as with Mars being in its fall in Cancer) and strengthens the two planets in question.

With mutual receptions, the two planets in each others' signs are tied together, so to speak, by cross-rulership ties. It can be another way in which planets interrelate without an aspect between them. Some astrologers consider each planet to be as if in two places at once in the chart, one being the actual placement, and the other being the same place as the other mutually received planet. They then have two sets of aspects and sign and house placements for those planets. For example:

1) Moon in Aries and Mars in Cancer, square each other. Being in mutual reception, the square is not considered stressful and the way between the planets is eased, so if that is the final aspect (or next aspect), you may read it as a trine or sextile.

2) Uranus in Capricorn and Saturn in Aquarius are in mutual reception. With the Moon in Libra, it will eventually square Uranus. But you need a trine between them. Then you just switch Saturn and Uranus and the Moon then trines Uranus at the time it would have trined Saturn. You can consider the trine to Saturn as also being in effect. Like having your cake and eating it, too. It does not really work the other way, acting as if the Moon squares both Uranus and Saturn. It only makes things better, it does not spread around unfortunate or stressful influences. It's like astrological sweetness and light.

3) Mercury in Pisces and Neptune in Gemini are in mutual reception. (If Neptune were in Virgo, it would also be considered mutual reception.) The Moon is in Scorpio and moving to trine Mercury. You need an aspect (classical) between Moon and Neptune, but that won't happen while the Moon is in Scorpio. However, with the mutual reception, you can read Neptune as if it were in Pisces, and then you have a trine formed between the two.

4) Saturn in Scorpio and Mars in Capricorn are considered to be in mutual reception, as Mars is the old ruler of Scorpio. With this configuration, a Moon in Taurus could be considered to be moving to trine Saturn, instead of opposing it.

Hopefully you get the idea by now. If you are having trouble getting at a particular aspect between two planets, check out mutual reception. It may provide an out. Actually this works best when the transiting Moon is applying to aspects of mutually received planets. But you can also use it with other planets. If in Example 4, Venus in Taurus was applying to an opposition of Saturn, you could also consider it to become a trine through mutual reception. However, this only works with faster planets applying to slower ones. If, in Example 4, it was Jupiter in Taurus, it wouldn't count, as Jupiter cannot ever apply to an aspect with Mars, because Mars moves on the average faster than Jupiter. The order/hierarchy of planets aspecting each other is Moon (☽), Mercury (☿), Venus (♀), Sun (☉), Mars (♂), Jupiter (♃), Saturn (♄), Uranus (♅), Neptune (♆), Pluto (♇).

If the planets in question are in actual aspect also (as Mars in Cancer and Moon in Aries can be square to each other), the influence of the mutual reception is considered a mitigating influence, and can soften the harshness of a stressful aspect and make more wonderful the influence of an easy aspect.

Be this as it may, mutual reception is another way you can get to the energies of a planet without it having a direct aspect from the Moon or other planet in question. This is another of those strange archaic rules of horary which seems weird, but actually works. You have to have a thorough grounding in the sign rulerships, both archaic and modern. It works with old as well as new rulerships (more crazy-making). It can also transmute an unfortunate aspect into a fortunate one by allowing you to "move" the two planets around to each others' positions and then calculate the Moon aspects. It causes the planets to act cooperatively.

If you need two people to act cooperatively, then plan a working using a mutual reception where those planets represent the people in question. This is an advanced application and not easy to set up without a full electional chart. But if you can manage it, and be sure you have a good final aspect and all the rest, it can be extremely effective.

If you only get the idea of two planets being in each others' signs creates a feedback loop between them, and allows you to interchange the two, then you will have grasped enough of mutual reception to make it effective.

OTHER PLANETARY ASPECTS

This section will be short. Basically, you decide what you want to accomplish with your working. You then find the planets which rule the things involved, and see if you can get a favorable aspect between those planets, and time accordingly, paying attention to the Moon's final aspect, the signs the planets in question are in, and the Moon sign.

With aspects between planets (not including the Moon), you will have to wait longer. Some aspects will occur very rarely, Jupiter conjunct Saturn happens once every 20 years, or so. Some will never happen in your life-time, Neptune and Pluto were conjunct in 1891–1892 and will not conjunct again for about 400 more years. Sun aspects happen yearly, on the average, depending upon the speed of the other planet involved.

Look ahead in the ephemeris or calendar to see which aspects are coming up in the next month, season, or year. If one major aspect lends itself to a working you are contem-plating, then try to time things with that in mind. For exam-ple, the Uranus-Neptune conjunction in February, August, and October of 1993, blended energies that were very potent and magickally related, so planning workings with this aspect in mind really added oomph to the working. When you try to combine strong energies, however, just be careful you can handle the energies involved.

Most almanacs highlight the major aspects in the com-ing year in the front, along with eclipses, and stations of the planets. They are also listed in the daily section with Moon aspects. Although these major aspects are exact on a certain day, their influence "builds" over a month or more before they are exact. Ideally, you want to time your working so that no other planet is in aspect to either of the planets in the major aspect you are using before the aspect you want becomes exact. The Moon doesn't count in this case, though you can count the Moon also if you want to be most precise and have the most pure energies from the aspect. This may not be possible if you need a certain Moon sign or final Moon aspect (never neglect the Moon's final aspect in these timings). That's OK, it just means 1) it may take longer for the result to manifest and 2) other persons or influences may aid in the manifestation. If it's important and worth waiting for, you can be patient and put up with these extras.

In our sample almanac on page 67, we show three major planetary aspects. Venus conjunct Pluto was exact at 7:58 A.M. Sun trine Jupiter was exact at 11:27 P.M. and Saturn parallel Neptune was exact at 4:37 A.M. Using these aspects, you could do a working which started on the day of the aspect, or you could do the working a day or two earlier, provided no other planet (other than the Moon) aspected either of the planets in question. In the Venus conjunct Pluto example, you couldn't start earlier than 2:13 A.M., because at 2:12 A.M., Mercury opposed Venus. So you have a "window" of 2:13 A.M. to 7:58 A.M. to start this working, revitalizing a sexual relationship. This is over five-and-a-half hours, so you could also coordinate a favorable planetary hour (preferably Mars, or, secondarily, Venus), if it fell within that time period.

With the Sun trine Jupiter example, the Moon does aspect both the Sun and Jupiter, but Moon aspects don't count, so you could start your prosperity spell before 10:59 A.M., and take advantage of the waxing Moon, which is good for things which should increase. If no other planet aspected either the Sun or Jupiter for a week before the trine, you could start then. Whether you choose to count minor aspects is your call. Most correctly, only the major, classical aspects count for this example (conjunction, sextile, square, trine, opposition).

With Saturn parallel Neptune, say four days beforehand Mercury sextiled Neptune at 10:05 P.M. You would have a "window" lasting from the minute after that trine until the time the parallel was exact, at 4:37 A.M. on our hypothetical day. Any time within that four day "window" would be acceptable for you to start your Saturn parallel Neptune working, charging your wand. You have a choice of the Moon in Aries or Taurus, and various days and lots of planetary hours. If the last aspect of the Moon in Aries was a trine to Uranus, and you know the last aspect of the Moon in Taurus is an opposition to Venus, you can pick the one most favorable to your Saturn parallel Neptune working. My choice would be the Aries Moon final aspect of Moon trine Uranus, as Uranus is another magickal planet, and the trine a favorable aspect. Venus is not a particularly magickal planet, and an opposition is a separative aspect, which you do not want when bringing energies into an object. You could then choose a Mercury hour (Mercury ruling tools in general), and if it was on a Wednesday (a Mercury day), you would have a "double whammy" Mercury hour. The Moon would also be waxing—good for things which should increase—you want to increase the magickal energy in the wand. In this example I would definitely count minor aspects, as the parallel is a minor aspect itself. So if during the four-day window, Mars was sesquiquadrate Saturn at 8:42 P.M. the evening before our hypothetical day, your window would be shortened. Now your window is from 8:43 P.M. the evening before to 4:37 A.M. on the day in question. You lose the Aries Moon and its good final aspect. But if the day before is Wednesday, and you can get a Mercury hour, you still get your "double whammy" hour. Your final aspect of Moon opposite Venus isn't good, but you have a "double whammy" hour to offset that. Not too bad a time, but it could be better. Certainly it is worse than if there was no Saturn sesquiquadrate Mars. This is how we electional astrologers work these things out. Sometimes the magic works, sometimes it doesn't.

Again, once the aspect becomes exact, it is most potent. Once it has passed, you have missed the bus, and have to wait for the next bus (or miss the bus altogether). These are buses which don't run very often. Think of them as special excursion tours and you need a reservation to take this tour. So, especially with the infrequent outer planet aspects, give yourself as big a window as possible, and time your start with plenty of leeway in case of any last minute emergencies. You will have plenty time to get the optimal final Moon aspect, Moon sign, and house placement when energies between the planets you want build over a month or more. Think of it as making your reservations early, paying for your ticket in advance, and showing up at the terminal an hour before departure. And don't forget to pack your toothbrush. With so much advance planning, you can really plan everything perfectly and guarantee a really successful trip. These are the aspects to do your really big workings with.

These major aspects are what fictional sorcerers are waiting for when they use the Necronomicon to open the gates between the dimensions, and other fantastic world-shaking workings. While I do not advocate these exact things, the energies are still there. Can you imagine an initiation timed with the Uranus-Neptune conjunction? The person would certainly not have an ordinary career in the craft. Aleister Crowley and his contemporaries were acutely aware of this type of influence, and made full use of the energies created by less-often potent outer planet transiting aspects. Believe it. If it was good enough for them, why not do it yourself?

OTHER METHODS

There are three other methods you can use to fine-tune timings for your magickal workings. All require you be able to cast an astrological chart (or have access to a computer which will do it for you). I will outline them briefly here, for those interested. Feel free to ignore these paragraphs if they seem too complicated.

Ascendant/Midheaven Degrees

This method has the magickal practitioner timing the start of a working so that a certain degree of the zodiac is on the Ascendant or Midheaven. If you are figuring it by hand, you have to know how to figure backward from the table of houses to the time of day. But, even though it is a pain, it can add little nuances and influences not obtained other ways. I find that having a degree on the Ascendant or Midheaven is of similar influence. Technically, the Ascendant degree causes you to experience the influence more personally and in your daily life, and the Midheaven degree causes you to experience the influence more openly, in public or the world-at-large, or in your professional life. But in practice, in our modern society, there is little distinction between one and the other.

There are a number of reasons you would want to have a certain degree highlighted in a chart for a working.

1) You might want to have a planet or point in your natal chart highlighted by placing it on the transiting Ascendant or Midheaven.

2) You could have a transiting planet highlighted in the same way.

3) You could try to have the influence of a certain degree highlighted. There are many reasons for this, using "strong" or critical degrees, or because of the Sabian Symbol a certain degree denotes. Sabian Symbols are a system of word-pictures and influences by degree which were "channeled" at the turn-of-the-century, and described in Dane Rudyhar's book, *An Astrological Mandala*.[1] They have been likened to an astrological tarot in scope and influence, except there are 360 different word pictures. Sabian Sym-

---

[1] Dane Rudyhar, *An Astrological Mandala* (New York: Vintage Books, 1973).

bols are but one of several systems of degree influences and word pictures. They are the most popular and easily accessible. If you find one of the others, try it also, if you are of a mind to.

4) You might want to place a certain fixed star or astronomical object on the Ascendant or Midheaven, to partake of its influence. Fixed stars and other astronomical objects of astrological influence are covered in Part Four of this book, Additional Studies. The ancient astrologers made much of these fixed stars, so why not you, too?

5) You could try to evoke the influence of a certain day of the year at a different time by highlighting the degree the Sun would be in on that day. Like using your birthday degree (where the Sun was when you were born) or the degrees (classical) of the Sabbats and equinoxes. Like having Samhain at Lughnasadh. Oestarra 0 Aries, Beltane 15 Taurus, Midsummer 0 Cancer, Lughnasadh 15 Leo, Mabon 0 Libra, Samhain 15 Scorpio, Yule 0 Capricorn, Imbolc 15 Aquarius.

6) Think up your own reason for highlighting a certain degree by placing it on the Ascendant or Midheaven.

A subset of this is tailoring the Moon's transiting degree to match any of the above criteria. While each degree is on the Ascendant and Midheaven once each day, the Moon is in a certain degree only once each month, so for that you will have to wait longer, but it stays in that degree for about two hours, as opposed to about four minutes for an Ascendant or Midheaven degree.

All this degree tailoring is also done while considering all the previously mentioned techniques, and includes paying attention to a void Moon, the Moon sign and the Moon's final aspect. So getting it all right is more complicated than it would at first seem. Rate how much trouble it is worth with how important your working is.

Moon House Placement in the Transiting Chart

This leads to calculating a chart for the time for your working and placing the Moon in a certain house in the chart you are creating for the working. You can easily tell what sign the Moon is in by looking in your almanac, but you have to do some figuring (or have a computer do the figuring) to get the time when the Moon will transit a certain house in the chart. The Moon does transit (or move) through each house during a day, so if you need a certain house or sign influence and you cannot wait for the Moon to move into the correct sign, you can at least get the Moon in the correct house for about two hours each day. You have to be able to figure this out—and this involves math, which is why this is called another advanced method. While the houses and signs do not correspond exactly to a planet's energy, they are similar enough that a Pisces Moon and a 12th house Moon will have similar effects, at least enough for the level of sophistication outlined here.

An explanation is required here. The word transit is used in several ways in astrology. There are daily transits, which refer to the planets and signs moving around the sky each day as the Earth rotates on its axis. The rising and setting Sun is an example of this. Daily transits are also used to refer to the positions of planets in the sky as they move around a natal or other fixed-time chart, and make aspects to the planets and points in that specific chart. A Solar return (the Sun's yearly return to the degree at birth) is an example of this. There are other types of transits to a natal (or other) chart which are calculated by various methods (primary and secondary progressions, contra-progressions, solar arc progressions and others.) Suffice it to say, in this sub-section we are talking about the transits caused by the Earth rotating on its axis and the daily motion of signs and planets.

Remember, you still have to pay attention to Void Moon, Moon sign (try not to sabotage the house with an incompatible sign, if at all possible), next and final aspects and so forth. (This all begins to sound like a broken record, but it is a progressive system, with each technique affecting all the others. And you can all too easily sabotage your efforts if you have a Void Moon or an incompatible final aspect. This is why electional astrologers have to have a strong masochistic streak to put themselves through all these hoops for just one event chart!)

Electional Chart

All this discussion leads to doing a full electional chart for a particular working. This necessitates that you pay attention to all the techniques outlined earlier. You will also use a number of rules and other stuff which will not be included here. You could go to your local electional astrologer and tell them what you want your working to accomplish, the time frame you have in mind, and then have the astrologer go crazy trying to get everything to work out to the optimal advantage. Even for the professionals, no chart is perfect. You can only do the best you can with what you are given. Everything depends upon how important you think the thing is you are after, and what kind of energy you have to work with.

Personal Example

Included here is a chart for a working I did in April, 1992. It illustrates a number of points discussed, and I will include my rationale and why I used this chart.

In March, 1992, I rearranged furnishings in my house and moved my ritual space from upstairs into my living room. This necessitated a re-consecration of my ritual space and also some tools, particularly a new athame. I wanted to get a good time for this, and really didn't have forever to wait. I wanted to do it on my day off, and with other considerations picked April 2. (See Chart 4.)

The first thing which should stand out is the Moon moving to conjunct the Sun in Aries in the 9th house. The

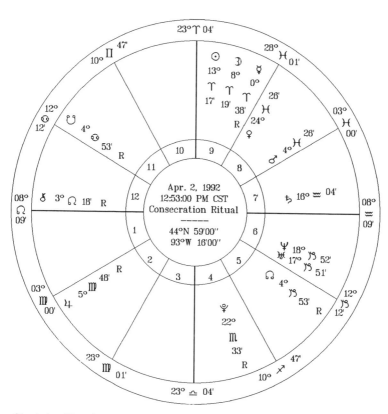

Chart 4.   Temple space and tool consecration ritual. April 2, 1992. 12:53 P.M. CST, 93 W 16, 44 N 59. Koch houses.

9th house rules temple space (organized religion). With Cancer on the 12th cusp, and Leo on the ascendant, the Sun and Moon rule the 12th of magick and the 1st of the individual, in this case, me. So you get the symbolism of me consecrating a magickal space. Aries is the sign of beginnings, and this was in some ways a new start for my magickal career. I like to use fixed stars, and I chose a time when I would have 23 Libra (Spica) on the 4th cusp, for a magickal altar. Also the 4th rules the end of the matter, and it would make a good end to the working. (This end of the matter is an advanced electional consideration.) The Moon's final aspect is a square to Neptune, which might seem strange, but a square incites to action, and I definitely wanted to get things going for myself. I call the square the "kick in the butt" aspect. Neptune also rules the 8th of initiations and other magickal things, so it works well. Venus, exalted in Pisces in the 8th (making no aspects), disposes of Neptune in the 6th, so they are tied nicely. Saturn and Uranus are in mutual reception, so the Moon square Uranus is transmuted into a sextile because the Moon sextiles Saturn. Uranus and Neptune are in the 6th of tools, adding magickal energy to tools in this chart, and the Moon aspects both, which is favorable. (Technically, it is called Translation of Light, which is another advanced electional concept.) Mars (of an athame) is in the 8th, but it opposes Jupiter ℞ in Virgo (of tools) in the 2nd. The opposition isn't all that wonderful, but if I want the energy to get out there (opposition is separative), that's not as awful as it would seem, and Jupiter is in Virgo (of tools), though it is retrograde and in its detriment. Still, for a re-consecration Jupiter and Mercury retrograde aren't bad. The transiting Moon in Aries is moving through a house in my chart favorable for a working such as this. The New Moon at 14 Aries is also favorable to things in my chart for such a working. Mercury in Aries is in its esoteric sign of rulership. Mercury will also conjunct Venus at 29 Pisces, the last degree of the last sign, which adds some nifty symbolism. Technically the aspect doesn't count, as Mercury changes sign before the conjunction, but in advanced electional astrology, it does count, after a fashion. Mercury rules the 2nd house of possessions, and it is in the 9th of religion and consecration. As an icing on the cake, the Part of Fortune is in the 12th of magick. I used a waning Moon, a dark Moon, because I also used Pluto, Hecate, and Persephone in the working, as patron deities. Some would avoid that Moon, but I had my reasons for using it. Remember this is a system by which you can personalize your workings.

As a disadvantage, Saturn and Pluto are applying to a square, but there are many intervening aspects before the square is exact, so it isn't as awful as it would seem. The Sun is the chart ruler (ruler of the sign on the ascendant) and it is in Aries (exalted), so that adds power to the chart. The Sun also applies to a sextile of Saturn, and as Saturn rules the 6th of tools, it adds to the consecration of tools aspect to the chart. Because of the mutual reception between Saturn and Uranus, you could also read that sextile as Sun sextile Uranus, which is also favorable: more magickal energies involving the chart ruler. Pluto is in Scorpio intercepted in the 4th of altars. This is really nice, as I have my altar in the living room, but I am not "out," so it doubles as just another piece of furniture. This intercepted Pluto helps with the "hidden in plain sight" type of magickal altar I have. The retrograde Pluto helps with that also. Venus and Mars, both ruling the 4th of the altar (Libra on the cusp and Scorpio intercepted) are in the magickal 8th house in the magickal sign of Pisces. As another icing, Taurus (ruled by Venus) is intercepted in the 10th of public image, so it adds to the "hidden in plain sight" aspect of the altar.

Hopefully this helps illustrate how an electional chart can tie many elements together to get at energies in varied ways. When I do an electional chart, there comes a point when the elements just fall together and things really click. I may have done the chart with one specific aspect in mind (the Moon conjunct Sun in the 9th house and 23 Libra on the 4th cusp), but once the chart is done, I find all sorts of other wonderful things which I didn't plan for, and which tie in with my intent. This is where the art of astrology comes into play. Synchronicity helps make these charts resonate well to the energies of the universe and allows you to tap into them, enhancing what you intend to do.

SUMMARY

If you want to use astrology to enhance your magickal workings, you need to remember three things. 1) Timing is important; don't miss the bus. Get to your stop in plenty of time before the bus is due to arrive. Allow for leeway in timing. 2) Perfection is impossible, so just do the best you can, and be satisfied with that. Planning for perfection is the path to madness. 3) KISS—Keep It Simple, Stupid! Work with the level of sophistication you are comfortable with. Experiment with the more advanced stuff, but if it is beyond you, or you aren't sure of the energies you will be dealing with, let it drop. I would feel bad if I heard someone released Chthulu by accident, using these guidelines. You wouldn't want to hurt my feelings. I'm a really blubbery crier.

Oh, and one more thing—HAVE FUN! Enjoy yourself, think of this as a new magickal toy, another tool in your magickal arsenal. Play with it, experiment.

PART THREE

MAGICK AND
YOUR NATAL CHART

INTRODUCTION

In Part One we explored the 52 astrological words and how they related to magick. Now we will explore astrology from a general viewpoint to see how each sign, house, and planet relates to magickal things, and life in general when seen from a magickal perspective. For this you will need a copy of your personal chart. Go back to Part One if you are uncertain which hour wedge is which house and what all those squiggles are representing in the way of signs and planets. Armed with all this wonderful information, and this section, you should be able to get a handle on your personal chart, and get some idea of what you are like in a magickal way. The definitions I use are not the usual astrological definitions. That stuff you can get in many other wonderful astrology books. These definitions are specially slanted for people who are interested in psychic and spiritual development, and who use magick and other psychic and mystical disciplines to help attain soul growth.

The definitions are short phrases, word lists, and correspondences. They are meant to give a definite flavor for each sign and house, so readers can get a general idea of what each is about and perhaps go on to formulating a definition or two of their own. The definitions are not exhaustive, but are inclusive and hopefully suggestive of other things. These phrases and word lists can cobble together a mix-and-match of definitions that will correspond to various signs and house placements as shown in personal charts.

So get out your natal chart, and start finding out about yourself in a magickal way. Think of this section as one of those *MAD Magazine* fill-in-the-blank articles. Be creative. Pick weird word combinations and see if you can't think of ways to make them work. Be silly. Have fun.

MAGICKAL NATURE OF THE SIGNS AND HOUSES

We will start these definitions with the signs and houses. In this section, planets are not individually important except as pointers as to which sign/house paragraphs to read. To best use these definitions, read the paragraphs which correspond to the sign and house placements of your Sun, Moon, Ascendant sign, and sign and house placement of your Ascendant ruler. Then blend the meanings. All of us have all the signs and planets in our charts. But some are more prominent than others, and that is what makes for the differences in styles and expressions of magickal abilities.

You must "do" your Sun by sign and house to shine. You need to "do" your Moon by sign and house to be happy, and also look to the Moon by sign and house for the most natural modes of magickal expression. You need to "do" your Ascendant ruler by house and sign to be fulfilled. The sign upon the Ascendant itself is the "mask" you wear in public and with those who don't know you well— casual acquaintances. If your Ascendant sign is complementary to the sign of your Sun, you project a personality that is compatible to the "real" you. If your Ascendant sign is not complementary to your Sun sign, you project a personality which is at cross purposes to the "real" you. By complementary I mean signs of the same element or a complementary element (fire and air are complementary, earth and water are complementary). If you have signs which are of the same quality but non-complementary elements, there is less compatibility, but there is still a common theme. It's just the manner of expression which is at cross purposes. If the signs are not related by element or quality, there is the least compatibility and the most difficulty integrating the modes of expression. Here is where the person needs to get creative in blending meanings to come up with modes of expression which satisfy the needs of both signs.

This may seem like a lot, but if you take it in pieces, say starting with the chart ruler, you can get a handle on that, and then move on to the Sun by sign and house and so on. Many times you will find you are already expressing these energies in ways that are compatible. This is natural. You instinctively know all this, and all the chart is doing is pointing it out and allowing you to see what you already "know," and offering alternatives to the ways you have already worked out.

You may discover that certain expressions seem to be at odds with each other. This is not uncommon. How many people are always consistent or predictable? It is these incompatibilities and forces which seem at odds with each other which make for character. People with these inconsistencies tend to be more interesting. The struggle to blend energies that—on the surface—seem incompatible, requires creativity, persistence, patience, and a willingness to learn from past mistakes. The end of this process is wisdom. Besides, if we all were perfect, then the Gods would give us some real work to do.

Once again I am blending the influences of the signs and houses. They aren't exactly the same, but the meanings and expressions are close enough to work. We are mainly magicians, not hard-core astrologers. We'll leave the fine distinctions for others and get on with the magickal stuff. Our overall goal is to introduce the practicing magician to astrology so it can be used to aid the practice of magick. One endpoint of magick is soul growth and awareness of psychic potential, so this section helps address that.

For example, say a person has a Capricorn Ascendant and the ruler of that ascendant, which is Saturn, is in Sagittarius in the 12th house. This person may have magickal experiences as a leader of a religious group which uses magick in its ceremonies, or this person may secretly be a traditional practitioner of High Magick and Alchemy, or this person may establish a new formal magickal tradition or discipline using channeled information. All these definitions blend Capricorn, Sagittarius, and 12th house energies. It's a cosmic mix and match.

THE FINAL SIGNATURE

If you have a final signature indicated with your chart, that can be very important also. A final signature is the collective compilation of planets (and the Ascendant) by elements and qualities and elements and qualities of house placements of planets. Here are the charts of six famous dead people. You may also want to refer back to Uncle Al's charts (charts 1–3 pages 26–28). These charts will be used to calculate final signatures, but they also will be good for practice to see how they stack up "magickally." Refer back to them when you read the rest of this chapter. Each chart has a couple of astrological goodies, and these people are very interesting mundanely and possibly magickally. Study them and see for yourself how each person was connected with psychic and magickal energies. To figure final signature, I make a little graph which looks like this:

C (cardinal)	F (fire)	A (angular)	L (life)
F (fixed)	E (earth)	S (succedent)	P (possessions)
M (mutable)	A (air)	C (cadent)	C (communications)
	W (water)		E (endings)

The words in parentheses are the keywords which correspond to each letter. Go back to Part One and look at table 1 (p. 36), and the mundane wheel (figure 2 on p. 22). Each sign is "created" by combining an element and a quality. Each house is "defined" by a placement (angular, succedent, or cadent), and a type (life, possessions, communications, endings). The final signature is determined by singularly adding up those elements in a chart, and deriving a sign and house. That shows the style and life area expressed in the chart. You can use only the ten traditional planets and the ascendant, or include Chiron and/or the big four asteroids. Some people count the sign on the midheaven also in the sign category. Some weight the Sun and Moon with two points each, and all other things with one. If you end up with no preponderance because two or more categories are equal, you can live with it, or weight the Sun, Moon and/or Ascendant extra to break the impasse. Or take less weight for Chiron and/or the asteroids (like a half point each). Whatever works. I ignore the Moon's Nodes and the Part of Fortune when figuring final signature.

The final signature in these charts will be figured two ways; one more conservatively, using only the ten standard planets and the ascendant as one point each. The other system weighs the Sun and Moon with two points each, the other planets (including Chiron) one point each, and the midheaven (10th house cusp) one point. These are indicated as "plain" and "weighted." In figuring the final signature of the sign (CFM and FEAW), I include the Ascendant (and Midheaven if using weighted figuring). In figuring the final signature of the house (ASC, LPCE), I use the planets' placements only, weighted or not. This is because the Ascendant and Midheaven do have signs on them, and those signs gain prominence in the chart by being on those two prominent houses. In determining the final signature house, the Ascendant and Midheaven are always connected with the same houses, so it would weight the 1st and 10th more heavily to include them. Another check is to add down each column, to make sure you have counted the correct number of points. In the plain system, you should get 11 points for each sign category (CFM, FEAW) and 10 points for each house category (ASC, LPCE). In the weighted system, you have a total of 15 points for the sign categories (CFM, FEAW), and 13 points for the house categories (ASC, LPCE). If you add down and do not get those

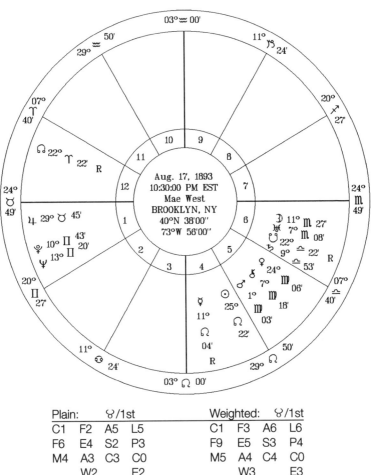

03° ♒ 00'

50'
29° ♒

11° ♑ 24'

07° ♈ 40'

20° ♐ 27'

☊ 22° ♈ 22' R

10 9

8

11

12 Aug. 17, 1893
10:30:00 PM EST
Mae West
BROOKLYN, NY
40°N 38'00''
73°W 56'00''

24° ♉ 49'

24° ♏ 49'

7

♃ 29° ♉ 45'

1

♀ 10° ♊ 43'
♆ 13° ♊ 20'

☽ 11° ♏ 27'
♅ 7° ♏ 08'
☋ 22° ♏ ♎
♀ 9° ♎ 22' R

6

2

☿ 7° ♍
♂ 24° ♍ 06'

5

20° ♊ 27'

3 4

07° ♎ 40'

☿ 11°
♌ 04'
R

☉ 25° ♍
1° ♍ 18'
22° ♌ 03'

50'

11° ♋ 24'

29° ♌

03° ♌ 00'

Plain:		♉/1st	
C1	F2	A5	L5
F6	E4	S2	P3
M4	A3	C3	C0
	W2		E2

Weighted:		♉/1st	
C1	F3	A6	L6
F9	E5	S3	P4
M5	A4	C4	C0
	W3		E3

Chart 5.   Mae West. She was born August 17, 1893, at 10:30 P.M. in
Brooklyn, NY. Placidus houses. Birth data from Debbi Kempton-Smith,
Secrets from a Stargazer's Notebook (New York: Bantam, 1982) p. 224.

numbers, go back and re-check your figuring; you made a mistake somewhere. I have all sorts of those little checks built into my calculations. They save wear and tear down the road. Even computer charts can have mistakes (remember, people must enter the data and program the computers), so I never assume anything is absolutely correct unless I have checked it here and there myself.

We'll start with Mae West. (See Chart 5.) Starting with Mae, we see she has one item (Saturn) in a cardinal sign (Libra); six items in fixed signs (Ascendant in Taurus, Jupiter in Taurus, Mercury in Leo, Sun in Leo, Uranus in Scorpio, Moon in Scorpio); and four items in mutable signs (Pluto in Gemini, Neptune in Gemini, Mars in Virgo, Venus in Virgo). She has two items in fire signs (Mercury in Leo, Sun in Leo); four items in earth signs (Ascendant in Taurus, Jupiter in Taurus, Mars in Virgo, Venus in Virgo); three items in air signs (Pluto in Gemini, Neptune in Gemini, Saturn in Libra); two items in water signs (Uranus in Scorpio, Moon in Scorpio). She then has five planets in angular houses (Jupiter 1st, Pluto 1st, Neptune 1st, Mercury 4th, Sun 4th); two planets in succedent houses (Mars 5th, Venus 5th) and three planets in cadent houses (Saturn 6th, Uranus 6th, Moon 6th). She also has five planets in life houses (Jupiter 1st, Pluto 1st, Neptune 1st, Mars 5th, Venus 5th); three planets in possessions houses (Saturn 6th, Uranus 6th, Moon 6th); no planets in communications houses (3rd, 7th or 11th); two planets in endings houses (Mercury 4th, Sun 4th). This makes for a preponderance of fixed earth and angular life which translates to Taurus and 1st house.

Think about Mae West. Was she not an archetypal earth-mother? From her big bosom and generously rounded figure to her earthy sensuality and sexy humor, she was all woman. And very pleased and proud of it. That Leo Sun added to her looks, blonde hair and flashy style, but her earthy sensuality is pure Taurus. Her chart needs that outlet of having that mask (1st house) of earthy expres-

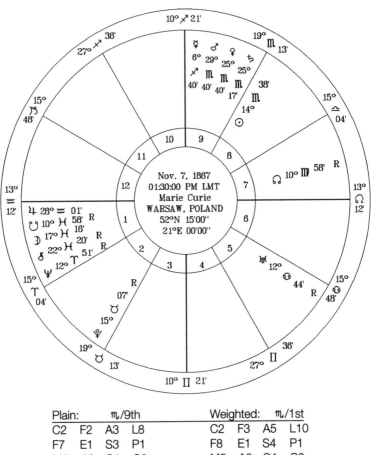

Plain:		♏/9th		Weighted:		♏/1st	
C2	F2	A3	L8	C2	F3	A5	L10
F7	E1	S3	P1	F8	E1	S4	P1
M2	A2	C4	C0	M5	A2	C4	C0
	W6		E1		W9		E2

Chart 6.   Marie Curie. She was born November 7, 1867, at 1:30 P.M., in Warsaw, Poland. Placidus houses. Birth data from Lois M. Rodden's *Profiles of Women* (Tempe, AZ: American Federation of Astrologers, 1979) p. 226.

sion (Taurus). Using her Leo Sun, she made a career for herself on the stage, but she could have as easily used those energies to become a farmer, or a call-girl, or musician (she was a singer), or a couch potato. The rest of the chart will show in more detail how those energies of the final signature will be supported or modified and help refine the choices.

Adding Chiron and the Midheaven and weighting the Sun and Moon with two points each, we will look again at Mae's final signature (the weighted numbers). She has one point for cardinal (Saturn in Libra); nine points for fixed (Midheaven in Aquarius, Ascendant in Taurus, Jupiter in Taurus, Mercury in Leo, two points for Sun in Leo, Uranus in Scorpio, two points for Moon in Scorpio); five points for mutable (Pluto in Gemini, Neptune in Gemini, Mars in Virgo, Chiron in Virgo, Venus in Virgo). She has three points in fire (Mercury in Leo, two points for Sun in Leo); five points for earth (Ascendant in Taurus, Jupiter in Taurus, Mars in Virgo, Chiron in Virgo, Venus in Virgo); four points for air (Pluto in Gemini, Neptune in Gemini, Saturn in Libra, Midheaven in Aquarius); three points for water (Uranus in Scorpio, two points for Moon in Scorpio). She has six points in angular houses (Jupiter 1st, Pluto 1st, Neptune 1st, Mercury 4th, two points for Sun 4th); three points succedent (Mars 5th, Chiron 5th, Venus 5th); four points cadent (Saturn 6th, Uranus 6th, two points for Moon 6th). She has six points for life houses (Jupiter 1st, Pluto 1st, Neptune 1st, Mars 5th, Chiron 5th, Venus 5th); four points possessions houses (Saturn 6th, Uranus 6th, two points for Moon 6th); no points for communications houses (nothing 3rd, 7th, 11th); three points endings houses (Mercury 4th, two points for Sun 4th). This adds to a preponderance of fixed earth and angular life. Taurus 1st again.

Do not assume that the final signature will be the same with different weightings. Let's look at Marie Curie. (See Chart 6.) Plain figuring (ignoring Midheaven and Chiron).

2 points cardinal (Neptune Aries, Uranus Cancer);

7 points fixed (Ascendant Aquarius, Jupiter Aquarius, Pluto Taurus, Sun Scorpio, Saturn Scorpio, Venus Scorpio, Mars Scorpio);

2 points mutable (Moon Pisces, Mercury Sagittarius);

2 points fire (Neptune Aries, Mercury Sagittarius);

1 point earth (Pluto Taurus);

2 points air (Ascendant Aquarius, Jupiter Aquarius);

6 points water (Moon Pisces, Uranus Cancer, Sun Scorpio, Saturn Scorpio, Venus Scorpio, Mars Scorpio);

3 points angular (Jupiter 1st, Moon 1st, Neptune 1st);

3 points succedent (Pluto 2nd, Uranus 5th, Sun 8th);

4 points cadent (Saturn 9th, Venus 9th, Mars 9th, Mercury 9th);

8 points life (Jupiter 1st, Moon 1st, Neptune 1st, Uranus 5th, Saturn 9th, Venus 9th, Mars 9th, Mercury 9th);

1 point possessions (Pluto 2nd);

0 points communications;

1 point endings (Sun 8th).

This makes a preponderance of fixed water and cadent life, Scorpio 9th. This is the final signature of one who delves into higher learning. Deep research into abstract things. She discovered radium and other elements. She also held a chair in physics at the Sorbonne.

Weighting the chart the second way, including Chiron, Midheaven, with Sun and Moon getting 2 points each, you get another set of values.

2 points cardinal (Neptune Aries, Uranus Cancer);

8 points fixed (Ascendant Aquarius, Jupiter Aquarius, Pluto Taurus, Sun Scorpio) [two points], Saturn Scorpio, Venus Scorpio, Mars Scorpio);

5 points mutable (Moon Pisces [two points], Chiron Pisces, Mercury Sagittarius, Midheaven Sagittarius).

3 points fire (Neptune Aries, Mercury Sagittarius, Midheaven Sagittarius);

1 point earth (Pluto Taurus);

2 points air (Ascendant Aquarius, Jupiter Aquarius);

9 points water (Moon Pisces [two points] Chiron Pisces, Uranus Cancer, Sun Scorpio [two points], Saturn Scorpio, Venus Scorpio, Mars Scorpio);

5 points angular (Jupiter 1st, Moon 1st [two points], Chiron 1st, Neptune 1st);

4 points succedent (Pluto 2nd, Uranus 5th, Sun 8th [two points]);

4 points cadent (Saturn 9th, Venus 9th, Mars 9th, Mercury 9th);

10 points life (Jupiter 1st, Moon 1st [two points], Chiron 1st, Neptune 1st, Uranus 5th, Saturn 9th, Venus 9th, Mars 9th, Mercury 9th);

1 point possessions (Pluto 2nd);

0 points communications;

2 points endings (Sun 8th [two points]).

This makes a final signature fixed water and angular life-Scorpio 1st. Note the sign preponderance has stayed the same, but the house has changed. This is not uncommon. I

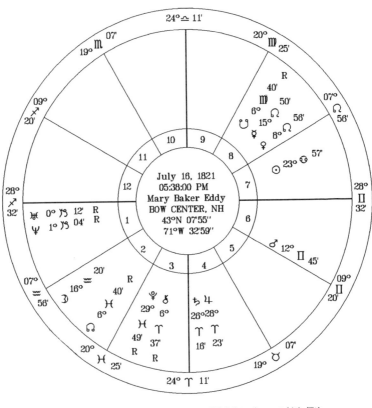

Chart 7.   Mary Baker Eddy. She was born July 16, 1821, at 5:30 P.M., in
Bow, NH. Placidus houses. Birth data from Lois M. Rodden's *Profiles of
Women* (Tempe, AZ: American Federation of Astrologers, 1979) p. 120.

stay with the same method for determining final signature, and keep with it for all charts I do. Pick whichever you like and then stick with it.

Let's check out Mary Baker Eddy. (See chart 7.) The plain final signature:

5 cardinal (Uranus Capricorn, Neptune Capricorn, Saturn Aries, Jupiter Aries, Sun Cancer);

3 fixed (Moon Aquarius, Venus Leo, Mercury Leo);

3 mutable (Ascendant Sagittarius, Pluto Pisces, Mars Gemini);

5 fire (Ascendant Sagittarius, Saturn Aries, Jupiter Aries, Venus Leo, Mercury Leo);

2 earth (Uranus Capricorn, Neptune Capricorn);

2 air (Moon Aquarius, Mars Gemini);

2 water (Pluto Pisces, Sun Cancer);

5 angular (Uranus 1st, Neptune 1st, Saturn 4th, Jupiter 4th, Sun 7th);

3 succedent (Moon 2nd, Venus 8th, Mercury 8th);

2 cadent (Pluto 3rd, Mars 6th);

2 life (Uranus 1st, Neptune 1st);

2 possessions (Moon 2nd, Mars 6th);

2 communications (Pluto 3rd, Sun 7th);

4 endings (Saturn 4th, Jupiter 4th, Venus 8th, Mercury 8th).

This makes a final signature of cardinal fire and angular endings, Aries 4th. This woman founded the religion of Christian Science, which is like founding a tradition, and Aries 4th expresses that well. Using weighted points, it works out differently.

cardinal 8 (Uranus Capricorn, Neptune Capricorn, Chiron Aries, Saturn Aries, Jupiter Aries, Sun Cancer [two points], Midheaven Libra);

fixed 4 (Moon Aquarius [two points], Venus Leo, Mercury Leo);

mutable 3 (Ascendant Sagittarius, Pluto Pisces, Mars Gemini);

fire 6 (Ascendant Sagittarius, Chiron Aries, Saturn Aries, Jupiter Aries, Venus Leo, Mercury Leo);

earth 2 (Uranus Capricorn, Neptune Capricorn);

air 4 (Moon Aquarius [two points], Mars Gemini, Midheaven Libra);

water 3 (Pluto Pisces, Sun Cancer [two points]);

angular 6 (Uranus 1st, Neptune 1st, Saturn 4th, Jupiter 4th, Sun 7th [two points]);

succedent 4 (Moon 2nd [two points], Venus 8th, Mercury 8th);

cadent 3 (Pluto 3rd, Chiron 3rd, Mars 3rd);

life 2 (Uranus 1st, Neptune 1st);

possessions 3 (Moon 2nd [two points] Mars 6th);

communications 4 (Pluto 3rd, Chiron 3rd, Sun 7th [two points]);

endings 4 (Saturn 4th, Jupiter 4th, Venus 8th, Mercury 8th).

This gives cardinal fire, Aries again, and angular emphasis, but both communications and endings have 4 points each. This is seen fairly often, two houses weighted equally. I deal with it in two ways. One is that I see if either of the weighted categories includes Sun, Moon (or Ascendant for sign weightings). If one house does, and the other does not, then

I go with that one. Mary Baker Eddy has in communications Pluto, Chiron and Sun (2 points). In endings she has Saturn, Jupiter, Venus and Mercury. One category, communications, has Sun, and the other, endings, does not have Moon, so I go with communications, which changes the final signature to Aries 7th. She did need that audience for her ideas.

The other way is to go with two signs or houses—Aries 4th/7th, and acknowledge there are two equally strong sign and/or house influences in the life. Occasionally you will have three categories equally weighted. I then just leave it and do not give a final signature in that category, except by partial indication (for example, as fixed, or just air, or just cadent, or possessions only), by whichever category does have a preponderance. You also find charts which don't resolve to any sign or house—fixed and life, for example. These individuals have no strong direction indicated by final signature. They can be versatile but also may have trouble finding a direction because of the wide range of possibilities of expression. Which is better, a generalist or a specialist? Depends on what you're doing. This lack of pre-ponderance is neither good nor bad (as is any indicator in any chart), it just is something the person will have to deal with in his or her life. HOW the person deals with it may then determine whether it is good or bad. Remember, there are many possibilities for each word (and word element), and the optimum method of expression can vary with lifestyle, national, and socioeconomic factors.

There is a famous case in astrology of astro-twins. Astro-twins are two people born in the same city at the same time, who then have the same chart. Fictionally, the Prince and the Pauper is an example. Anyhow, the two real people were two men. One ended up being George III of England (the guy who we fought against in the American Revolution), and the other a prominent middle-class baker in London. The socioeconomic situations were very differ-ent, but the life changes and conditions were remarkably similar in their respective circumstances. Each married on the same day, each inherited the family business from his

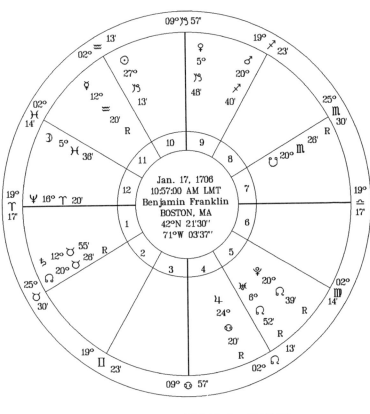

Plain:	♈/9th			Weighted:	♈/♂/9th		
C5	F5	A3	L5	C7	F5	A4	L5
F4	E3	S4	P1	F5	E5	S4	P2
M2	A1	C4	C1	M3	A2	C5	C2
	W2	E3			W3		E4

Chart 8. Benjamin Franklin. He was born January 17, 1706, at 10:57 A.M., in Boston, MA. Placidus houses. Birth data from Debbi Kempton-Smith's *Secrets from a Stargazer's Notebook* (New York: Bantam, 1982) p. 126.

father in the same month, each had the same number of children, each died in the same month, each became prosperous and well-thought-of in his respective circle. The similarities go on, but it helps to illustrate how different circumstances can change the mode of operation for a chart.

We'll do one last example of figuring final signature. In Ben Franklin's chart (see Chart 8), using plain figuring, he has:

> 5 cardinal (Neptune and Ascendant Aries, Jupiter Cancer, Venus and Sun Capricorn);
>
> 4 fixed (Saturn Taurus, Uranus and Pluto Leo, Mercury Aquarius);
>
> 2 mutable (Mars Sagittarius, Moon Pisces);
>
> 5 fire (Neptune and Ascendant Aries, Uranus and Pluto Leo, Mars Sagittarius);
>
> 3 earth (Saturn Taurus, Venus and Sun Capricorn);
>
> 1 air (Mercury Aquarius);
>
> 2 water (Jupiter Cancer, Moon Pisces);
>
> 3 angular (Saturn 1st, Jupiter 4th, Sun 10th);
>
> 3 succedent (Uranus and Pluto 5th, Mercury 11th);
>
> 4 cadent (Mars and Venus 9th, Moon and Neptune 12th);
>
> 5 life (Saturn 1st, Uranus and Pluto 5th, Mars and Venus 9th);
>
> 1 possessions (Sun 10th);
>
> 1 communications (Mercury 11th);
>
> 3 endings (Jupiter 4th, Moon and Neptune 12th).

This gives an Aries 9th final signature. Using a weighted tabulation, Ben has:

7 cardinal (Neptune and Ascendant Aries, Jupiter Cancer, Venus, Midheaven and Sun [2] Capricorn);

5 fixed (Saturn Taurus, Uranus and Pluto Leo, Chiron and Mercury Aquarius);

3 mutable (Mars Sagittarius, Moon [2] Pisces);

5 fire (Neptune and Ascendant Aries, Uranus and Pluto Leo, Mars Sagittarius);

5 earth (Saturn Taurus, Venus, Midheaven and Sun [2] Capricorn);

2 air (Chiron and Mercury Aquarius);

3 water (Jupiter Cancer, Moon [2] Pisces);

4 angular (Saturn 1st, Jupiter 4th, Sun [2] 10th);

4 succedent (Uranus and Pluto 5th, Chiron, Mercury 11th);

5 cadent (Mars and Venus 9th, Moon [2] and Neptune 12th);

5 life (Saturn 1st, Uranus and Pluto 5th, Venus and Mars 9th);

2 possessions (Sun [2] 10th);

2 communications (Chiron and Mercury 11th);

4 endings (Jupiter 4th, Moon [2] and Neptune 12th).

This gives us an Aries/Capricorn-9th final signature. Pretty convoluted, huh? See how the sign emphasis has changed. Aries to Aries/Capricorn? We could refine it down, but with Sun-earth and Ascendant-fire, we have no extra weighting here. So we leave the dual signs. Ben published *Poor Richard's Almanac*, a first-of-its-kind publication; the 9th rules publishing, Aries rules new ideas. He was a Renaissance Man, also from the 9th-house emphasis. Note Ben's Pisces Moon in the 12th, which shows he probably did get good results with magick, which he allegedly practiced. His "boudoir politics" can be attributed to Mars and Venus in the 9th. Ben made political acquaintances through mistresses of influential men: Venus sextile a Pisces Moon, Mars trine Neptune and Pluto gave irresistible charm. The epithet, "father of our country," can be used as he reportedly fathered over 100 bastards. Scientific abilities can be traced to ℞ Mercury conjunct Chiron, opposite Uranus, all square Saturn. The fact that he didn't kill himself with his experiments probably traces to Mars (chart ruler) in Sagittarius (9th) and Jupiter exalted in Cancer. He was lucky!

The final signature is seen as the sign and house expression of the chart as a whole, sort of the overall "style" indicated by the chart. It can explain the way a person seems to others, especially if the final signature is of a sign and/house not represented by Sun, Moon, Ascendant or Ascendant-ruler. This can indicate a person who may be a lost soul—one who has no readily available outlet for personal expression. If he or she starts doing the sign and house of her or his final signature, he or she may get in touch with the self, and feel more complete and fulfilled.

The last two charts I leave to you as an exercise. Edgar Cayce, the Sleeping Prophet, was a man of modest education who made his living as a photographer. When in trance he was able to access the Akashic records and did life readings for thousands of individuals, diagnosing and prescibing remedies for health problems which baffled the best medical minds of his day. Records of these readings are kept at the Association for Research and Enlightenment in Virginia Beach, VA. Mark Twain is one of America's greatest writers, but he was more than that. Possessed with an insatiable curiosity (note the Mercury in Scorpio on the Ascendant), Twain kept an open mind about nearly everything. He was known to explore psychic and paranormal phenomena. He was not afraid to say just what was on his mind, and used his writing to tweak the noses of those in the establishment, having his characters say things that might not have been otherwise accepted in polite society.

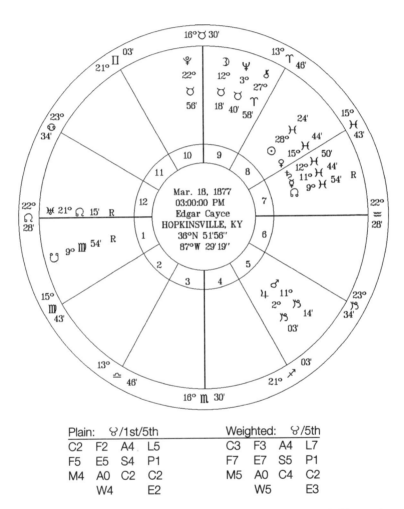

Plain:	♉/1st/5th			Weighted:	♉/5th		
C2	F2	A4	L5	C3	F3	A4	L7
F5	E5	S4	P1	F7	E7	S5	P1
M4	A0	C2	C2	M5	A0	C4	C2
	W4		E2		W5		E3

Chart 9.   Edgar Cayce. He was born March 18, 1877, at 3:00 P.M., in Hopkinsville, KY. Placidus houses. Birth data from Debbi Kempton-Smith's *Secrets from a Stargazer's Notebook* (New York: Bantam, 1982) p. 123.

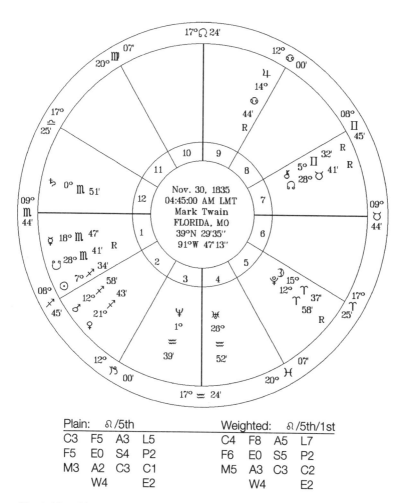

Plain:	♌/5th			Weighted:	♌/5th/1st		
C3	F5	A3	L5	C4	F8	A5	L7
F5	E0	S4	P2	F6	E0	S5	P2
M3	A2	C3	C1	M5	A3	C3	C2
	W4		E2		W4		E2

Chart 10.   Mark Twain. He was born November 30, 1835, at 4:45 A.M. LMT, in Florida, MO. Placidus houses. Birth data from Lois M. Rodden's *Astro-Data II* (Tempe, AZ: American Federation of Astrologers, 1980) p. 380.

SIGN AND HOUSE DEFINITIONS

The Aries or 1st House Magician: Pioneers, innovators, people who like to be first. They are good at energy work. They start lots of projects but aren't too good at carrying through and finishing those projects. They can be psychic warriors, preferring action to diplomacy and negotiation. They may prefer to work solo, or want to be leaders of groups. They can get bored quickly and need encouragement in their workings. Feed their egos and they will do most anything for you. They don't like doing anything which has nothing in it for them. They may have an interesting collection of athames and swords (magickal weapons). They like to wear red a lot and may play with fire. These people are quick to anger but just as quick to forgive and move on. Impatience may be a problem and they may neglect precautions or even court danger. They can be effective in emergency situations, unless they are challenged and then they can become belligerent. They have enormous courage. They also have a tendency to act first and think later. They may start their own traditions. They like to be first, and even in established groups, they often come up with innovations or new techniques which can be highly effective.

The Taurus or 2nd House Magician: Sensualists, Earth Mother worshippers. They can be into music and dance. They have enormous patience and appreciate beauty and harmony. Sometimes they may be indolent, impossible to get going, but if they are motivated to action, they become the irresistible force. They like to have a bunch of magickal toys, their things. Food and drink are important. It should be tasty and something they like, possibly sweet. And preferably enough to satisfy their appetites. They like flowers and plants, pretty but preferably edible or usable as herbs or perfumes or providing pleasant sensations. They have green thumbs if they put their hands to Earth. They stay with one tradition because it is familiar, they like routine and stability. Ethics are important and they spend time formulating their own ethical codes. These ethics can become rigid if they are pushed too far. They prefer to stay near home, with their creature comforts and familiar surroundings. Anger comes slowly and after much provocation, but when they blow, beware of being in the way, for this is the placement of the bull in the china shop and they don't slow down until all their anger is spent. They do well with money spells. They love sensual things, things which make them feel good both inside and out.

The Gemini or 3rd House Magician: Jacks-of-all-trades, trivia experts, they keep an amazing amount of information about the strangest things in their brains. They are wonderful with words. They are the true eclectics, following the creed that "the eclectic only steals from the very best." They go with the flow and are adaptable to whatever style is prevalent in their area. These people like to be members of several magickal groups and/or traditions so as to have a variety of magickal expressions. They are the networkers in their communities, and also possibly the worst gossips. Telepathy comes easily. They like to write and communicate about magickal experiences. They like to travel to different areas to experience other styles of magick. They read voraciously and probably have a library which is the envy of many. They don't like to stay still, and if you tie their hands behind their backs they cannot talk. They are almost never solitaries and may have a number of partners and/or groups that they work with. Sometimes only they know who all their contacts are. They are lost without a telephone or mail service.

The Cancer or 4th House Magician: Empathic, sensitive, able to divine the motives of others. They can be "mother hens," worrying about people who may be hurting or in trouble. They like to cook and probably practice a wonderful brand of kitchen magick. They are reverent to the past and tradition and may be community historians. Mediumistic abilities can be pronounced, and they are good with divination and scrying. They prefer to do magick at home, and their homes may well be fortified with substantial shields. They can be shy and retiring, but also make effective leaders, for they organize activities. They need time alone to recharge and can become psychic chameleons, soaking up the vibes of any gathering. They need to learn shielding and detachment, or they can become psychic victims, mirroring the feelings and attitudes of their groups. They like doing house blessings. They are collectors. They may make the magickal community their family. They can be simultaneously extremely effective in some areas and helpless in others. They need hugs and cuddles.

The Leo or 5th House Magician: Show-offs, revel in being the center of attention. They are happiest being "Witch Queens," having people acknowledge their accomplishments and abilities. They like parties and fun. They can be artistic and need to be able to express themselves in their own unique creative ways. They like children and relate well to them, but do not always become parents because they are really just big children themselves. They have a talent for theatrical ceremonies and circles. They are good with namings and Wiccanings. They have a talent for love spells. They are the showpeople and clowns in the magickal community, and can become disruptive and petty if they feel their contributions aren't given proper recognition. They can be generous to a fault, and really enjoy the "grand gesture." They like games and can treat magick as a game. They have strong will. They can use fine arts in magick, expressing themselves through ritual painting or sculpture. They are honest and loyal, though if you hurt their pride, they will never fully trust you ever again.

The Virgo or 6th House Magician: Craftspeople who like working with their hands creating things. They are good at gardening, growing herbs and medicinal plants and things which are useful. They like making tools and other objects which they may or may not sell. They want things to be perfect and may denigrate their own work, pointing out miniscule flaws and imperfections. They are good with details and numbers and are micro-managers. They need to keep busy or they can decide that you will be their next project. They have a reputation for being nit-picky and drive people crazy, pointing out reasons why things cannot be done or are impractical, or finding fault with everything. Everyday magick is their forte, making magick for practical everyday ends. They are shamans, relate well to animals, and probably have familiars and/or spirit guides. They are into health and diet and may become vegetarians. They like the idea of ritual purification and may fast to cleanse the body and/or achieve spiritual enlightenment.

The Libra or 7th House Magician: Peacemakers and diplomats. They like working with a partner and do not like being alone. They love handfastings. They like truth and beauty and other pleasant abstracts. Balance and harmony are important, and they dislike discord. They are also good at cutting away spells. They are the quintessential "Devil's Advocate," and will take the other side in an argument just so all sides will be represented. They can be the advocate for those who are unwilling or unable to speak. They like rituals where women and men are equally represented. They generally believe in honoring the Goddess and God together, because each needs the other, in their eyes. They tend to believe in good, and can become sweetness and light. They like music and dance, with a partner or as part of a group. They like to wear pretty things—ritual garb or jewelry. They have trouble making up their minds and may delay initiations or commitments because they feel irrevocable steps cut them off from their options. They like to give and receive hugs and cuddles.

The Scorpio or 8th House Magician: likes to delve in the depths. They are intensely interested in matters concerning sex, death, and transformation. They like to explore sex magick and Tantra. They probably have very intense and interesting initiatory experiences, but these may not be the usual initiations. They also like ritual weapons and probably have a nifty collection of "toys." They can be good with money and prosperity spells, and may be able to successfully do these types of workings for others. They are fascinated with the "dark side" and seek to embrace the depths in themself and encourage others to do so. They are more interested in villains than heroes because the villains are more complex, driven characters. They either need to work with a partner or are fiercely solitary. They have enormous courage and will power and these are the people who are most likely to try and "conjure Chthulu," just to see if it can be done. They can be psychic warriors, and will guard their communities from real and perceived threats. They have many secrets, but will try to uncover the secrets of others, because they want to know. Research is a hobby.

The Sagittarius or 9th House Magician: Really likes to do rituals in grand style, with all the bells and whistles. They are philosophers and get into comparative studies and obscure disciplines. They are good at predicting the future and divination in general. Dreamwork is one field of study which can bring effective results. They are good with languages and enjoy rituals with non-English words or from other cultures or traditions. They are most likely to become accredited ministers. They like to travel and probably go to festivals in other parts of the country, "just to see how the other guys do it." They love to learn and can become eternal students, learning one tradition or discipline after another, or studying one subject for years, becoming expert in all phases. They can become pompous and overbearing, and in extreme cases be like misplaced old-time preachers. They can become adept at astral travel. They think of magick (and life) as an adventure.

They like physical disciplines such as martial arts, or any discipline that hones the body as well as the mind.

The Capricorn or 10th House Magician: archetypal Elders. They have wisdom beyond their years. They are good at organization and pay close attention to the mundane running of the religious group and are the best people for dealing with real world concerns. Recognition of achievement is important. They may "collect degrees" to validate their knowledge and training. The more mature ones know that experience and wisdom are the only degrees needed by true adepts. They like Ceremonial Magick, the stuff which all has to be done according to formula with no words mispronounced or actions done incorrectly. They like to be High Priests/esses of their groups. They may become hermits for a time, as solitude can be healing for these people. They like the mountains. They like working with rocks and crystals. They believe in working at Magick; an honest, properly done effort generates an appropriate return. They try to use magick in their careers, or even make magick their careers. They may tend to allow the end to justify the means. They are result-oriented; they do not believe in well-meaning but ineffectual efforts. They can be the "wise ones" in their communities.

The Aquarius or 11th House Magician: the Tricksters of the Zodiac. They like to stir things up, create change, make chaos, upset the hierarchy, lead a revolution. They have incredible flashes of insight, but if they don't write these wonderful ideas down, can lose them as quickly as they came. They are very concerned for the community as a whole, and can forget the needs of the individual if they aren't careful. They prefer to work in groups or in a coven rather than in pairs, though occasionally one is a solitary. They like new, far out ideas and rituals and techniques. They may use astrology. They have a talent for spotting truths, though they may not communicate these truths in a comfortable or fashionable way. They can be the voice in the wilderness. They are ahead of their time. There are some who are really rigid and traditional, but eventually they loosen up and become as weird and far-out as they were establishment. They like things they can prove, although their idea of proof is not always something which can be replicated in a laboratory. They like to make up the rules as they go along. They demand freedom for themselves and can rebel against dogmatic traditions that limit freedom of action and speech.

The Pisces or 12th House Magician: These people are combinations of all the other types. They believe in Magick and their personal belief systems are what powers their workings. They can be mediums, or psychics, or exhibit most any or all of the psychic talents catalogued at present. They have a tendency to lose themselves in the magick, and so can be subject to possession if precautions aren't taken. They can achieve good results using drugs or other mood-altering substances, but ultimately the best method is just pure meditation or other mind-altering techniques that do not rely upon outside catalysts. They can make and use oils, incense, and perfumes. They aren't known for their grounding and centering abilities. They may want to have someone watching over them when doing their thing to help bring them home, if needed. They are most likely to want to live entirely in magickal realms and just leave the real world entirely. They can write beautiful poetry. They excel at dance and song. They are able to see through the material into the ethereal. They can develop the talent to be able to "go between the worlds" at will. They can be effective psychic barometers.

MAGICKAL NATURES OF THE PLANETS

While the signs and houses are the set and costumes of the play that is your life, the planets are the actors. The planets move around, and interact, and bring focus to the houses. They act in the manner of the signs. Without planets, everyone would be the same. The planets (and their placements) are what makes each of us unique.

Your birthchart is, in effect, a snapshot of the solar system at the time and place of your birth. If you change the time of your birth, the Ascendant degree and all your house placements (of your planets) will change. Keep the same time, but change the place, either east/west or north/south and the chart will change in a similar manner. The amount of change will depend on the distance you move away from the exact spot of birth. This "exact spot" is practically the size of a city or town. You can get really exact with super-precise degree, minute, and second measurements of latitude and longitude, but as birth times are not always measured that exactly (to the second and insuring the clock is precisely on time), and because there is still controversy as to when "birth" actually occurs (from the head showing in the birth canal to the head emerging—and what about breech births?—to the first cry, to cutting the cord), being super-exact with place measurements becomes moot. In math there is a concept called "fewest significant digits," which roughly translates to "your measurements can only be as good as the least precise one, no matter how precise the others are." So using the longitude and latitude of the city or town of birth is precise enough. And generally, birth is timed from the first cry, which is first breath, for those who were wondering.

The birthchart is a "snapshot" of the solar system but the planets do not stop moving. They are continually moving, and that is what accounts for the ebb and flow of the events of everyday life. Add to that the precession of the equinoxes and other longterm cycles and you can theoretically account for the life of the Earth and the Solar System. There is even a nascent galactic astrology being formulated which takes into account the rotation of the Milky Way around the Galactic Center, and probably there will also be developed a universal astrology which goes beyond this galaxy and charts the universe as a whole.

Natal placements set up energy potentials. Planets are interrelated by aspect, by sign and house placement, and by sign and house rulership. How these potentials will manifest in life is up to the people who use the energy. Some respond the same way all the time. Some learn from the negative expression of energies and then choose to operate more positively. Some are really creative (or chaotic) and respond differently every time. And some never respond at all for various reasons. It is an observable fact that some people never respond to the energies of certain planets. They may not be ready to deal with the energies (especially if the planet is a trans-personal planet—Uranus, Neptune, or Pluto), the wavelength may be too high for their mode of expression in this life. If a personal planet is not expressed, these people may have already dealt with those energies in a former life (if you buy into the reincarnation theory) and don't need to repeat those lessons. Or maybe the focus in this life is elsewhere, and those energies are superfluous.

When it comes down to it, natal placements and transits operate in a similar manner. Both set up energy potentials and need to be expressed by some mode of behavior. The natal placements are fixed, they are the themes that will be present throughout the life. The transiting influences become variations on the theme of the natal chart. The transits bring the day-to-day changes of circumstance which color the modes of expression present in the natal chart. They can enhance or hinder the natal expressions. Astrology provides the road map of basic energies and also changes in energies which are experienced, changes that provide opportunity for planning and awareness of what may be happening in the future. Foreknowledge can enhance positive opportunities or soften the blows of negative happenings. Knowledge of a natal placement can provide insight into changing the expression of that energy so it becomes more comfortable and less stressful.

In the following discussion, planets can pertain to either natal or transiting planets. The theory for expression of energies is the same. The difference between the two is that the energies of natal placements will always be there, while the energies of transiting placements are transitory. Transits are in effect for a specific time and overlay the basic natal modes of expression.

There is a school of thought that believes that a transit cannot have an effect unless the transiting planet is already having a relationship (in natal chart) with the planet. For example: transiting Mars opposing natal Venus. Unless natal Venus is aspecting natal Mars, or is in a sign or house ruled by Mars, or is in the 1st or 8th house (mundanely ruled by Mars), or is in some other way affected by Mars, then it is considered that the opposition will have no effect. Personally I do not go this far. Certainly, if there is no tie between these two planets, it will be more difficult to deal with this transiting opposition, as the person has developed no natal coping mechanisms for Venus / Mars energy. And with no natal mechanisms in effect, then the way the person experiences this aspect may well be a "negative" one. But it does not have to be negative. As long as the person is aware of both Venus and Mars in the natal chart, and how each operates, he or she can work out a way for dealing with the blended energies. It just takes more conscious awareness of coping with the energies. This may sound really "California Feelgood," but it does work. This is what the free will part of astrology is all about. You can just muddle along, and life will bring ups and downs, whether or not you pay attention to transits and the like. And paying attention to the transits does not guarantee that you will never be surprised unpleasantly by life again. There are no guarantees. Astrology may be infallible, but we astrologers are not. And anyone who claims to be is just feeding you a line.

The planets bring change into the life and when they contact natal placements by aspect, potentials are set up for energies to be experienced according to the nature of the planets involved, the type of aspect, the signs and houses involved by placement and rulership. This is what prediction is. The astrologer can see which planet is aspecting which natal placement and how, and by blending the meanings of the planets, aspect, signs, and houses involved, the astrologer makes a prediction of possible response to the energies being experienced. The part about seeing which planet is aspecting what is easy. So is seeing which houses and signs are brought into the mix. The blending of energies is more difficult, and the actual prediction of possible response by the client in question is very difficult. Some astrologers refuse to make predictions. There is a school of thought which feels that making predictions is unethical, that you predispose a person to a certain mode of action or behavior and that becomes a form of control over the life of another. Certainly the days of Mars square Uranus always indicating an accident which will cause injury are over. The concept of free will allows the individual to choose the mode of expression of the energies involved. If the individual refuses to choose or even acknowledge the energies are there, then you may end up with the injury-causing accident scenario, but there is no guarantee of that. The astrologers who make the most accurate predictions are using three things (in addition to astrology):

1) common sense and a good understanding of human nature;

2) a thorough knowledge of the client and how she or he has reacted in the past;

3) intuition (or psychic abilities).

The third element is currently frowned upon as a basis for prediction unless it is clearly pointed out and made clear to the client that intuition is the basis for the prediction. In reality, all three elements are often used equally. Each planet, sign, and house means so many things that the astrologer can be overwhelmed by the multiplicity of choices of action available. An astrologer can make a prediction and look to the chart and justify the prediction by the elements involved, but why a specific prediction was made as opposed to the many other possibilities often comes down to intuition. Theoretically, intuitive predictions are the ones which "come out of the blue," but in reality, the astrologer can usually find justification for the prediction. This is not to say that an astrologer can justify anything from any placement (though it can seem that way sometimes), but that each placement has so many different possible modes of expression that the possibilities seem endless.

When I make predictions, I try to let the client know what the energies are which are being brought into focus. From the general statement of what the pure energies are (neither positive or negative, merely modes of expression), I then give a number of possibilities to express the energies, some positive, some negative, some absurd (I like the absurd ones—humor puts a lot of things in perspective). I see planetary placements and transits as a buildup of energy, like when you scuff your feet on a carpet. The expression comes when you then touch an object and make the spark. The energies are there before you make the spark, and the longer you delay and keep scuffing before you touch something, the greater the spark will be. You can make one big spark, waiting as long as possible to act, or you can make a number of small sparks, touching things frequently as you go along. The choice is yours.

One way I suggest to magickal practitioners to experience the energy of natal placements and transits, is to do a circle and confront the energies head-on. Call on the deities of the planets and talk to them, acknowledge their power and influence in your life, and ask them how they would have you react. You don't have to take their advice, but it does provide another viewpoint. In Part Five of this book, there is an astrological circle which I developed to do just such a thing for myself when confronted with a particularly

powerful eclipse. Just meditating on the planets and archetypes involved can also bring insight. Using tarot trumps,
which correspond to the signs and planets, is another
method of focus. You get the idea. Be creative, have fun
(that word again!), do your own thing. That is what astrology is all about—your own thing. This chapter will hopefully give you new ideas of what your own thing is or could
be. Growth means change. Live a little, try something new!

PLANETARY DEFINITIONS

Rather than take a cookbook approach to magickal indicators in your natal chart, I will just present some definitions
and keywords associated with the planets and how each
might work magickally. The reader is then encouraged to
look at his or her natal chart and see which planets (if any)
are in the 4th, 6th, 8th and 12th houses and how they may
interreact (easily, stressfully, cooperatively, in an either/or
fashion). Check out the rulers of the signs on your natal 1st,
4th, 6th, 8th and 12th houses, and the natural rulers of these
houses; Mars, Moon, Mercury, Pluto and Neptune and also
Uranus, which also may have to do with magick.

   Play with this stuff. Pick a day and "do your Mars" in
as many ways as you can think of. Experiential astrology
uses role-playing to get in touch with the energies and
modes of expression of planets and aspects. Do what seems
right to you.

   The Ascendant shows how people project themselves
and what masks they may wear. Any planets in the Ascendant (the 1st house) color that expression with their nature;
the closer they are to the actual Ascendant degree, the more
powerful the expression. Planets in the 12th house within
seven or eight degrees of the Ascendant are also considered
to influence the Ascendant. Read about those planets also, if
you have any, but keep in mind that the influence of these
planets is more unconscious than the influence of those

which are actually in the 1st house. You may not be aware of how these 12th house planets influence the way others see you. If you doubt their influence, ask a good friend or two and see what their impression is of how you project yourself. You may be surprised at how others see you.

And the chart ruler is also important. The chart ruler is the planet that rules the sign upon the Ascendant. Read about that planet and how it operates. See where it is by sign and house, and blend those energies to discover a comfortable magickal mode of expression. Check out old rulerships if your Ascendant is Aquarius, Pisces, or Scorpio, and see how you might blend the energies of the old and new rulers of your Ascendant by signs and houses. Look also at the esoteric ruler of the Ascendant by sign and house for alternative and more spiritual modes of expression.

This will add up to a lot of reading and thinking and acting out energies. Take it slowly, planet by planet. Blend energies and get at two or more planets at once. This is a lifetime work. Expressing and dealing with your personal chart is the work of your life. It is why you chose to be born at the place and time you were. That chart gave you the best opportunity for doing what you needed to do. And realize that when you master one mode of expression, the Gods then come and give you new things to deal with and ponder. As you advance, your abilities and insight grow and mature, your work becomes more complex, and the workload increases to accommodate your expanded abilities. Which then further expands your abilities as you master the new modes of expression so then you are given more complex tasks and so on, and so on. Life—we all keep at it until we die. Then we can rest.

The following paragraphs may make it seem as if it is impossible for a person to be devoid of psychic ability or talent. In a way, that is so. Theoretically what are termed paranormal abilities are really inherent in each of us. But some people manifest these abilities more easily and better than others. If you are reading this book, it is a good bet you are interested in exploring these abilities and honing the psychic skills you possess. This section gives you a way, through astrology, to determine what those abilities might be, and in what areas they may manifest.

SUN ☉

The Sun is the Will (as in to Will, to Know, to Do, and to be Silent), life, it is the center of the solar system and the most personal body in the chart. The house and sign of your natal Sun is where you "shine." The house placement shows the area of life where you need to shine. The sign shows the style you need to do the things of that house. Play with keywords to help discover how you can shine—if you do those things you should feel more fulfilled. This need not mean a change of career or lifestyle, but possibly the addition of a hobby or new pastime or leisure activity. The Sun is the basic identity of the personality, the other planets modify and color this basic expression. How the Sun ties into the chart as a whole shows how easy or challenging it will be for you to be "yourself." The Sun by house, sign, and aspect can show how strong the will is. A Sun which is prominently placed by sign or house, or involved in a lot of close strong aspects, shows a person with a strong will and self-identity. Challenging aspects to the Sun, squares or oppositions, and also conjunctions with challenging planets (Mars, Saturn, Uranus, Pluto, and Chiron), show a life which is one of challenges to the self. Challenging aspects indicate a person who has to fight for individuality and self-expression, and thereby develops a strong will. Trines and sextiles and conjunctions to other planets show the skills and gifts which aid the personality in developing the will. No aspects to the Sun (which is rare) show a person who has difficulty expressing individuality because there are no outlets (or ties) to the rest of the chart. A mutual reception with the Sun can then become highly significant. Again, trying to understand the Sun by house and sign can be extremely beneficial in helping discover outlets for an unaspected Sun. The Sun is the main yang planet of the chart. It shows where the person can be assertive and make a mark. It has been elevated to a position of importance over all other astrological factors. When someone asks, "What's your sign?" that person doesn't mean the Moon, or ascendant, or Saturn. That person means your Sun. The Sun sign does define the basic personality, but it also has to do with the society in which we live, which values all those yang things—assertiveness, will, identity, self-expression, individuality, self-reliance, and all that stuff. That yang stuff is important, but it should be considered equally important as the yin stuff, not moreso. The Sun represents the God as King of the Heavens, Light of the World, consort of the Goddess (as Moon). The Sun determines the seasons of the year.

Moon ☽

The Moon symbolizes the memory, unconscious, emotion, habit, instinct, the "soul" of the person. While your Sun by sign and house shows where you will shine, the Moon by sign and house shows what you need to do to be happy. Again, it is not necessary to change lifestyles or vocation, but using keywords for the sign and house in question will help you discover some possibilities for expression. Adding hobbies or the like to your life can bring happiness and satisfaction. The Moon is also the planet of psychic abilities in general. Looking to the Moon by sign and house and aspects to other planets can give indications of areas of latent psychic talent. If the Moon is tied to any of the magickal houses (4, 6, 8, and 12), by position, rulership (Cancer on the cusp), or aspect to planets in those houses, or planets ruling those houses, there is a likelihood of psychic and magickal ability. How those abilities manifest depends upon the houses, signs, planets involved, and also the climate in which the individual lives. If the individual is in an environment which highly discourages any psychic self-expression, then the abilities will probably be latent or repressed. Our modern society is not honoring of psychic talent, so abilities may not be explored or developed. Using the Moon by sign, house, and aspects can show ways of getting in touch with one's unconscious and ways of exploring emotion, psychic ability and yin energies. The Moon sign is as important as the Sun sign in magick and psychic work. The Moon can indicate the magickal style of the person.

Difficult aspects, oppositions or squares and also conjunctions to planets which cause intensity or turbulence (Sun, Mars, Jupiter, Saturn, Uranus, Neptune, Pluto, and Chiron), show a possibly active and/or turbulent magickal life. The aspects can bring problems and possible pitfalls relating to the nature of the planets aspected, but by meeting the challenges posed, magickal practitioners become stronger and more experienced and (hopefully) wiser in their magickal dealings. Easy aspects show talents which don't necessarily have to be developed. Planets aspecting the Moon by easy aspects can indicate potential magickal allies.

The Moon also represents the Goddess in all her aspects, but most purely as Queen of the Heavens, the Queen of the Night, and also through the Moon's phases the Triple Goddess. Venus also represents the Goddess, though in different forms. How the person serves the Goddess can be determined by looking at the Moon. The Moon also rules the altar, the magickal home base which magickal practitioners create for themselves. In many ways, when people practice magick, they are operating through the Moon. People who have very different magickal personas from their "regular" personalities, have the Moon in a sign which expresses itself differently from the Sun sign. A strong Moon can indicate empathic abilities. Mediumship and scrying are Moon disciplines. The Moon rules children in general as well as childbearing. It also rules fertility (with Venus). The Moon rules midwifery, and all those attendant skills, as well as the menstrual cycle and Women's Mysteries. The Moon rules the tides and day-to-day changes of mood, emotion, weather, and climate.

ASCENDANT

The Ascendant is not a planet, but a point determined by calculation. However, in determining psychic ability, and understanding the self, the Ascendant is extremely important. Where the Sun is the Self, and the Moon is the Soul, the Ascendant is the Mask worn by the personality. It is the "public face" a person shows to the world, the persona which is encountered upon casual social contact. Have you ever met a person at a party or wherever, and gotten an impression of what that person was like, only to learn later, upon more sustained and closer contact, that the person is really very different from that first impression? This is the sign of someone whose Ascendant and Sun are in signs which are very different in style. At the party you met the Ascendant—the mask. Later, as you get to know the person better, the Sun has a chance to come through the mask and shine unimpeded. But it takes a while for the Sun to shine through. There are people who are acutely aware of the difference and jealously guard the Sun's expression, almost never letting anyone get past the mask. Those people are the ones who feel that the more you know about them, the more of a handle you have upon them. Often they are afraid of something, usually a loss of control, and really it only matters to them.

The Ascendant, along with the Sun and Moon, defines people as they operate in the world. Of course, the other planets are important too, but contained within these three energies is about 30 to 50 percent of the person. If there are planets within 8 degrees of the Ascendant, itself, then that planet, or planets are also added into the mix of the mask and the persona, itself. With respect to magickal and psychic expression, if the planets in or near the Ascendant are any of those which have magickal ties (Moon, Mercury, Uranus, Neptune, Pluto, and also Chiron), then the abilities are enhanced. Also, to a lesser extent, any planets which aspect (other than by conjunction) the Ascendant also color the outer persona, and contribute to abilities. The sign upon the Ascendant itself is important, and if it is one of the signs associated with the magickal houses (Cancer, Virgo, Scorpio, or Pisces), it can also be an indicator of magickal and/or psychic abilities. Then the planet which rules the sign upon the Ascendant (the chart ruler), can also be an indicator of talent depending upon the house and sign it is in.

Look at your chart ruler by sign and house as another way of being fulfilled and satisfied with your life. Check out old rulerships if your ascendant is Scorpio or Aquarius or Pisces. Also check out esoteric rulers for more spiritual modes of expression. The esoteric rulers are most effectively used with the ascendant.

MERCURY ☿

Mercury is the Magus, the magickal practitioner. Mercury is neutral, neither yin nor yang. Mercury partakes of the sign it is in and planets in aspect to it for its style of expression. It is also dual (or multiple) by nature. Mercury is a chameleon, adapting itself to the environment. Mercury rules the mind and mentality, speech and communication of all kinds. It rules manual dexterity, wit, cleverness, and movement in general. If the Sun is the Will, Mercury is the Knowledge. Mercury also rules tools and things that are used to gain ends. Mercury shows the kinds of tools and trappings that magickal practitioners will utilize in their magickal self-expression. Mercury also indicates the words (if any) that will be used in magickal workings. Mercury shows what books will be read or created (grimoires). A well-connected Mercury can insure magickal success, even if there is little psychic sensitivity, so long as the practitioners follow directions and go through the proper motions. Mercury/Moon ties can indicate telepathy (psychic communication).

Mercury is the trickster and a thief. Stressful aspects to Mercury, especially by Neptune, can indicate people who delude themselves, who refuse to face up to truths or who allow themselves to be deluded or tricked by others. Once these individuals get past the negative expressions, they can then easily tap into "other worldly" energies. They just have to be careful to remain grounded and be sure to return fully to the "real world" after each exploration.

Mercury-Pluto aspects indicate a penetrating mind which needs to get to the bottom of things, to discover the secrets of life. The person can also be extremely stubborn. Mercury-Uranus aspects indicate a person who has a predilection for practicing astrology. These aspects also indicate someone who has an unusual mind, who comes up with wacky ideas and gets inspirations out of the blue. Mercury-Uranus thinks in leaps of logic, often getting from A to Z without going through B, C, D, and the rest; non-linear thinking is common. Mercury-Chiron indicates one who can be a teacher or mentor, but who also can be a maverick, someone who does not necessarily follow the rules. There can be healing ability, especially by "laying on of hands."

Mercury rules cards, and can incline to a study of tarot. Palmistry also relates to Mercury's rulership of the hands. A strong Mercury gives endless curiosity and a sense of wonder. The mind is always working, and can be occupied with more than one thing at once. There is a danger of over-intellectualization and over-rationalization. But there is a quick wit and a quick tongue. In fact everything is speeded up as Mercury is the quickest planet, it moves forward and back around the Sun. Where Mercury is by sign and house shows where the curiosity lies. When Mercury is retrograde by transit, strong Mercury people are strongly affected, they are thrown into another gear. If natal Mercury is retrograde, the mind is able to think forward and backward simultaneously. There is a marked ability for mathematics. But the retrograde Mercury person may take a while in life to get in touch with curiosity and/or intellect. There may be communications problems. The person could also choose not to exercise the intellect unless interested in a subject, which can make schooling difficult.

Aspects to the Sun, Moon, Ascendant or Mercury by the outer planets (Uranus, Neptune, Pluto, and also Chiron), show an individual who can communicate with the universal, tap into the collective unconscious, work with archetypes, become a channel for the Gods. How this manifests depends upon the planets aspected and where they are by sign and house and the nature of the aspects. In this case, any aspect is better than none. As our modern society is not especially understanding of these abilities, this can lead to being labelled weird, or co-dependent, or (in extreme cases) insane, because these people can exhibit behavior that is not considered normal, and therefore is considered threatening and possibly "deviant." Learning to honor and acknowledge these extraordinary abilities can bring self-esteem and a feeling of acceptance by the self. This type may not be "normal" but it is also not insane. Alcoholism, drug abuse, co-dependent behavior, and some forms of mental illness can be symptoms of being tied into the Universal, but afraid and unable to either cope or turn-off the impressions received. Tobacco and other drugs can blunt or block impressions and possibly "turn off the voices." This is not at all meant to imply that the cause of alcoholism, drug abuse, or mental illness is thwarted psychic expression or a tap into the Gods which is not understood. However, in a society which considers a person who "hears voices" as a possible schizophrenic, it can be detrimental for someone who receives impressions from the great beyond to mention or act upon them, no matter how helpful or benign they may be. Just finding out that one is not alone, that there are others who also have these extra-normal experiences, who can cope and live (mostly) normal lives without being considered "crazy" is often immensely comforting. And being able to learn to control and use those experiences and abilities for the general good can add a feeling of usefulness and purpose, where there was only fear and alienation before.

VENUS ♀

The other Goddess planet is Venus. It has to do with yin energies and also feminine energies. Venus is not psychic or magickal by itself, but in aspect with psychic planets or in magickal signs or houses it can add an aura of glamor and femininity and allure to the magickal persona. Venus likes things to be aesthetic, pretty, well-mannered, cooperative. Venus likes possessions and wealth, so a magickal practitioner with Venus aspecting another magickal planet will have nice things, aesthetic altar trappings, a valuable athame (or other magickal devices/tools). Venus likes growing things and may have a fine garden, either with herbs and vegetables or just beautiful flowers for decoration and/or aromatic oils. Venus is the Goddess of Love. Love, romance, attraction, companionship are all Venus manifestations. And all manifestations of love are of the Venus domain—familial, platonic, sensual/sexual, unrequited, societal, universal. Even hate, which is inverted love pertains to Venus (how you act upon that hatred has to do with Mars). Venus is sensual and this can lead to massage or touching in other ways. Sex is a blend of Venus and Mars energies, Venus for the attraction and sensuality and sensation, and Mars for the sex act, itself. Tantra as a magickal discipline is a Venus/Mars function, because the sensations and touching are as important as the actual sex itself, and Saturn is also included, as there is a measure of control needed to hold off orgasm so as to maximize the buildup and direct the energies to be used in specific ways. The Goddess as symbolized by Venus is the female who is fertile and attractive, who revels in her own sensuality and wants to share her pleasures with others. She can be the Maiden—who is just becoming aware of her sexuality, and her body, and is learning to please herself and others—and the Mother—who is fully awakened to her sexuality, fertility, is skilled, and who is willing to share and pass on those skills. She can be the pregnant Mother (along with the Moon), with wide rounded body bursting with new life and the mysteries of reproduction. She can also be the Hetaera, the skilled courtesan who lives independently and has devoted her life to expressing bodily pleasure and shares and also passes on those skills. Venus is not really a Crone, except as an echo of beauty and fertility.

MARS ☿

Mars is the other main yang planet along with the Sun. Mars is energy, action, and ego. Mercury may be the awareness and intelligence, but Mars is the ME, the I AM. Mars is the me first, I want, pure self-directed ego. Mars can appear selfish, but that's because Mars' main bent is for survival. It takes forethought and awareness (not Mars qualities) to realize that survival may depend upon others and doing with less now may increase chances later. Mars is not a psychic or magickal planet in itself, but Mars can provide drive, energy, and impetus for action. Sun is the Will, Mercury the Knowledge and Mars is the Doing. Misdirected or repressed action manifests as anger, a thwarted Mars. Anger in itself is not a bad thing, a controlled and directed anger can be the catalyst for great actions. But the control and direction have to come from other planets—

like Saturn—Mars is not known for control or discretion. Mars is conflict, war, and aggression. An unaspected Mars in a natal chart is very difficult to deal with. There is no tap into action, no way to motivate and get things going, no outlet for anger. Thwarted Mars can also manifest as frustration. That's why it can be so satisfying to go and do something when angry or frustrated. Mars is physical action and when doing something active you are expressing the Mars energy, thereby alleviating the anger and/or frustration. Mars co-rules Scorpio which rules the 8th house, so it can indirectly tie into magick. Mars is energy, pure, and unmodified. At its most basic, magick is just energy manipulation through controlled visualization. Mars is the energy, the other planets provide the controlled visualization. Also with Mars aspecting a magickal planet, the practitioner can have great courage, to go "where angels fear to tread," but also can be impulsive and incline to action before fully prepared or researched, or even act before full precautions are made. Mars can incline to acting first and thinking later. Mars can also indicate one who is an "energy worker" or fire walker. Phrenology is a Mars phenomenon. Where your Mars is by house and sign shows where you have lots of energy, where you will expend energy. It also shows where your anger buttons are, and how you express that anger. Mars is the sex act itself, independent of love or sensuality. Mars is the God as symbolized by the phallus, a primal force for reproduction and fertility. He is also the God of War, but more generally the God of Action or Energy.

JUPITER ♃

The greater benefic expresses the principles of expansion and increase. Jupiter also deals with philosophy and higher thought. Mercury is the thoughts themselves, and how the mind works, Jupiter is what is contained in the mind.

Jupiter signifies religion and persons "of the cloth." Jupiter also rules the law, courts, and judges. Kempton calls Jupiter "merciful fatso," which sums up a lot of what he is about. Jupiter is considered male or yang in nature, but is not a planet which signifies males in general as the Sun and Mars do. Jupiter may pertain to Men's Mysteries, but that could also be said of the Sun and also Mars. Jupiter certainly rules the studies and philosophies of Men's Mysteries. Whatever Jupiter touches, he expands or causes to increase. Good for money, bad for your waistline. Jupiter transiting over your Ascendant can bring about weight gain. Jupiter can also be pompous and superior. Jupiter likes the grand gesture, going first class, philanthropy, conspicuous consumption. He classically rules physicians and institutional medicine. Jupiter co-ruling Pisces has some magickal influence. He likes big ritual, impressive ceremonies, ecclesiastical rank and hierarchy. Jupiter aspecting a magickal planet will increase that planet's expression, for good or ill. It can incline to trust and optimism. Jupiter in magick can give the capacity for great learning and study. One possible manifestation is someone who reads and learns a lot about magick and the ideas and philosophy of magick, yet may not necessarily practice magick. Jupiter loves learning for learning's sake, but does not always put that learning to practical use. Faith and trust and hope and charity are also Jupiter things. Jupiter is the God as King of Creation, master of all he surveys, bestower of largesse and material benefits. Jupiter as ruler of established religion is not comfortably expressed in Pagan groups. Jupiter is religion, faith and grace, but Neptune is spirituality. So Jupiter's expression of religion is more of what Christians seek nowadays, than that which Pagans seek. Many preachers have strong Jupiters. Jupiter rules languages and foreign cultures and travel. Jupiter in a magickal context can give an aptitude for Rune magick, I Ching, astral travel, dream interpretation, founding one's own tradition (along with Saturn), speaking in tongues.

SATURN ♄

Where Jupiter expresses the principles of expansion and increase, Saturn (Jupiter's father) expresses the principles of decrease and limitation. Jupiter is mercy; Saturn severity. Saturn is the letter of the Law; Jupiter the Spirit. Saturn rules the skin, the largest organ and also that which separates us from the rest of the world. The skin is our boundary, it holds us in, it covers us and protects us from what is outside of us. Saturn rules boundaries and limitations in general, which in themselves are not bad. Saturn also has a lot to do with psychic boundaries, shielding. Saturn can be pessimistic, gloomy, sorrowful, but it is also realistic, grounded, responsible, reliable. Saturn is the great teacher. He brings the hard lessons of life, where we must work hard, where we have a chance for failure, for loss. But if we do work hard and learn the lessons he sets before us, accept our failures and determine not to repeat them, he then eventually rewards our efforts. Jupiter's rewards can come unearned. Saturn's rewards are always worked for, and because of that, they are appreciated more. Saturn is also our fears, limitations, handicaps, doubts, lack of confidence. Look to Saturn by sign and house to see what you fear and where you will meet those fears. Overcome those fears and you will gain self-confidence, wisdom, and maturity—Saturn's gifts.

Saturn is Father, in contrast to the Moon as Mother. Saturn is male and yang, but like Jupiter, does not signify men in general. Saturn is a God, yet Saturn symbolizes the Crone aspect of the Goddess. Saturn is the age and wisdom gained through life and hard work and experience. Saturn can then turn around and teach those hard-learned lessons to those who are younger, less mature, less experienced. Saturn is not fertile, like the Crone, it is past the fertility of youth and cannot have bodily offspring, though Saturn can have children of the mind or intellect. This is where the teacher function of Saturn comes into play. As a God, Jehovah is one of

Saturn's aspects. Jehovah is a stern, severe demanding God-the-Father who punishes disobedience and puts his followers through trials and tribulations. He lays down the law and demands his followers follow it to the letter. He rewards devotion and hard work, yet can also take away that which he has given, leaving the follower with nothing, yet still demands devotion and adherence to ritual and tradition. This version of Saturn/Jehovah has unfortunately given poor Saturn a lot of bad press over the centuries. Saturn was also closely associated with Satan, but the brooding cold malevolent Satan who got people to sign away their souls. The hot passionate impulsive Satan, the "Devil made me do it" guy is Mars.

Saturn does not have to do with magick directly, but it embodies many principles that are essential for successful magickal activity. Sun is the Will, Mercury the Knowledge, Mars is the Doing and Saturn the Silence. Saturn is discipline, hard work, the material world, stones and rocks, the binding of energy, the earthing of power, the "so mote it be." Without Saturn we could not manifest our energies and desires in the material world. We could dream up spells all day, but wouldn't have the discipline to write them down or work on them until they were the best they could be. Saturn aspecting magickal planets can indicate one who has to work hard to become adept, yet once learned, the lessons are never forgotten. Saturn can delay magickal participation, or cause the person to work with people older or younger. Kabbalah and other Judeo-Egyptian type disciplines may be of interest to a Saturn magickal type. They will probably like routine and memorization and solid preparation, rather than just "winging it" in the ritual. Saturn can also indicate a High Priest/ess type personality, or one who is an elder. Working with rocks and crystals is Saturn as is working with gems, along with Venus.

The Saturn Return is a phrase which astrology has made popular, yet few people truly understand what it is. Although most people know only enough to dread its coming, which is a shame. Saturn has a cycle of about 29 years. This means that every 29 years Saturn makes one revolution around the Sun, and returns to the place it was 29 years ago. When Saturn, after it has moved all around the zodiac, returns to the degree where it was at birth, it is called the Saturn Return and is extremely significant for all people. Because of retrograde motion, that period can vary from age 28 to 31 years. The Saturn Return forces people to examine their lives closely, up to that point. They must look at opportunities, how the opportunities were handled, whether they did the work necessary to establish themselves and grow, or if they learned the lessons which life brought. Were they able to learn from or own up to mistakes, or did they do the same stupid things over and over again? Did they accept the consequences for actions, both good and bad, or did they scapegoat and take credit for what was not their efforts? Did they pull their own weight or did they expect others to do for them? Did they think the world owed them a living, or did they forge their own path, as best they could? Did they pay their bills on time and live within their means, or are they in debt up to their eyeballs? Were they grasshoppers or ants? This is the Cosmic Reckoning Time. If people have worked hard and done all the responsible-hard-work-Saturn-things, then they are allowed to take satisfaction in what they have created and reap the benefits of their efforts. If they just played and took what was handed them and have not been responsible or real world, then they are going to have their nose rubbed in all of it and be forced to face up to their prodigality and the waste of their youth. It will not be pleasant. As our society is more play and credit and youth-oriented, many people do not come to their Saturn Returns prepared to answer those hard questions successfully. They are then forced to start over and will hopefully learn those lessons the second time around. Hence the dread. Saturn may delay, but you cannot escape Saturn's evaluation of your cosmic progress. The Hindus consider Saturn to be the most spiritual planet.

Work hard and you will attain enlightenment. People who have strong Saturns in their birthchart may have a hard life up to the Saturn Return, but they have also probably worked hard and been responsible and paid their bills and so the Saturn Return becomes a time of appreciation and enjoyment of their accomplishments.

One person I know was able to attain her dream and, with help, was able to buy a house during the Saturn Return. It was a lot of work, but it also paid off.

There is another Saturn Return at about age 58 and yet another at about age 87. They bring up similar issues. If the first return was successful, or if not and the individual finally got her or his act together, then the later returns can bring societal recognition and material reward from the life's work. With successful Saturn returns, you gain and grow and prosper materially and spiritually. Each Saturn return can be either a "high water mark" of achievement and growth or a "time to pay the piper" for waste and prodigality. Hopefully the new Saturn cycle brings new work and issues into the life, and marks a new life stage. Sadly, for some each Saturn Return just serves to point up all the failures and mistakes and these people are forced to repeat the same lessons until they finally get them right. And starting over at 58 (or 87) is lots harder than starting over at 29. The ancient Greeks did not consider a person an adult until the first Saturn Return had been completed. These Saturn return issues contrast Jupiter (fun, play prodigality) with Saturn (hard work, responsibility, paying bills). Guess which is the stronger of the two planets, and in the end, a better friend and ally?

THE OUTER PLANETS

The outer planets (or modern planets) are more magickal and mystic by nature. They are transcendental and transpersonal. Not everyone will be able to resonate to their energies. And their energies are most easily misunderstood, as they operate not personally, but societally, and often in an overwhelming manner. Having a personal planet in aspect to one of these planets is like having a "nine ampere tap into God." People may be quite psychic and able to transcend the material world easily, but can also get caught up in energies far greater than they can ever handle alone, or even with a group. With these planets it is especially important to pay close attention to all the magickal precautions. Shielding and grounding and centering are also very important. These planets, when natally afflicted, can indicate a potential for "possession," the taking over (or sharing) of the body by discarnate beings. This can happen voluntarily or otherwise. All three planets are also chaotic, in their own ways. They are higher octaves of other planets and so resonate well with the planet which they are associated with, but they are also like supercharged versions of those other planets, and can become overwhelming. The transits of these outer planets are long-lasting and life-changing. When aspecting the Sun, Moon, or Ascendant they can cause permanent personality and/ or life changes, according to their natures. Or they can cause no effect at all, if people are not able to resonate to the energies. Most people will not experience a full cycle of these planets. Their periods of 84, 186, and 248 years are longer than our average lifetimes. Most all people will experience the squares of Neptune and Pluto and the opposition of Uranus. All three of these aspects are considered to be triggers for the midlife crisis, with changes according to the natures of each. Depending upon the year born (Pluto having an elliptical orbit) the Pluto square can occur from age 37 to 58 (or older). The Uranus opposition occurs about age 42, and the Neptune square occurs at about the same time. For people who were born from 1950 to 1956, all three happen at about the same time. Lotsa fun! (I have a strange idea of fun.) I am not trying to frighten people, but to make people aware of the energies which are manifest in these three planets. Each is a powerhouse in its own right.

URANUS ♅

Uranus is the higher octave of Mercury, and so all those Mercury things also have an affinity for Uranus. But Uranus is also electric—literally. Uranus rules electricity and electromagnetic communication. The chaos of Uranus is the most pure chaotic expression. It is the chaos of true randomness. It is explosion and anarchy and revolution and new strange and radical ideas. Uranus is sudden insights which come from the blue and are not necessarily provable by linear logic. Uranus corresponds to the Tower card, Trump 16 of the tarot. In magick, Uranus does not rule a magickal house or sign (it rules Aquarius and the 11th house), but it is manifest in the magickal energy constructs that go out and make manifest the magickal practitioners' will and workings. Mars is tangible energy, fire and the like, but Uranus is intangible energy. It is the bolt from the blue which can strike without warning. Uranus electrifies whatever planet it aspects and house it is in. In transits, Uranus can cause sudden unexpected change, but whatever Uranus takes away, it gives back twofold. It can cause explosions and upsets. Uranus energy is not easily controllable in intensity, but it can be shaped and directed like a lightning bolt. Once discharged, it has to build up again to discharge level. Uranus is the sudden enlightenment of genius, the urge for anarchic social change, democracy and the voice of the people, the political power of groups of activists, the energy built up in a working coven, the industrial revolution and the coming of progress, science fiction and the future.

NEPTUNE ♆

Neptune is the most spiritual and elusive of the planets. As it rules Pisces and the 12th house, it can probably be termed the ruling planet of magick. Mercury was the classical ruler of magick. Neptune is an insubstantial, elusive planet. It rules fog, illusion, dance, oils, and perfumes, poisons, alcoholism, and spirituality. It dissolves whatever it touches, and allows contact with the divine, however that may be perceived. Jupiter rules religion, but that is organized religion—a concrete solid stated faith with rules and codes of behavior. Neptune rules spirituality and the indescribable feeling of union with the universal. Neptune deals with karma and reincarnation—a nice theory but not really empirically provable by tangible means. Neptune's spirituality is somewhat at odds with Jupiter's religion. Neptune allows each to directly perceive the divine, which is at odds with—and directly challenges—a number of established religious practices. The New Age is a Neptunian phenomenon, arising out of the spirituality movement of the 19th century, which was also Neptunian in nature. Mars is ego and survival, and Neptune dissolves the ego so the individuality can merge with the divine. Neptune sacrifices individuality in service to the divine. People with a strong Neptune have trouble in our material success-oriented society. Jesus was a Neptunian figure, his emphasis being on the divine and not having a strong stake in the material world. Neptune's chaos is the chaos of formlessness. Neptune dissolves structure and solid things, and converts them to the spiritual. In magick, Neptune rules the unseen realms, the spirit worlds, the divine presence which can be felt by the adept, the subtle elusive changes and perceptions which occur while magick is being worked, and the subtle but profound changes which come about from practicing magick over a period of time. It is the adept's sensitivity to all which is not solid or tangible nor even of this world, but which is the body and soul of magickal working. Art and music and dance are realms where Neptune's subtle elusive enlightenments can be made manifest. Neptune is the higher octave of Venus, causing Venus' love to be transformed and made universal.

PLUTO ♀

Pluto's chaos is the chaos of upheaval and transformative change. Urban renewal is a very Pluto phenomenon. Pluto tears down and destroys old forms and structures, and then rebuilds from those ruins a new reality. The phoenix is very much a Pluto symbol. Pluto does not bring renewal without destruction, but some people only see the destruction and do not perceive the rebuilding as the second half of the Pluto cycle. The cyclic fertility, death, dormancy and rebirth of the God is a Pluto image. Persephone's journey into the underworld and transformation thereby is also a Pluto image. Where Neptune is dissolving and insidious, causing change so subtly as to be imperceptible, Pluto causes upheaval and its actions are always strongly apparent. Living through a Pluto transit is not fun, or even enjoyable, but after it is all over, the transformed person often has the feeling of being glad it happened, but also being glad the change is over. It is like a purgative cleansing, yukky and unpleasant while it is happening, but it sure feels good once all the toxins are all gone. Pluto is the higher octave of Mars. Where Mars is energy, Pluto is power. Nuclear power is another Pluto phenomenon. Often, Pluto operates in the underworld, making changes and building pressures, and when the pressures have built to a peak, then the energies explode into the outer, conscious world. A volcano is another good Pluto image. You can't see the magma rising or feel the pressures building until it is about to blow up, and when it does blow it is always something of a surprise. You know the pressures are building but cannot exactly predict when it will blow. Pluto rules Scorpio and the 8th house. In magick, Pluto rules the transformations which initiations bring about. Pluto is the power that can be summoned and wielded by the adept, but this power can also become too great to be manipulated by mortals, and then it can end up manipulating those who sought to control it. Pluto has to do with the overwhelming forces of nature which cause upheaval and change, but which are also cleansing.

MUTUAL RECEPTION

Mutual reception is another concept used in horary and electional astrology. It can provide another means of "getting at" certain energies in a chart. In natal astrology, mutual reception is also used in interpreting planetary influences. Mutual reception occurs when two planets are in each others' signs of rulership. Like Mars in Cancer and the Moon in Aries. What this sets up is a sort of feedback loop. Mars is in Cancer, so the Moon has influence over Mars as Moon rules Cancer in the mundane wheel. With the Moon in Aries, Mars has influence over the Moon as Mars rules Aries. With both these planets in each others' signs, each has influence over the other, and referring to one gets you the other which refers you back to the original which then refers you to the other etc., etc., ad nauseum. It then becomes an endless loop. The two planets, being in each others' signs, are considered to support each other. This can erase debilities (as with Mars being in its fall in Cancer) and strengthens the two planets in question.

This becomes important when determining a "final dispositor" for the chart. There can be no single final dispositor if there are two planets in mutual reception in a chart. A single final dispositor is a planet in its own sign, to which, through chains of rulership, all the other planets lead. It is fairly rare and becomes a focal determinator in the chart in question. In a natal chart, a single final dispositor can have more influence than the chart ruler (ruler of the Ascendant). This will be discussed in depth in the next section.

With mutual receptions, the two planets in each others' signs are tied together, so to speak, by cross-rulership ties. It can be another way in which planets interrelate without an aspect between them. Some astrologers consider each planet to be as if in two places at once in the chart, one being the actual placement, and the other being the same place as the other mutually received planet. They then have two sets of aspects and sign and house placements for those planets. If the planets in question are in actual aspect also (as Mars in Cancer and Moon in Aries can be square to each other), the influence of the mutual reception is considered a mitigating influence, and can soften the harshness of a stressful aspect, and make more wonderful the influence of an easy aspect. Some astrologers go so far as to interpret the placements of the two planets as if exchanging places, instead of being in the places they are in the chart, and then they interpret each planet as if it were back in its own sign, by aspect, sign, and house placement.

In natal charts, mutual receptions can have another application. Two planets which are in mutual reception can be considered to be in "fortunate aspect." Those planets may or may not aspect each other, but because they are in mutual reception, they are sometimes read as if in favorable aspect to each other. It is considered a good thing. The two planets in mutual reception are always tied together in the person's life, even if you don't consider them in favorable aspect.

There is a book published some years ago which took the idea of mutual reception even further, considering house rulership as well as sign rulership, and intermixing and cross-correlating them.[1] So Saturn in Scorpio could (in this system) be considered to be in mutual reception with Pluto in the 10th—Pluto ruling Scorpio and Saturn ruling the 10th. Or Mars in the 3rd is in mutual reception with Mercury in the 1st, Mars naturally ruling the 1st and Mercury ruling the 3rd. It gets really confusing.

---

[1]Anne Ryan, *Planets in Mutual Reception* (South Euclid, OH: The House of Astrology, 1980).

If you only get the idea that the two planets being in each others' signs creates a feedback loop which allows you to interchange the two, then you will have grasped enough of mutual reception to make it effective. You can also have pairs of planets which, when in mutual reception, erase debilities or detriments of both planets. Below is a list:

Sun in Aquarius—Uranus in Leo

Moon in Scorpio—Mars in Cancer (old Mars rulership of Scorpio)

Moon in Capricorn—Saturn in Cancer

Mercury in Sagittarius or Pisces—Jupiter in Gemini or Virgo (modern and old rulerships of Jupiter)

Mercury in Pisces—Neptune in Virgo

Venus in Aries or Scorpio—Mars in Taurus or Libra (modern and old rulerships of Mars)

This can be a way of getting your influence and bypassing unfortunate placements. Some of these pairs are not often in effect (Neptune was in Virgo from 1929 to 1942, roughly), but some are fairly common—Venus-Mars, for example. If it's available, then take advantage of it.

FINAL DISPOSITOR

Related to the concept of mutual reception is the concept of a single final dispositor (or final dispositor for short). This is a condition where one planet is in its own sign of rulership (and I tend to use modern rulerships only), and all other planets, through chains of rulership reference (or disposition), end up at that single planet in rulership. If there is a mutual reception, there can be no final dispositor, for those two planets will refer to each other endlessly in a closed loop. If no planets are in rulership signs, there can be no final dispositor. If two (or more) planets are in rulership signs, there can be no single final dispositor, for there are two (or more) planets in rulership, and therefore two (or more) endpoints of reference (or disposition).

It is like the planet in its own sign (final dispositor) is the "boss" and all the other planets lead to that planet through chains of command—like in the military, or at a large corporation. Eventually the chain of command ends up at one big boss—"the buck stops here." In a chart—natal, horary or electional—a single final dispositor is an extremely strong planet and becomes the dominant planet in the chart, moreso than the chart ruler (ruler of the Ascendant). It is as if you have to deal with that final dispositor in the end, all roads lead to it, so it becomes the big boss of the chart. You might as well just deal with it directly and cut out all the middle men. In an electional chart, it becomes the big high focus of the chart, and so anything you do will have the influence of that planet all over it, no matter how you approach the matter. Even if there are no direct aspects to that planet in the chart, it is still the big boss, only more behind the scenes than out front. Using a final dispositor gets you mega-influence of that planet, regardless of the aspects.

Unfortunately, from 7 February 1991 to 7 April 1996, there can be no single final dispositor in any chart at all. First Saturn and Uranus are in mutual reception and then Saturn and Neptune are in mutual reception. As these planets move slowly, they remain in a sign for years. And so the mutual receptions are in effect for years. This also continues into the next century, with long times of mutual receptions due to the outer planets being in the last five signs which are ruled by the slower moving outer planets. More times of long mutual receptions are:

11 March 2003 to 15 September, 2003;

31 December 2003 to 28 May, 2010;

15 August 2010 to 12 March 2011
(all Uranus in Pisces and Neptune in Aquarius).

6 October, 2012 to 23 September, 2014;

16 June 2015 to 18 September 2015,
(both Saturn in Scorpio and Pluto in Capricorn).

27 October 2005 to 24 November, 2006,
(Jupiter in Scorpio and Pluto in Sagittarius.
This is concurrent with the Uranus/Neptune mutual
reception).

This is unusual to have so much of these 24 years (roughly
60%) being times of mutual receptions.

The concept of a final dispositor works in natal charts
also. The final dispositor becomes the big boss of the
chart and then usurps the influence of the chart ruler
(ruler of the Ascendant). If the final dispositor and chart
ruler are the same, it becomes a double whammy of influence. In any case, the final dispositor becomes the most
important planet in the chart, and the sign and house it
occupies is the area where the life will be played out. It
focuses energy immensely on that planet, sign, and
house. Everything a person does eventually leads back to
that planet sign and house. It creates a single focus, but
can also lead to obsession and narrow-mindedness. It
depends upon how the person relates to the energies of
that planet sign and house, and if the rest of the chart
supports that influence. If the rest of the chart is not in
tune with the final dispositor, then the person feels torn;
the dispositor being the major influence is the strongest,
yet the rest of the chart doesn't support that expression so
the person feels unable to cope with the needs and focus
of the final dispositor.

Example 1

When checking a chart for a final dispositor, I look at each planet and see if the complimentary ruler is in the others' sign. For example, you have a chart with Sun in Aries, Moon in Virgo, Mercury in Pisces, Venus in Aries, Mars in Leo, Jupiter in Capricorn, Saturn in Pisces, Uranus in Aquarius, Neptune in Capricorn and Pluto in Sagittarius. See figure 5 on page 188. (These placements were made up and do not correspond to any actual placements.)

First off, I see that Uranus is in Aquarius, its own sign, so we have the possibility for a single final dispositor. I will keep this in mind as I check the rest of the planets. Sun is in Aries, and as Mars is the ruler of Aries and the Sun the ruler of Leo, I would need Mars in Leo for the Sun and Mars to be in mutual reception. Mars is in Leo, so the Sun and Mars are indeed in mutual reception. This ends the possibility of Uranus, being a single final dispositor, as there is mutual reception between other planets. I will continue checking mutual reception, however; Moon is in Virgo, and so Mercury, the ruler of Virgo would have to be in Cancer, which the Moon rules. It is not. Mercury is in Pisces, and so Neptune, the ruler of Pisces or Jupiter, the co-ruler of Pisces will have to be in Virgo or Gemini, the signs ruled by Mercury. Neptune is in Capricorn and Jupiter is also in Capricorn, so there is no mutual reception with either. Venus is in Aries, so Mars the ruler of Aries will have to be in Taurus or Libra, and as it is in Leo and already in mutual reception with the Sun, we again find no correlation. We already checked Mars (through the Sun). Jupiter is in Capricorn, so we would need Saturn, ruler of Capricorn, in either Sagittarius or Pisces. And Saturn is in Pisces, so Jupiter and Saturn are in mutual reception. Saturn is in Pisces, and we then would need Neptune or Jupiter (co-rulers of Pisces) to be in Capricorn or Aquarius (signs ruled by Saturn). And both Neptune and Jupiter are in Pisces, so Saturn is in mutual reception with BOTH Jupiter and Neptune. (It would also work if either or both Jupiter and Neptune were also in Aquarius.) This then ties all three planets together and becomes a very powerful stand-out in the chart, be it natal or electional. You are able to "get at" all three planets through any one of them. We have dealt with Uranus at the beginning, and being in its own sign, it cannot be in mutual reception at all. We dealt with Neptune when we looked at Saturn (but we can look again and see Neptune is in Capricorn, and Saturn is in Pisces, so they are in mutual reception). It works starting with either planet—it has to. If not, you made a mistake somewhere. Pluto is in Sagittarius, and as Jupiter is not in Scorpio, there is no mutual reception between them.

So after all that we get: Uranus is in its own sign, Aquarius. Sun and Mars are in mutual reception. Jupiter and Saturn are in mutual reception and Saturn and Neptune are also in mutual reception. So Saturn, Jupiter and Neptune are all tied by mutual receptions. All other planets are not affected by rulership or mutual reception at all. Uranus is not a single final dispositor, as there is mutual reception.

If Uranus (or any other planet) was a single final dispositor, it would mean that to "get at" the energies of the chart, you would have to go through Uranus (or whichever planet). Since all planets lead to the final dispositor, you have to go there to get to the energies of the chart.

Example 2

Let's look at another example. Sun in Taurus, Moon in Pisces, Mercury in Aries, Venus in Gemini, Mars in Aquarius, Jupiter in Aries, Saturn in Scorpio, Uranus in Aquarius, Neptune in Capricorn, and Pluto in Sagittarius. See Figure 6, page 188.

We see that of all the planets, Uranus is in its own sign, Aquarius, a possible final dispositor. We will keep this in mind. Sun is in Taurus, so we look to see if Venus is in Leo;

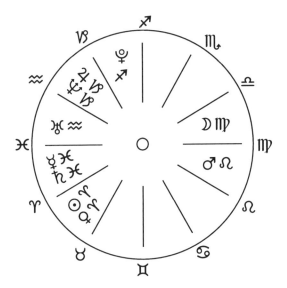

Figure 5.   Final dispositor example 1.

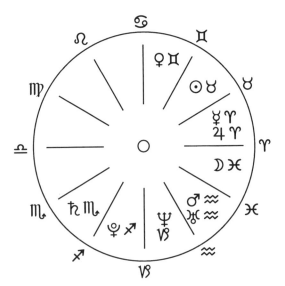

Figure 6.   Final dispositor example 2.

it is not. Moon is in Pisces so we look to see if Neptune or Jupiter is in Cancer; neither is. Mercury is in Aries, so we look to see if Mars is in Gemini or Virgo; it is not. Venus is in Gemini, so we look to see if Mercury is in Taurus or Libra; it is not. Mars is in Aquarius, and we know Uranus is in its own sign, so there is no mutual reception there. Jupiter is in Aries, and Mars is in neither Sagittarius nor Pisces. Saturn is in Scorpio, and Mars is not in Capricorn. It is in Aquarius, however, so mutual reception *can* exist. But Scorpio is also ruled by Pluto, and Pluto is in neither Capricorn nor Aquarius. This brings up a tricky question. In determining final dispositors, I personally like to use the modern rulerships, and let the older dual rulerships go. There are those who will disagree with me. Some will consider it fudging. However, with Saturn in Scorpio and Mars in Aquarius we are using *two* secondary rulerships. (Saturn co-ruling Aquarius and Mars co-ruling Scorpio.) Personally, I feel this can be a bit of a stretch. I will reserve judgment until I have finished with the rest of the planets, and make my decision then. Uranus is in its own sign. Neptune is in Capricorn, and Saturn is not in Pisces. Pluto is in Sagittarius and Jupiter is not in Scorpio.

So we end up with one planet in its own sign, and one possible weak mutual reception. Now comes the part where we see if all roads (planets) lead to Uranus. The Sun is in Taurus so it disposes of (refers us to) Venus, which is in Gemini, which refers us to (disposes of) Mercury, which is in Aries, which refers us to Mars, which is in Aquarius, which refers us to Uranus, which is in its own sign so the road stops there. We have tied a chain of rulerships to Uranus, all five planets (Sun, Venus, Mercury, Mars and Uranus) end up with Uranus in Aquarius. So far so good. Jupiter is in Aries and refers us to Mars. Since we know Mars already leads us to Uranus, we need go no further (though we can for practice—Jupiter is in Aries and refers us to Mars, which is in Aquarius which refers to Uranus, which is in its own sign, Aquarius.) Saturn is in Scorpio. With planets in signs of dual rulership, I prefer to use the modern rulership, when checking for a final dispositor. It is the more pure, less muddied expression of energy. It does set up a condition where you could have a final dispositor *and* a mutual reception. Some would consider it heresy, or fudging and trying to have your cake and eat it too. So far, it has worked for me. Anyhow, Saturn is in Scorpio which refers us to Pluto in Sagittarius which refers us to Jupiter in Aries (which refers us to Mars in Aquarius and then leads us to Uranus in Aquarius). Moon is in Pisces which refers us to Neptune in Capricorn, which leads us to Saturn in Scorpio (which refers us to Pluto in Sagittarius, which leads us to Jupiter in Aries, which refers us to Mars in Aquarius, which ends up leading to Uranus in Aquarius). So all ten planets end up leading us to Uranus in Aquarius. All roads lead there, so we can say Uranus in Aquarius is the single final dispositor in this chart. All attempts to do anything with this chart end up at Uranus, so it is best to deal with Uranus directly. We are in the position of having a possible mutual reception (Mars in Aquarius and Saturn in Scorpio), but with the single final dispositor I will just toss out the weak mutual reception, and deal with Uranus, who ends up being the boss. My judgment call. You can operate differently. In determining the chain of references (or chain of dispositors) I always use modern rulerships. Always.

Example 3

Another Example: Sun in Scorpio, Moon in Taurus, Mercury in Libra, Venus in Libra, Mars in Cancer, Jupiter in Leo, Saturn in Cancer, Uranus in Pisces, Neptune in Aries, and Pluto in Sagittarius. See Figure 7 on page 191.

We see that Venus is in Libra, its own sign, a possible final dispositor. Sun is in Scorpio, and neither Pluto nor Mars is in Leo. Moon is in Taurus, and Venus is not in Cancer. Mercury is in Libra and Venus is not in Gemini or Virgo. We dealt with Venus already. Mars is in Cancer and Moon is not in Aries or Scorpio. Jupiter is in Leo and Sun is

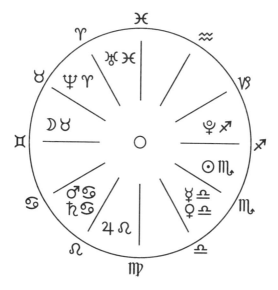

Figure 7.   Final dispositor example 3.

not in Sagittarius or Pisces. Saturn is in Cancer and Moon is not in Capricorn or Aquarius. Uranus is in Pisces and neither Neptune nor Jupiter is in Aquarius. Neptune is in Aries, and Mars is not in Pisces. Pluto is in Sagittarius and Jupiter is not in Scorpio.

So far, so good, no mutual receptions. Now we will trace the "roads" (references, dispositions) and see if they all lead back to Venus in Libra. Moon and Mercury are in Taurus and Libra so both lead directly to Venus in Libra. Mars and Saturn are both in Cancer, which refer to the Moon which leads directly to Venus. Neptune is in Aries and leads to Mars, which leads (through the Moon) to Venus. Uranus is in Pisces which refers to Neptune, which eventually leads back to Venus. The Sun is in Scorpio, which leads to Pluto in Sagittarius, which refers to Jupiter in Leo which refers to the Sun is Scorpio which leads to Pluto in Sagittarius. Oh dear. These three planets, while not in mutual reception, form a closed loop. Each refers to the other in a closed loop of three, endlessly. Using modern rulerships, you cannot break out of this loop. So where we have a single planet in its own sign, and no mutual receptions, we *do not* have a single final dispositor, because of that closed loop. This happens fairly often, which is why you have to trace back the rulerships and references and leads.

Hopefully these examples illustrate how the concept of mutual reception and final dispositors work. If there is no planet in its sign of rulership, there can be no final dispositor. If there are two or more planets in their signs of rulership, there can be no single final dispositor (because there are two or more possible endpoints of leads, or references, or dispositions). And if there are planets in mutual reception, again there can be no final dispositor. Go back to Charts 5–10 on pp. 133, 135, 139, 143, 146, 147 of the famous dead people. One of these has a single final dispositor.

It's fun to go through charts and trace mutual receptions and final dispositors. At the very least you really learn your rulerships. And they provide different ways of getting at planetary energies which you can then use in your workings. And if you have a single final dispositor in your natal chart, then you are well advised to become friends with that planet and explore the various ways of expressing its energies by sign and house placement.

NORTH AND SOUTH NODES OF THE MOON

The Moon's Nodes are astronomical points which are considered to be of importance in astrology, in natal and also horary and electional work. What they are have several applications.

The Sun follows the exact same path through the sky year after year. This is called the ecliptic. *Ecliptic* is a word derived from eclipse, and the two are interrelated. The

Moon moves along a much broader path in the sky, moving north or south of the ecliptic by as much as 24+ degrees. This placement north or south of the ecliptic applies to all the planets, and adds the third dimension of up or down to the two-dimensional astrological chart.

When planets are within one degree of each other in this north or south dimension (both planets being either north or south), they are considered to be parallel in declination, which is an aspect similar in influence to a conjunction. If two planets are within one degree but in opposite declinations (one north and the other south), they are considered to be contra-parallel in declination, which is an aspect similar to an opposition. These aspects cannot be easily determined by looking at a standard astrological chart. Looking at the planets in signs and houses gives no indication of declination and whether or not they are parallel or contra-parallel. Declinations are often listed in a ¡able somewhere on the horoscope sheet among the numbers and other gobbledygook. In the aspectarian, they are depicted along with any other aspects. (See chart 11, page 195.) Planets may be parallel or contra-parallel irrespective of any other aspects which may or may not be in effect. Many astrologers do not consider these aspects, because they require extra calculations, and are not readily apparent. But they are valid and can show planetary blending of energies which may not show up otherwise.

The Moon's Nodes are astronomical points, one directly opposite the other, which show where the Moon will cross the ecliptic. Why is this important? When the Moon crosses the ecliptic and either conjuncts or opposes the Sun, an eclipse will occur. Actually if the new or full Moon is within a maximum of $18\frac{1}{2}$ degrees (or a minimum of 12 degrees) of the nodal axis, an eclipse will occur. Now, just because an eclipse is occurring doesn't mean it will be total or visible in your area. A solar eclipse which occurs while it is night in your location will not be visible for you. Even if it is daytime, the eclipse may be only partial for

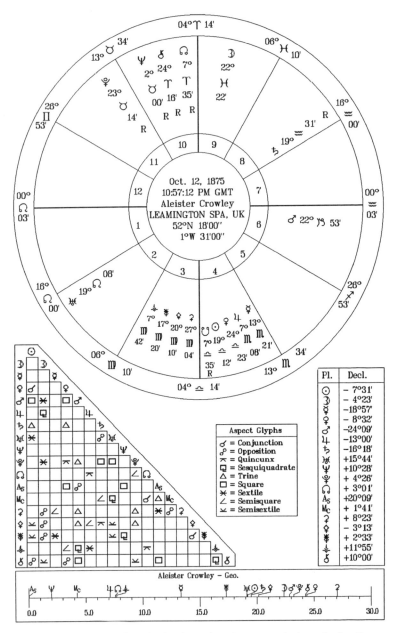

Chart 11. Aleister Crowley's chart showing aspectarian, declinations, planet and house longitudes, element/quality tally, a 30° strip chart, plus a key to planet, sign, and aspect symbols for beginners.

Aleister Crowley — Natal Chart

Planets in Elements and Modalities

Fire	♅ ☊ As Mc ⚷	Total = 5	Weighted Score = 8
Earth	♂ ♆ ♇ ⚳ ⚴ ⚵ ⚶	Total = 7	Weighted Score = 8
Air	☉ ♀ ♄	Total = 3	Weighted Score = 6
Water	☽ ☿ ♃	Total = 3	Weighted Score = 6
Cardinal	☉ ♀ ♂ ☊ Mc ⚷	Total = 6	Weighted Score = 11
Fixed	☿ ♃ ♄ ♅ ♆ ♇ As	Total = 7	Weighted Score = 10
Mutable	☽ ⚳ ⚴ ⚵ ⚶	Total = 5	Weighted Score = 7

Weights Used: ☉=3, ☽=3, ☿=2, ♀=2, ♂=2, ♃=1, ♄=1, ♅=1, ♆=1, ♇=1, ☊=0, As=3, Mc=3,

Planetary Dignities (Modern)

Planets in Rulerships	♀
Planets in Exaltations	♂
Planets in Detriments	♅ ♇
Planets in Fall	☉

There are no Mutual Receptions.

Planet		Geo. Long.	G.Trav.	Geo. Lat.	Antiscia	Rt. Asc.	Decl.	Hel. Long.	Hel. Lat.
Sun–Earth	☉	19°♎12′17″	+ 0°59′	+ 0°00′	10°♓48′	197°43′	− 7°31′	19°♈12′	+ 0°00′
Moon	☽	22°♓22′15″	+14°01′	− 1°28′	7°♎38′	353°35′	− 4°23′	19°♈12′	+ 0°00′
Mercury	☿	13°♏21′	+ 0°36′	− 3°14′	16°♒39′	219°51′	−18°57′	16°♒43′	− 7°00′
Venus	♀	24°♎23′	+ 1°15′	+ 1°00′	5°♓37′	202°57′	− 8°32′	1°♏32′	+ 2°22′
Mars	♂	22°♑53′	+ 0°38′	− 2°41′	7°♐08′	295°11′	−24°09′	6°♓58′	− 1°44′
Jupiter	♃	7°♏08′	+ 0°13′	+ 0°57′	22°♒52′	215°06′	−13°00′	10°♏23′	+ 1°07′
Saturn	♄	19°♒31′R	− 0°01′	− 1°24′	10°♏29′	322°24′	−16°18′	24°♒33′	− 1°19′
Uranus	♅	19°♌08′	+ 0°02′	+ 0°40′	10°♉52′	141°47′	+15°44′	16°♌27′	+ 0°41′
Neptune	♆	2°♉00′R	− 0°02′	− 1°49′	28°♌00′	30°27′	+10°28′	1°♉34′	− 1°46′
Pluto	♇	23°♉14′R	− 0°01′	−14°36′	6°♌46′	54°29′	+ 4°26′	22°♉34′	−14°21′
N. Node	☊	7°♈35′R	− 0°03′	+ 0°00′	22°♍25′	6°58′	+ 3°01′	19°♈12′	+ 0°00′
Ascendant	As	0°♌03′		+ 0°00′	29°♉57′	122°14′	+20°09′		
Midheaven	Mc	4°♈14′		+ 0°00′	25°♍46′	3°53′	+ 1°41′		
Ceres	⚳	27°♍04′	+ 0°27′	+ 7°52′	2°♈56′	180°28′	+ 8°23′	18°♍30′	+10°37′
Pallas	⚴	20°♍10′	+ 0°29′	− 7°44′	9°♈50′	167°56′	− 3°13′	7°♍04′	−10°37′
Juno	⚵	17°♍20′	+ 0°24′	− 2°40′	12°♈40′	167°19′	+ 2°33′	5°♍41′	− 3°28′
Vesta	⚶	7°♍42′	+ 0°26′	+ 3°29′	22°♈18′	160°43′	+11°55′	21°♌45′	+ 4°26′
Chiron	⚷	24°♈16′R	− 0°03′	+ 0°38′	5°♍44′	22°14′	+10°00′	23°♈59′	+ 0°36′

Aleister Crowley — Midpoints in Planetary Order — Modulus = 360.00 — Geo

♈ 00°♈00′	☉/♇ 06°♌13′	☿/♂ 18°♐07′	♀/⚷ 24°♋20′	♄ 19°♒31′	♆/⚳ 14°♋32′	As/⚷ 12°♊10′
♈/☉ 09°♋36′	☉/☊ 13°♋24′	☿/♃ 10°♏14′	♂ 22°♑53′	♄/♅ 19°♏20′	♆/⚴ 11°♋05′	Mc 04°♈14′
♈/☽ 26°♍11′	☉/As 09°♍38′	☿/♄ 01°♑26′	♂/♃ 15°♐00′	♄/♆ 25°♍45′	♆/⚵ 09°♋40′	Mc/⚳ 00°♋39′
♈/☿ 21°♋40′	☉/Mc 11°♋43′	☿/♅ 01°♎14′	♂/♄ 06°♒12′	♄/♇ 06°♎23′	♆/⚶ 04°♋51′	Mc/⚴ 27°♊12′
♈/♀ 12°♋12′	☉/⚳ 08°♎08′	☿/♆ 07°♌40′	♂/♅ 06°♏00′	♄/☊ 13°♍33′	♆/⚷ 28°♈08′	Mc/⚵ 25°♊47′
♈/♂ 26°♌26′	☉/⚴ 04°♎41′	☿/♇ 18°♌18′	♂/♆ 12°♍26′	♄/As 09°♏47′	♇ 23°♉14′	Mc/⚶ 20°♊58′
♈/♃ 18°♋34′	☉/⚵ 03°♎16′	☿/☊ 25°♋28′	♂/♇ 23°♍03′	♄/Mc 11°♍53′	♇/☊ 00°♉25′	Mc/⚷ 14°♈15′
♈/♄ 09°♍46′	☉/⚶ 28°♍27′	☿/As 21°♍42′	♂/☊ 00°♍14′	♄/⚳ 08°♐18′	♇/As 26°♊39′	⚳ 27°♍04′
♈/♅ 09°♊34′	☉/⚷ 21°♋44′	☿/Mc 23°♋47′	♂/As 26°♎28′	♄/⚴ 04°♐51′	♇/Mc 28°♈44′	⚳/⚴ 23°♍37′
♈/♆ 16°♈00′	☽ 22°♓22′	☿/⚳ 20°♎12′	♂/Mc 28°♌33′	♄/⚵ 03°♐26′	♇/⚳ 25°♋09′	⚳/⚵ 22°♍12′
♈/♇ 26°♈37′	☽/☿ 17°♑51′	☿/⚴ 16°♎45′	♂/⚳ 24°♏58′	♄/⚶ 28°♏37′	♇/⚴ 21°♋42′	⚳/⚶ 17°♍23′
♈/☊ 03°♈48′	☽/♀ 08°♑23′	☿/⚵ 15°♎20′	♂/⚴ 21°♏31′	♄/⚷ 21°♍54′	♇/⚵ 20°♋17′	⚳/⚷ 10°♋40′
♈/As 00°♊02′	☽/♂ 22°♒37′	☿/⚶ 10°♎31′	♂/⚵ 20°♏06′	♅ 19°♌08′	♇/⚶ 15°♋28′	⚴ 20°♍10′
♈/Mc 02°♈07′	☽/♃ 14°♑45′	☿/⚷ 03°♌48′	♂/⚶ 15°♏17′	♅/♆ 25°♊34′	♇/⚷ 08°♉45′	⚴/⚵ 18°♍45′
♈/⚳ 28°♊32′	☽/♄ 05°♓57′	♀ 24°♎23′	♂/⚷ 08°♍34′	♅/♇ 06°♋11′	☊ 07°♈35′	⚴/⚶ 13°♍56′
♈/⚴ 25°♊05′	☽/♅ 05°♐45′	♀/♂ 08°♐38′	♃ 07°♏08′	♅/☊ 13°♊22′	☊/As 03°♊49′	⚴/⚷ 07°♋13′
♈/⚵ 23°♊40′	☽/♆ 12°♎11′	♀/♃ 00°♏46′	♃/♄ 28°♐20′	♅/As 09°♌36′	☊/Mc 05°♈55′	⚵ 17°♍20′
♈/⚶ 18°♊51′	☽/♇ 22°♎48′	♀/♄ 21°♐57′	♃/♅ 28°♍08′	♅/Mc 11°♊41′	☊/⚳ 02°♋20′	⚵/⚶ 12°♍31′
♈/⚷ 12°♈08′	☽/☊ 29°♍59′	♀/♅ 21°♍46′	♃/♆ 04°♌34′	♅/⚳ 08°♍06′	☊/⚴ 28°♊53′	⚵/⚷ 05°♋48′
☉ 19°♎12′	☽/As 26°♏13′	♀/♆ 28°♋11′	♃/♇ 15°♌11′	♅/⚴ 04°♍39′	☊/⚵ 27°♊28′	⚶ 07°♍42′
☉/☽ 05°♑47′	☽/Mc 28°♍18′	♀/♇ 08°♌49′	♃/☊ 22°♋22′	♅/⚵ 03°♍14′	☊/⚶ 22°♊39′	⚶/⚷ 00°♋59′
☉/☿ 01°♏16′	☽/⚳ 24°♐43′	♀/☊ 15°♋59′	♃/As 18°♍36′	♅/⚶ 28°♌25′	☊/⚷ 15°♈56′	⚷ 24°♈16′
☉/♀ 21°♎48′	☽/⚴ 21°♐16′	♀/As 12°♍13′	♃/Mc 20°♋41′	♅/⚷ 21°♊42′	As 00°♌03′	
☉/♂ 06°♐02′	☽/⚵ 19°♐51′	♀/Mc 14°♋19′	♃/⚳ 17°♎06′	♆ 02°♉00′	As/Mc 02°♊09′	
☉/♃ 28°♎10′	☽/⚶ 15°♐02′	♀/⚳ 10°♎44′	♃/⚴ 13°♎39′	♆/♇ 12°♉37′	As/⚳ 28°♌33′	
☉/♄ 19°♐22′	☽/⚷ 08°♎19′	♀/⚴ 07°♎17′	♃/⚵ 12°♎14′	♆/☊ 19°♈47′	As/⚴ 25°♌06′	
☉/♅ 19°♍10′	☿ 13°♏21′	♀/⚵ 05°♎51′	♃/⚶ 07°♎25′	♆/As 16°♊01′	As/⚵ 23°♌41′	
☉/♆ 25°♋36′	☿/♀ 03°♏52′	♀/⚶ 01°♎03′	♃/⚷ 00°♌42′	♆/Mc 18°♈07′	As/⚶ 18°♌53′	

Symbols of the Planets and Signs

☉ = Sun	♅ = Uranus	⚴ = Pallas	♈ = Aries	♎ = Libra
☽ = Moon	♆ = Neptune	⚵ = Juno	♉ = Taurus	♏ = Scorpio
☿ = Mercury	♇ = Pluto	⚶ = Vesta	♊ = Gemini	♐ = Sagittarius
♀ = Venus	☊ = N. Node	⚷ = Chiron	♋ = Cancer	♑ = Capricorn
♂ = Mars	As = Ascendant	R = Retrograde	♌ = Leo	♒ = Aquarius
♃ = Jupiter	Mc = Midheaven		♍ = Virgo	♓ = Pisces
♄ = Saturn	⚳ = Ceres			

your location or not even visible at all. Determining where exactly the eclipse is visible is a job requiring higher mathematics and other calculations. Stonehenge and other similar structures were constructed to aid in determining eclipses. They are giant calculators which are used to measure the position of the Sun and Moon, and other astrological and astronomical things.

The Moon's Nodes (or nodes for short) move around the sky at a fixed rate and have a period of about 18.6 years. They move in a retrograde motion (backward) and this accounts for eclipses being in earlier degrees and signs than the previous ones, generally. In any calendar year there can be as many as seven and as few as two eclipses. By eclipses I mean both lunar and solar eclipses. Generally they come in groups of two or three, a lunar eclipse followed by a solar eclipse two weeks later followed possibly by another lunar eclipse. It could also go solar-lunar-solar, or be just solar-lunar or lunar-solar or be just solar or lunar alone (though this is rare). Four eclipses is the average in most years, two pairs of solar-lunar or lunar-solar eclipses, at roughly six month intervals (six lunar month intervals). You can see when an eclipse will occur just by looking in an ephemeris. You find the New Moons and Full Moons and if the conjunction or opposition is within 12 (or 18) degrees of the nodes, it will be an eclipse. More astrologickal magick.

Eclipses are of several types. The solar eclipses can be partial, total or annular. A partial eclipse is one which is a bit off-center, where the orb is 10 degrees or more (these are approximate figures; for more accurate and complete analysis consult *Interpreting the Eclipses*, by Robert Carl Jansky).[2] The Moon does not totally obscure the Sun. A total eclipse is one where the Sun is totally obscured by the Moon, and there is darkness in the daytime somewhere on Earth, the orb is 10 degrees or less. An annular eclipse is one where

---

[2]Robert C. Jansky, *Interpreting the Eclipses* (Van Nuys, CA: Astro-Analytics Publications, 1977).

the Moon is farther from the Earth making its apparent diameter smaller than the Sun, so it passes completely in front of the Sun, but because it appears smaller than the apparent diameter of the Sun, it does not totally obscure the Sun, and a ring or annulus (ring in Latin) of sunlight is visible around the Moon. There is no darkness, but there is a dimming of light. Lunar eclipses are of three types also, partial, total (umbral) and penumbral. A partial lunar eclipse has the Moon in a partial shadow as cast by the Earth upon the Moon. A total lunar eclipse is just that, one which has the Moon totally darkened by the Earth's shadow. A penumbral eclipse is one where the Moon is farther from the Earth in its orbit and it does not enter the deeper umbral shadow cast by the Earth, but the lesser penumbral shadow, and so is only partially darkened. Any basic astronomy book will give more complete explanations of the types of eclipses and have diagrams of the planets and Sun and shadows cast.

So in astrology, the Moon's Nodes are eclipse markers. Incidentally all the planets (except the Sun) have nodes, but these other planetary nodes do not move as the Moon's Nodes do. They are fixed points. They are not generally considered in astrological interpretation.

The Moon's Nodes are also used in natal and horary and electional astrology as interpretive tools. In horary and electional astrology, they are considered a weakening influence, and any planet which is in the same degree as the nodes, regardless of sign, is considered to be weakened and its influence is lessened. It is an indicator of misfortune with regards to the nature of the planet and the sign(s) it rules and houses affected by rulership and placement. It can deny action or completion if coupled with other unfortunate indicators.

In natal astrology, the nodes are used to indicate several things. One is they are said to indicate karma, to show the native where the karmic purpose for this life lies with respect to sign and house placement, and aspects to the nodes show ease or difficulty of accomplishing these karmic goals. They are also said to indicate karmic teachers who come into the life and the aspects to the nodes show how the native will respond to those teachers—whether the native will learn the lessons offered or ignore the help. Sign and house placement can indicate the nature of the teachers and the areas of life in which they are encountered. Transits of the nodes to natal placements can indicate timing of teachers' arrival in the life.

In any case, the nodes can be useful for people who are interested in spiritual growth and karmic concerns, but they deal with those areas of life which are not readily scientifically provable. Not all astrologers consider the nodes, and they are a less important consideration, in the scheme of the chart as a whole, but they can add depth and confirm influences already apparent in the rest of the chart. It certainly can't hurt to consider them. Some astrologers feel that to misuse or ignore the nodes' influence in your life is to deny happiness or fulfillment. Try it for yourself and see how they work or don't work for you.

Another set of names for the nodes are Caput Draconis for the North Node and Cadua Draconis for the South Node, Dragon's Head and Tail (in Latin). Sometimes these are shortened to Caput and Cadua. These are probably from the ancient belief that eclipses were caused by a giant Dragon (or other animal depending upon the culture) which was swallowing the Sun (or Moon). When the Moon's Nodes were discovered, the names were probably given them in acknowledgment of their effect, that is causing eclipses (or rather, marking when eclipses would occur). Prediction of eclipses was one of the original reasons for the development of astrology. Character interpretation and prediction of events other than eclipses came later.

In Hindu Astrology, the Moon's Nodes are treated as planets and are interpreted in the same way as the other planets are. The North Node is called Rahu and the South Node is called Ketu. They are placed in the chart as are the rest of the planets, and are always opposite each other. They have signs of exaltation and fall, gemstone rulerships, and all the other stuff that "real" planets have. The use of the nodes in Western astrology probably stems from this tradition.

In the astrological chart, generally only the North Node is shown. That is because the South Node is always directly opposite the North Node, so to show it is felt to be redundant. When interpreting the nodal axis, a pair of signs and houses are always considered, the signs and houses always being opposite each other.

The North Node is considered to be a fortunate point, a positive place where the destiny of the native lies, by sign and house. It is said to show where the karma lies. It must be done by sign and house for the native to benefit from the incarnation, and if done will bring fulfillment and satisfaction, and also possibly happiness. It requires work and can never be fully mastered; once one level of accomplishment has been gained, there are presented other new modes of expression to be mastered. But keeping in mind the ideals presented by this placement can act as a personal guide as to what the soul's work is for this life.

The South Node is considered to be an unfortunate point, a place of difficulty or troubles. This interpretation can be misleading. More specifically, the South Node is said to show the soul's gifts which have been granted in this life through application in past lives. It is what we have earned as karmic rewards. It is also a place where the individual is comfortable expressing energies. The only problem is that if we stay in the South Node mode of expression, we are "resting on our Laurels," so to speak. The concept of karma demands that the soul keep working to perfect itself through successive incarnations, and resting on laurels is not working toward perfection. So although it may "feel comfortable" to act out the South Node, it is theoretically hindering our soul growth, by preventing us from exploring the North Node, which is where we should be.

In application, most people exhibit a blend of North and South Node energies. Certainly, we should be able to take advantage of the gifts earned in past lives, but we should also work on the tasks presented in this present life. Ideally we use the gifts of the South Node to aid in expressing the North Node. These expressions can be either lofty or mundane. I have the North Node in my 3rd house, and I am somewhat unsuccessful in dealing with automobile repairs. A broken car can drive me nuts faster than anything else. However, I have tried to compensate for this by assiduously keeping my car in as good repair as possible (mechanically—body damage and rust don't count). I try to get the oil changed regularly and before a trip I always set aside time and money for any maintenance which may be needed, so as to avoid breakdowns during the trip. It doesn't always work, but I have fewer car problems than friends who are less stringent about preventive maintenance. On the other hand, when I am traveling by common carrier—bus or train or plane—I have few problems. I usually get my pick of reservations; I have never lost luggage; I have never missed a flight or been denied access to transportation when I really needed it. Even snowstorms and the like have only slowed me down, never denied travel totally. This is the gift of a 9th house South Node. All this may seem petty and mundane, but this sort of stuff is what the Nodal Axis is all about. More spiritually, I have always had a relatively easy time learning astrology, and other lofty philosophical disciplines (9th house). Finally getting down to it and writing this book (3rd house) took a major "boot to the head" from the Gods. Think about the meanings of the houses and signs and I think you will discover a number of ways you operate to compensate for your nodes. Here are more succinct capsule definitions of the nodes.

☊ *North Node*: Karma, what you are to accomplish in this life by sign and house, what you need to learn to do, not easy but satisfying.

☋ *South Node*: Karmic rewards which you have already earned, line of least resistance, easy to do but no rewards attached, unconscious talents, stuff you rely upon but don't think about.

In interpretations, I am again blending the meanings of the signs and houses. It's more efficient and we don't need to be picky.

☊ ♈ *North Node in Aries or the 1st House*
☋ ♎ *South Node in Libra or the 7th House*
These people need to pay attention to themselves. They need to learn to be more assertive, to work to get their own way, to express themselves in their own way, not to live up to others' expectations of behavior. They are more inclined to let the other guy make the decisions, to not rock the boat if their interests may cause friction, to go along with the partner or peers. They are good diplomats and peacemakers, they are able to make others feel comfortable and at ease. They may be inwardly unhappy while outwardly conforming and polite and polished. Self-assertion and expression of personal wants and needs is imperative. Just expressing preferences can be enough, but using compromise to work out mutually agreeable solutions which satisfy both personal and others' inclinations will better satisfy the expressions of these placements. These people need to be first in something. They need to take time for themselves, spend money on themselves, buy a toy which isn't necessary, start something new, take an idea and try it out to see how it works. Enlightened self-interest is something which should be explored. Survival instincts may be weak. Magickally it can indicate the need to work solo or to do their own magick rather than relying on partners or letting others do the magick for them. They should use swords or athames or other weapons in magickal workings. Become psychic warriors. Working with energy a lot can be helpful. Do something in the magickal community

which hasn't been done before, or do something in a new and different way.

☊ ♉ *North Node in Taurus or the 2nd House*
♆ ♏ South Node in Scorpio or the 8th House

This person needs to work on values and self-esteem. A less evolved expression is in the individual accumulating possessions and tangible assets which the person controls unilaterally. A set of personal values is imperative, and working to live by those values is the task indicated. Also sexual satisfaction is another mode of expression, that is making sure that the individual enjoys sex at least as much as the partner, rather than sacrificing self-satisfaction for the partner's pleasure. The inclination is to share all resources; to adopt the values of the partner, whether or not the values fit the individual; to put the partner's pleasure above the individual's; to sacrifice what the person feels is moral or correct to please the partner or keep peace in relationships. This person needs to learn to relax and just kick back now and again. The world will not stop spinning if this person takes time off. Patience and control of the temper are things which should be cultivated. The issue of values is paramount, sticking to one's principles no matter how uncomfortable or inconvenient is important, yet the person must also be able to compromise enough to maintain peaceful partnerships. Deciding where to draw the line is the key. Magickally, ethics are paramount, there is a need to formulate an individual ethical code and stick to it. Also this person should obtain her or his own tools, rather than borrowing or relying on other's generosity. Music and dance are ways of getting in touch with inner needs.

☊ ♊ *North Node in Gemini or the 3rd House*
♆ ♐ South Node in Sagittarius or the 9th House

The person with this placement needs to communicate person to person, rather than being walled up in an ivory tower of lofty philosophical study and contemplation. Dealing with the nuisances of daily life is one method of expression, rather than hiring others to do the little daily tasks which are considered unimportant. Learning practical everyday skills is beneficial, the inclination is to stay in the rarified air of higher studies and let the little stuff slide. This can be the placement of the eternal student, or the person who graduates with honors with a college degree which has little or no real world job value. Learning how to apply higher knowledge to everyday life is the balance needed. Mundane skills and tasks are as valuable as the more lofty disciplines. Also being active in one's local community or neighborhood is healthy, rather than disregarding local people in favor of the nation or the world. This can indicate the activist who crusades to end famine in Africa while totally disregarding the homeless at home. This person should take a vacation in the home city to discover the interesting things it has to offer. Magickally, this person should write the spells and ceremonies used, rather then copying from grimoires. Practical application of magickal knowledge is indicated, learning for learnings' sake is a dead end unless it can be used in everyday life. Informal everyday little magicks are preferable to ceremonial magick and big rituals. This person should stay active in the local community, rather than ignoring local concerns in favor of the greater Pagan community regionally or nationwide. Use people skills to network with others of like mind and share information. This person might try writing or publishing a newsletter.

♌ ♋ North Node in Cancer or the 4th House
♋ ♑ *South Node in Capricorn or the 10th House*
Home, family, roots, ancestry are the areas these people should explore and honor. Self-made people with no past are negative expressions of this placement. People who change their name because it is too ethnic, or people ashamed of their humble beginnings are avoiding the

lessons here. Keeping in touch with relatives, researching family history, being proud of roots are all things that should be cultivated. Also a career in the home can be beneficial. People who choose to stay home and raise children and maintain a nurturing nest for working partners is a choice not honored in our society as it should be. Those who choose to stay in the home, rather than merely conform to societal norms, should be commended. This can be the placement of "house husbands," or people who work at home. Having the home as a nontraditional workplace, using technology, is one way to express these energies. Just owning a home and keeping it nice and clean and comfortable and in good repair is a way to use this placement to best advantage. Fam-trads and lineage are important to magickal practitioners. Working magick at home is preferable to large public ceremonies. Nurturing and caring for people's comfort and needs is more helpful than being in charge or the power-behind-the-throne. Chasing titles or degrees is a dead end. Researching the past, or keeping histories as a legacy for future Pagans is the work indicated here. Psychometry is a possible talent. Cultivate empathy with others.

☊ ♌ *North Node in Leo or the 5th House*
☋ ♒ *South Node in Aquarius or the 11th House*

Having and raising your own children is an excellent way of using these energies successfully. But you must raise these children to be themselves, not little copies of the parents. Allowing self-expression is the wider issue confronted here. The inclination is to put society as a whole over individual self-expression or needs. Being in a theater group or managing your own investments also shows good utilization of energies. The needs of the whole do not outweigh the needs of the few or the one in this case. The trick is to determine when your needs can be expressed without causing major disruptions in society as a whole. This is the "Robert Mapplethorpe" placement. Hopefully self-expression will not be as "in-your-face" as his was, but the need for expressing the spirit in various media is healthy and desirable. The inclination will be to copy the expressions of the peer group, following fads, going with the in crowd, rather than deciding what is most satisfying. Dare to be different is a healthy phrase; just try to choose non-controversial or non-threatening ways to express yourself. Magickally theatrical circles are helpful. Putting your individual stamp on your workings, however small, is beneficial. Working with a few individuals rather than being one member of a large group is desirable. Raising children in the Craft can be a legacy for the future, but allowing the children to choose for themselves when they are old enough, and respecting their choices is the best action of all. Giving readings for others can be rewarding, and brings some recognition of talents.

☊ ♍ North Node in Virgo or the 6th House
☋ ♓ *South Node in Pisces or the 12th House*

Serve or suffer is the knee-jerk reaction to this nodal axis. Working to better conditions is the way to deal with these energies and becoming helpless and dependent can be the way to avoid the growth needed. Taking responsibility for health, work environment, and obligations are the things you need to address. Keeping fit, watching the diet, taking an active role in health care are all ways to avoid becoming an invalid, or being at the mercy of an impersonal uncaring healthcare system. Taking whatever jobs are available and trying to better your position is preferable to giving up and going on welfare. Realizing that all honest work is honorable, no matter how lofty or humble the position is an important lesson of this placement. Do something rather than just whining about how awful conditions are. Don't let yourself be overwhelmed by big institutions, do what you can to change things, however small. Getting your hands dirty is good therapy. Keep your little corner of the world neat and clean and you have done a lot toward learning the lessons of this placement. Magickally, low magick and shamanism are more desirable paths over high magick and ceremonialism. Food magick, herb magick, and working with familiars are good expressions of this energy. Doing the tasks that keep a community going are naturals for you. Attending to obligations should be given preference. Keeping diaries and notes on everything you have read or done or tried can drive others bonkers, but dealing with minutiae can be comforting and a way of managing the big overwhelming stuff. You can trip up demons by pointing out their mistakes and calling them on it. An herb garden can be a great way to benefit from your labors in the Craft.

☊ ♎ *North Node in Libra or the 7th House*
☋ ♈ *South Node in Aries or the 1st House*

You need to learn to deal with others cooperatively. You need to cultivate politeness, good manners, and diplomacy, hearing what others have to say before expressing your opinions. Let the other guy have his way at least half of the time. You are good at asserting yourself and making wants and wishes known. You are a fighter, but need to direct that energy toward fighting for the rights of others, particularly those who are not able or willing to stick up for themselves. This position is good for advocates for others. You catch more flies with honey than with vinegar is a catch phrase for this axis. Marriage is a challenge for this person, learning when to compromise for the sake of the relationship. You need to find the balance between compromise and assertion of your individual wishes, perhaps by thinking out what is really important and what is just insisting on your own way because of habit. Make the battles count and you'll get farther than challenging the partner at every turn. In magick you need a working partner. Using the balance of energies can teach valuable lessons on sharing power and other efficient modes of expression. Sometimes the other guy can do it better than you can. Try invoking the Goddess or God alternately, and experience directly the opposite flow of energies. Work cooperatively in your spells and ceremonies and make them joint efforts. Share the beauty of magick and working with others.

☊ ♏ *North Node in Scorpio or the 8th House*
☋ ♉ *South Node in Taurus or the 2nd House*

The person with this placement needs to learn to share—resources, possessions and yourself. You have had your own things for a while and need to share, to see how shared resources can bring pleasure to a partner. You also need to try to see things from the other guy's point of view. Ethics are strong, but can be single-minded, what you know is correct is not necessarily correct for everyone else. You need to learn situational ethics and become less absolutist in your beliefs. You need to realize everyone has an ethical system and you should honor it, even if (especially if) you do not agree with it. Trust is a big issue and placing your fate in the hands of another is difficult, but needs to be learned. In various measures we all hold each other's fates. Sex is important and you need to learn that if the partner is not pleased, then your individual pleasure is reduced. Pay more attention to your partner's enjoyment, and you will find that your own pleasure is enhanced. You are good at relaxing and just letting things go by, and need to be more energetic and assertive, to work for what you want for partner and self. You may need to be a little blunt to get your point across, if that is what it takes. This is the position for sex magick. Shared energy workings can be very liberating. Initiations can be difficult, trusting another and allowing the self to be placed in a relatively helpless position, but can also be extremely effective in opening up new doors. Working magick on behalf of others or for the common good, even against personal interests is also instructive. Beware of going overboard into extremism, or the "dark side." Research is a talent which should be cultivated.

☊ ♐ *North Node in Sagittarius or the 9th House*
☋ ♊ *South Node in Gemini or the 3rd House*

Deep philosophies and abstract thinking is needed here. The tendency is to learn a little about a lot of things, and you need to learn to specialize and go into depth in one or two subjects. The outlook may be provincial and a wider view of the nation and world needs to be cultivated. This is the "not in my backyard" axis, and if your backyard is not ok, then why should it be ok for someone else's backyard? Out of sight should not be out of mind. Relating local and regional concerns to the country or world-at-large is an effective way of handling these energies. Travel to or contact with persons of different cultures and backgrounds helps give a broader perspective and scope. This position can indicate you may have never traveled more than a day's drive from your birthplace. Higher education will be beneficial and broadening, especially if you have to leave home. Religious education will be helpful also, especially comparative religious studies. Take a cruise where you don't do the driving or have to attend to the day-to-day details of life. Magickally this is the placement for the Big Ritual ceremonial magician. All the smells and bells should be brought out and used. Take care to acquire only the best optimal tools for magick, even if they are more expensive than the garage sale stuff. A few good tools are better than lots of cheap but adequate stuff. Astral travel, dreamwork, divination, are all good things to study. Picking a magickal speciality and becoming an expert, studying for years, is a wonderful way to manage this placement. Dream work can be especially rewarding.

☊ ♑ *North Node in Capricorn or the 10th House*
☋ ♋ *South Node in Cancer or the 4th House*

This person should strive to have a career, a profession, to work at something outside the home. The tendency is to be shy and retiring and the lesson is to learn to live in the public eye. Personal honor should be cultivated, the word should not be given unless it is to be kept. This position also calls for the native to learn self-reliance—not to rely upon others for a livelihood, or help, or support in the things which the native can do, but would rather not. With unpleasant tasks, the philosophy should be, best to get it done quickly, then it is over. Otherwise the native will agonize over the task and try to get others to do it, and in the end expend more energy and effort than if he or she had just gone and done it. Professional attitudes and behavior are to be cultivated. Attention to rules and regulations and protocol are things which need to be learned. Dealing with the hard lessons of life, learning that nothing is free, that hard work brings rewards is difficult, but can be rewarding and profitable. The reputation should be guarded. Degrees and recognition of achievement can be valuable as a public affirmation of achievements, but should never become an end in themselves. In magick, this is the position of the adherent to an established hierarchical tradition. This person earns his or her place rather than being born into a situation which affords status. The rituals and ceremonies with complicated invocations which need to be done correctly will be what this individual needs. Wisdom can be attained, but only after years of study and work. Working for a magickal organization in an executive capacity is beneficial. Working with rocks and crystals is beneficial.

☊ ♒ *North Node in Aquarius or the 11th House*
☋ ♌ *South Node in Leo or the 5th House*

Friends should be treated as family by the person with this axis. Realizing that the commonality of humanity is as important as blood ties is the lesson taught. Adopting a child, or being a foster-parent rather than having one's own children can satisfy the needs of this placement. Children need and deserve love whether they have blood ties to the family or not. Putting the needs of society over individual preferences is needed. Selfish wants can cause damage to others immediately or in the future, and should be examined and eliminated. Acts that benefit the community should be cultivated—like recycling, or not being a conspicuous consumer, or becoming active in politics—rather than just bitching about conditions. Let the other guy shine, allow others to express individuality. Work for the common good, put some effort into larger social causes without thought of individual recognition. Magickally this is the placement for a person who should be in a coven or large group. Working cooperatively with others for a common goal will be advantageous. Planning for the future rather than living from day-to-day, putting off immediate rewards for larger future returns is another lesson of this placement. Learning astrology or other disciplines geared to helping others is one way to deal with these energies. Serving in some elected position in the community is another way to work with this placement. Participating in group workings designed to raise energy for group needs can be a way to learn about the needs which this axis brings. Precognition can be cultivated.

♋ ✕ *North Node in Pisces or the 12th House*
♋ ♍ *South Node in Virgo or the 6th House*

Learning to trust in the Gods and the inherent order of the Universe is what this position demands. The individual has to cultivate faith in the community, in the basic nature of humanity, in the way the Universe has been set up. There comes a point where the person can do no more and has to let go, trusting that things will turn out as they are meant to be. Micro-managing the native's life and the lives of others is misuse of negative energies. All that achieves is either more work needed to keep people on track, or resentment at not allowing others to do things for themselves. People have to do things to learn, and be allowed to do things imperfectly (or less well than you can) or make mistakes in order to be allowed to perfect their own skills. Be philosophical about your imperfections and the imperfections of others, taking the person as a whole as the measure, not the faults and foibles. Cultivate an awareness of the Gods and the Cosmos, kick back and put it all in perspective by seeing how small and insignificant you are in relation to the rest of Creation. If you are distressed by something which has happened (or not happened) think about how it will affect the world one hundred years from now. Give to charity, volunteer time and energies to those less fortunate. Count blessings instead of faults. Magickally this is the position of the potentially most effective magickal practitioner. If the person trusts in the Gods and works to keep faith and visualizations as pure as possible, much can be achieved. Learning to let go after doing all that can be done is the magickal lesson of this axis. Working with perfumes, oils, and incense is good. Mind altering techniques or substances can be effective, but can also become a crutch if used exclusively and without proper respect and precautions. Try to keep a perspective and don't rely exclusively on external stimuli. Meditation and creative visualization can be very helpful. Dance can be freeing of the soul.

ESOTERIC RULERS

Alice Bailey postulated a different set of planetary rulers for the signs than those we have been dealing with up to now. She felt these esoteric rulers tied in to spiritual and metaphysical issues for each sign. They helped lift the signs from the everyday mundane issues of survival in the world and provided added spirituality and depth. These esoteric rulers were seen as the key to unlocking the inherent spirituality and psychic abilities in each of us. Magick, of course, also addresses spiritual and psychic issues. In addition to focusing on the standard rulers of the signs and houses, why not try using the esoteric rulers and adding another level of interpretation?

One technique is to find the Sun/Moon midpoint in your chart. This is the point halfway between your Sun and

Moon. Use this as a new Ascendant for your birthplace (or present place of residence if you live away from your birthplace), and place your natal planets in this new chart. Using this "spiritual" chart can help define spiritual and psychic issues, perhaps not as obvious in your natal chart. You can use standard and/or esoteric rulers for interpretation. The planets will be in the same signs and degrees as in your natal chart, but the houses they are in will (probably) change. The aspects between the planets will also remain the same, but the aspects to the Ascendant and Midheaven will change, as well as any points based upon the Ascendant or Midheaven, such as the Arabic Parts.

Another technique is to interpret your natal chart paying special attention to the esoteric rulers of your Ascendant, and the signs of your Sun and Moon. The esoteric ruler of your Ascendant may give you a new chart ruler, and doing that ruler by sign and house can lead to greater spiritual fulfillment. It can also help highlight issues which aren't addressed by the standard ruler. When people are gripped by nameless longings, feelings that something is missing from an otherwise successful and fulfilling life, using this technique can help to bring deep satisfaction. It doesn't mean a change of career or residence, just perhaps the addition of a hobby or pastime in tune with the esoteric ruler by sign and house. Using this technique with the esoteric ruler of the Sun by sign can bring another dimension of spiritual fulfillment, and doing it with the esoteric ruler of the Moon's sign can bring another aspect of magickal ability to the fore.

In astrology, the Sun is seen as the present, what we are here to do and work on here and now; the Moon relates to the past, what we were or did in former lives, and what we have earned; and the Ascendant is the future, what we should be striving to achieve, goals we should be working toward. If the Sun, Moon, or Ascendant are in the same signs, it is said you are repeating lessons ignored or not learned completely in past lifetimes. Also if the sign on the

12th house cusp is the same as that on the Ascendant (due to interception) you are also said to be repeating lessons from your last life. This depends upon the house system used and can be the case for one house system and not the case for another, so it is not considered as reliable as the former. Of course this whole thing depends upon your belief (or lack thereof) in reincarnation. If you do—then it's a new toy to play with. If you don't, then ignore this paragraph altogether. Proof of these theories has been scarce. Still, it can be an interesting concept to play with. And meditation upon these ideas can bring interesting psychic issues to the fore. In the end, the real test is—does it work? If it does, then use it. If not, go on to the next technique.

All this stuff is being thrown out for your perusal. If something piques your curiosity then play with it. If it sounds too weird or far out, then just let it go. The idea for this whole book is to present a smorgasbord of astrological ideas and techniques for aiding magickal workings and psychic development. Whatever you choose to partake of is fine. And if you don't like the taste of certain ideas, leave them alone. Maybe next time you will be hungry for them. And maybe you never liked brussels sprouts no matter how they were prepared. But, if you never tried green eggs and ham, then do not knock them, Sam-I-Am. Take a bite and see.

Planning a magickal working using the esoteric ruler of the sign the Moon is transiting, in addition to the standard ruler, can bring in added issues and influences. You should always pay attention to the standard ruler, but adding the esoteric ruler can add depth and different influences which cannot be addressed by transiting aspects or the sign the Moon is in. It can also be a way of getting a needed influence without waiting.

Using esoteric rulers transmutes each sign into a more complete and spiritually fulfilling expression of energies. You are tapping into a higher energy level for the sign. Regular astrological rulers work well for the material world, the here and now of everyday existence. Using the esoteric rulers allows each sign a more spiritual mode of expression, as an alternative to the here and now of everyday life.

Each sign addresses certain issues and has certain talents and abilities. But taken to extremes, these specializations can lead to narrowing of possibilities or lack of expression in areas which the sign does not deal with effectively. Psychologically it can lead to dysfunctions with regard to things outside a field of expertise, leading to severe inability to cope with certain aspects of normal daily life or issues which an individual just chooses not to address in life. Then when these issues come to the fore, the individual is left either feeling powerless and unable to cope, or is acting at a severe disadvantage.

This is not to say that each sign cannot cope in the world as it is. But using esoteric rulers (especially of the Ascendant) can help add a dimension of depth and fulfillment, especially when the person is dealing with spiritual or magickal energies. You could say the esoteric rulers also help with integration of the feminine or yin energies which our modern society does not particularly honor or express.

A couple of explanations are in order. The list of esoteric rulers uses two "planets" which are not in regular horoscopes. For example, Earth refers to the Earth, the planet which we are living on. In a normal horoscope it is implied at the center of the chart, standard astrology being a geocentric system. In heliocentric astrology, the Earth is a planet and represented, but we aren't dealing with that here. Another technique is that the Earth is implied in every regular astrological chart, exactly opposite the Sun. So if your Sun is in Libra in the 10th house, your Earth is in Aries in the 4th house. Try this one and see if it works. Otherwise think of Earth as the element earth and look to the earth signs—Taurus, Virgo, Capricorn, and the planet Saturn, which is considered to be very much concerned with earth element issues.

Another planet used in esoteric rulerships is Vulcan or Hephaestus. It is a hypothetical intra-Mercurial planet. You can get ephemerides for Vulcan, but again we aren't dealing with that stuff here. There are a couple of ways to get around that. One is to look to where Virgo is in your chart, and interpret that as the house (or houses) to look to. Vulcan is supposed to become the exoteric ruler of Virgo, eventually. Another is to try dealing with Chiron, which is another extra planetoid, but more readily accessible as to placement and ephemerides. When you buy a computer generated chart, Chiron can be calculated for you if you ask for it. Astrologers are still fighting about/researching Chiron's rulership, but there is growing evidence that it rules Virgo and some of the issues addressed by Virgo are very similar to those of Vulcan. Try that, it can't hurt.

The mythology of Vulcan/Hephaestus is that he was one of the twelve Olympian gods, a son of Juno/Hera. Who his father was is explained in two ways: 1) that he was the son of Zeus and Hera; 2) that he was Hera's son alone by parthenogenesis. He was married to Aphrodite, but she was unhappy with the marriage. Hephaestus was ugly and maimed, and Aphrodite resented being married to an unattractive imperfect mate—the original Beauty and the Beast. But Hephaestus was the God of the forge and of smithcraft. He crafted Zeus' thunderbolts. He was a master artisan, creating all the jewelry and trinkets for the Gods. He even created a race of mechanical golden women to help him in his forge—the first robots. He also created magical three-legged carts with wheels which would move around at command and carry things from one place to the next. One author points out that Hephaestus was the only God to work for a living in the Olympian realm, all the others just sort of hung out. More anciently, Graves connects Hephaestus as the Sun God who was associated with Athena as Moon Goddess and patroness of smithcraft and all mechanical arts. In ancient times, a smith was also considered to be a magician/sorcerer who would imbue the weapons he created with magical properties. When the use of iron/steel in weapons became common, this magical attribute of the smith was reduced. That he was lame comes from several sources: 1) that ancient tribesmen purposely maimed their smiths so they could not run away to other tribes; 2) that a hobbling partridge-dance was performed in the erotic orgies connected with the mysteries of smithcraft. Mythologically he was lamed twice. First at birth when, disgusted by his sickly and unattractive appearance, Hera threw him down from Olympus. Second when he dared complain to Zeus about Zeus' humiliation of his mother when she rebelled against him. Zeus was so enraged that he threw Hephaestus down from Olympus a second time. When he landed he was not killed, being immortal, but his legs were so badly injured that Hephaestus had to create golden leg-supports for himself so he could walk again.

Esoteric astrology is dealing with the fuzzy ethereal realms, so things are not as cut-and-dried as in exoteric (regular) astrology. So we can be a little fuzzy around the edges and fudge here and there to try to make things work. After all, this is all hypothetical speculation anyhow, so we are just getting a little more hypothetical. Spiritualism is like that. You have to feel your way and use your intuition.

If all this is just too weird or strange, then ignore it. The KISS rule applies here also. What is presented here are various tools and techniques for you to try and see if they help. If you can't use the tool effectively, or it just doesn't fit your hand, then don't use it. Again, you are no worse off than before. This is really high-powered advanced philosophical astrological lore. It can be fun to play with, but it isn't at all the nuts-and-bolts astrology presented in the other sections of this book. This stuff is sort of the kabbalah of astrology—those weird higher realms where reality is not the same. But in the spirit of presenting all that there is, it is included here for the adventurous and curious. And also those completests who want to have it all spread out for them.

I have included a list of the esoteric rulers of the twelve signs that includes the signs and how, by using the energies of the esoteric ruler, each sign can become more effective and better able to cope with the world. See Table 5. Ideally, this process should occur naturally as each individual goes through midlife and matures and mellows. This midlife crisis occurs when Uranus opposes its natal place around age 42, and also when Pluto squares its natal position. This can occur between the age 37 and 52 (or later) depending on what sign Pluto was in when you were born. Those born with Pluto in Leo have the earliest Pluto square—before 40. The other signs have it later until people born with Pluto in Aquarius won't experience the Pluto square until well after 70. As Pluto was in Aquarius last in the 1780's, and won't be again until roughly 2025, we won't worry about that. All this happens because Pluto has an elliptical orbit and moves much faster in some signs (Scorpio being the fastest) than others (Taurus being the slowest). Most astrologers use the Uranus opposition to its natal place as indicator of the timing of the midlife crisis, but also pay attention to the Pluto square.

Table 5.   Esoteric Rulers.

Sign	Planet	Sign	Planet
Aries ♈	Mercury ☿	Virgo ♍	Moon ☽
Taurus ♉	Vulcan/Hephaestus (look to Earth, Saturn, Virgo and Chiron also)	Libra ♎ Scorpio ♏ Sagittarius ♐	Uranus ♅ Mars ♂ Earth ⊕
Gemini ♊	Venus ♀	Capricorn ♑	Saturn ♄
Cancer ♋	Neptune ♆	Aquarius ♒	Jupiter ♃
Leo ♌	Sun ☉	Pisces ♓	Pluto ♀

Aries: With Mercury as esoteric ruler of Aries, Aries is offered the opportunity to add thought and reflection to its unbridled enthusiasm and spontaneous action. Mercury allows Aries people to put themselves in others' shoes and try to see things from their viewpoint, which tempers the self-absorption of Aries pure ego. Aries is offered ideas by Mercury and becomes more adaptable and effective, thinking first where before there was usually just instinctive reaction to situations and life. Aries people can learn to plan ahead enough to pace themselves and therefore not burn out before a task is accomplished, and actually be able to finish things they start. With Mercury as esoteric ruler, it adds wisdom to courage, confidence, inspiration, and motivation.

Taurus: With Vulcan as esoteric ruler of Taurus, Taurus people can use work, creation, craftsmanship on a material plane, and use their sense of beauty and esthetics to create things rather than just sit cozily and watch, or revel in pure sensuality. By letting Taurus materially express their creativity and self-expression, Taurus people become less structured and set in their ways. Taurus can experience growth through creation and even encourage others to get out of their ruts to accomplish something, and benefit from the satisfaction derived from having a tangible product for their labors. Taurus can learn to innovate and do things in new and different ways, even create their own style of doing, rather than just following the routine which was established since time immemorial. Taurus gains self-esteem from creating, being innovative, developing ideas, and sharing those ideas and creations with others.

Gemini: Gemini has Venus as an esoteric ruler, and Venus can bring a personal value system and ethics to Gemini's world of ideas and words. Gemini gains depth from Venus' vision of the beauty and harmony in the Universe, seeing what is good and true and pleasing, and adding that to the unending flow of ideas and possibilities. Gemini gains the ability for synthesis, choosing the best, most beneficial solution from all the possible alternatives. Gemini can see the unity beyond the cold concrete facts, and can create a whole which is greater than the mere sum of its parts. Gemini then gains depth and can partake from the world of feelings as well as the world of pure ideas and mentality.

Cancer: Neptune is Cancer's esoteric ruler and Neptune's lesson for Cancer people is to trust their instincts and intuition, and let go of fears and inhibitions. Cancer gains a faith that what they do will provide the security they crave. Even when times are tough, just knowing that Cancer has done their best and let go, following the intuition Neptune provides, Cancer can then relax and feel comfortable with the way things are going. Cancer gains the faith that they can guide their own destiny and become the true intuitive they are destined to be.

Leo: Leo's esoteric ruler is the Sun—the Illuminated Sun. This Sun allows Leo to let go of the pure self, and allow others to shine as well. Leo can learn to acknowledge and honor the Divine spark in others and honor their worth as equal to Leo's. Leo can see that each expresses their divine spark differently, but that does not make them less important or valuable than Leo. Leo can tone down their flamboyant style which can overwhelm and drive away other less self-assured (some say self-absorbed) signs. Leo can use their sense of identity and self-assuredness to help other signs to see how to honor themselves and partake of the limelight—alongside Leo, who will not mind sharing.

Virgo: The Moon is the esoteric ruler of Virgo. Virgo people tend toward narrow specialization and analysis, and are most comfortable in their own special niche, doing their own thing, out of the limelight. The Moon allows Virgo to gain the ability to assimilate all of life's experiences and move beyond only what Virgo does well or feels comfortable and familiar with. The Moon goes with the flow and Virgo can learn to do this also, rather than stopping and trying to fix up or tidy up situations or people. With the Moon as esoteric ruler, Virgo can tune into feeling, emotions, the unconscious, and creativity so Virgo can use Mercury to create. With Mercury only, Virgo tends to be just a craftsman, with the Moon as well, Virgo can add to that being a creator, inventor, and artist, using their superb craftsmanship to make visions a concrete reality in the best way possible.

Libra: Libra's esoteric ruler is Uranus. Libra is the least objective air sign, being ruled by emotional and "other-oriented" Venus. Libra tends to live at one pole of being—all-thinking or all-feeling—or vacillates between the two extremes. Uranus gives Libra the ability to add objectivity to their feelings. Libra is able to cut to the core and tell the cold unadorned truth when necessary, without undue concern for the other's feelings. Uranus gives Libra balance, allowing them to live at the midpoint of the feeling/objectivity scale, rather than swinging from extreme to extreme. Libra gains the ability to make sudden radical change to restore balance and move to that center, if that is what it will take. Uranus lets Libra blend thinking and feeling and find the balanced center.

Scorpio: Mars is Scorpio's esoteric ruler. Mars brings conscious direction to Pluto's unconscious depths. Scorpio's will can be used to manipulate others unconsciously and Mars brings awareness to this process and the decisive ability to act and end the manipulation. With Mars, Scorpio can cut to the root of problems. Scorpio can become a psychic surgeon, a healer, a shaman and can use their will consciously to stimulate others to use their own will to fight back and transform themselves. Scorpio can use Mars energy consciously to achieve concrete results, transforming themselves and becoming catalysts for others' regeneration.

Sagittarius: The Earth as the esoteric ruler of Sagittarius grounds and adds solidity to Sagittarians' lofty ideas and ideals. Sagittarians gain stamina and determination and then can finish projects which have been started and end non-productive procrastination. Sagittarians are able to retreat inward from their outward adventuresome break-neck journey. Earth adds patience and an ability to proceed step by step. Earth keeps Sagittarius' feet on the ground while their visionary heads are in the clouds. It allows Sagittarians to put their ideas into practical use, to adapt their philosophies to the everyday life of the average person, bringing enlightenment to the mundane. They can apply the knowledge they have gained to everyday life, acting out the philosophies they have formulated.

Capricorn: Saturn is Capricorn's esoteric ruler as well as exoteric ruler. Capricorn, by heeding Saturn's esoteric message, can learn to relax and go with the flow, rather than trying to regiment their lives. Capricorn can relax and let their rigid adherence to duty, routine, and commonsense practical methods give way to compassion and understanding of the hardships life can bring. Capricorn can learn to celebrate survival and prosperity in an inhospitable climate. With Saturn, Capricorn can let the Cosmos carry the burdens for a while, lighten up, take themselves less seriously, and use Saturn's humor to lighten the way and brighten their outlook. Capricorn becomes less demanding on themselves and others and takes time to find joy, and can then play, laugh and meditate.

Aquarius: The esoteric ruler of Aquarius is Jupiter, which adds kindness and compassion to Aquarius' purely humanitarian urges. Jupiter's humor brings warmth and concern and vision to the purely reforming abilities Aquarius displays. Aquarius loves humanity as a whole, and with Jupiter, can also love individuals as well—warts and all. Jupiter lets Aquarius see the individuals who make up the group, community, society. Aquarius can understand that helping society as a whole does indeed start with helping individuals one by one. Jupiter allows Aquarius to get involved with the individuals they are helping without compromising their greater objectivity and vision of a better society. Aquarius can enjoy the fruits of their efforts in the present while still keeping the vision of a better future.

Pisces: Pluto, as esoteric ruler of Pisces, gives Pisces the ability to develop will, set limits and learn from their own and others' mistakes. Pluto can help set boundaries and develop shielding for Pisces empathy. Pluto can help Pisces perform psychic triage—to decide when enough is enough and stop the feeling of never having done all which can be done. Pisces learns to take a stand and even to stand alone. Pluto can plunge Pisces into the depths, but can allow Pisces to emerge newborn and regenerated stronger than ever. Bailey says Pluto dissolves the silver cord of attachment between the two fishes so that the spiritual fish is freed. Pluto allows Pisces to establish limits and boundaries between themselves and the world. This allows time to rest and recuperate, so Pisces emerge again, renewed and invigorated, and all the more effective for the rest and the will to forge ahead with compassion and love.

PART FOUR

ADDITIONAL STUDIES
AND ASTROLOGICKAL
RULERSHIPS

INTRODUCTION

This section is included as an area to throw out a number of ideas, techniques, and concepts that show different ways in which astrology, magick, and paganism interrelate. Among the topics covered here are some which everyone seems to expect from astrology (birth stones and sign correlation), areas of study new in astrology (Chiron and the asteroids) and other areas which are interesting, but not mainstream (The Great Astrological Year, world ages, The Eight Moon Cycles). Then there are the things I wanted to include which didn't fit anywhere else—syzygy, astrological ritual.

I called it additional studies in tribute to Llewellyn George because he has an additional studies section in his *A to Z Horoscope Maker and Delineator*.[1] (It's only in the older editions; the newer streamlined editions have eliminated this and other sections—a great shame.) For years, when there were few astrology books available and I was too poor to buy them anyway, I would amuse myself for hours reading that section over again and again. He threw out all sorts of strange ideas and correlations and gave me a glimpse into the philosophy and deeper truths of astrology, which were not encountered in standard natal astrological texts. It was deep stuff and each time I re-read the passages, I would come up with new ideas and concepts. Now the A to Z is dated and there are more contemporary and clearer texts which have usurped A to Z in popularity and modern validity. But I still have days

---

[1]Llewellyn George, *The A to Z Horoscope Maker and Delineator* (St. Paul, MN: Llewellyn Publications, 1972).

when it's gloomy and I'm lonely and so I go and get out old Llewellyn George and page through that additional studies section once again. I still find neat and interesting stuff.

Far be it for me to presume to be as deep or profound as Llewellyn George, but in his spirit of throwing out all sorts of strange stuff, I have named this section in tribute to him. Some information may be strange, some may upset you, some may seem just wrong, but it all is food for thought. Take some Pepto Bismol and chow down.

BIRTHSTONES

Assignments of birthstones to various signs and planets vary widely according to various sources. There seems a valid correspondence between astrology and certain stones and their uses, but there is little agreement as to which stones correspond to which signs or planets. These correspondences are the basis for the tables listing birthstones for the various months popularized by the jewelry industry since the early 1900's. Often these lists are altered depending on price, availability and popularity of various gemstones and materials. These lists are commercially driven and have little psychic or magical basis. There are older, less economically driven lists, but these, too, have an element of availability, workability and durability built into them.

Another factor to consider is that ancient names for materials may not correspond to modern equivalents. In the ancient world, the name "Lapis Lazuli" may have been applied to any gem material of a blue color, which includes what we nowadays call lapis lazuli, azurite, turquoise, blue sapphire, blue zircon, aquamarine and various other opaque and transparent materials of a blue color. In addition, the same name may have been applied to two different materials depending upon availability. And, conversely, the same material may have gone by two or more different names in neighboring localities (in space or time).

So most gemstone lists—both ancient and modern—are in varying degrees suspect. Generally, it is best to experiment yourself with various materials and decide upon your own correspondences and affinities. To include various lists from various sources would only engender confusion. I personally use stones and gems in various ways depending on how the material feels to me rather than to what sign it is attributed to. There are many good "rock books" available. Two of my favorites are *Cunningham's Book of Crystal Gem and Metal Magic,* by Scott Cunningham and Barbara Walker's *The Book of Sacred Stones.* Two different viewpoints of the same subject.

CADUCEUS

The wand of Hermes, sometimes said to be the sigil of Mercury and what Mercury symbolizes. Anciently it was a three-headed snake, but later it was changed to a single rod intertwined by two serpents, linked esoterically with the spinal column and kundalini energy. If Mercury is the Magus-magickal practitioner, the caduceus is either the Magus' magickal wand used to concentrate and direct magickal energy, or an esoteric symbol of the magickal energies generated within the Magus' body. In modern times, it has been co-opted by the medical professions, and has no other mundane modern connotations. Perhaps because healing was once a magickal process, the modern scientific medical practitioners want to show they too have the "magic" required to heal. Certainly scientific medicine has been very active over the past centuries in helping "stamp out" magic and superstition.

THE THREE MAJOR ASTROLOGICAL SYSTEMS

With respect to the three major systems of astrology—Hindu, Chinese, and Western: All are supposedly based upon an older purer form. Traditionally, Hindu is said to be the closest to the original. However, as each has evolved, each has adopted a mindset and worldview which mirrors the society it serves.

Hindu Astrology is highly predictive, yet extremely fatalistic—you cannot change your fate/karma. The possibility of bettering your lot in society is not considered— caste is caste and cannot be changed.

Chinese Astrology is based upon a Confucian world view. The family is paramount, individuality is de-emphasized, and harmony within the family and society is highly prized. So divorce is a non-option, marriage is expected of every young person, and family and children (perpetuation of the family) is paramount. One works to better the position of the family as a unit, each member contributing to the (hopefully) steady upward rise in position, wealth and status of the extended family unit. This rise may be over decades or centuries—Chinese Time. The consequences of actions are looked at with an eye to the effect decades or centuries in the future. Short term benefits are disregarded if they cannot be consolidated to make a favorable impact in the long term.

Western Astrology places emphasis upon the individual, individual initiative and actions. "The stars impel, they do not compel," is an axiom often stated in Western astrology to illustrate how one may avoid the negative impact of stressful transits or natal placements—the individual may choose to express these energies in a more constructive or beneficial form. If the individual ignores this possibility, then the full impact of these stresses will be felt. Individual initiative and self-improvement are considered desirable, one is encouraged to "make the most of" one's natal chart, and transits are opportunities for growth and challenges which provide possible upward mobility. Outworn and outgrown things are to be left behind, be it a mode of behavior, a bad habit, a relationship, a mindset.

Each system works, but with each comes a set of values you need to pay heed to, or the "magick" won't work as well. Hindu astrology is extremely precise in its predictions and timings, yet there is no mechanism for avoiding the consequences of a negative prediction, which doesn't sit well with people raised in a Western society where self-determinism is highly emphasized. Western astrology is excellent for determining personality and psychological characteristics, but if one's chart indicates difficulty in relationships and one is born into a society where each person is expected to marry and have children, knowing this will only cause unhappiness in the inability to fulfill one's expected societal role. The bottom line is: where each system has elements in common, and can borrow from the others, it is best to stick with the system which best fits one's society, warts and all.

COOKBOOK ASTROLOGY

This is a popular term used to designate astrology books that delineate planets by sign and house with a paragraph or two for each—(Saturn in the 1st, Saturn in the 2nd, etc., and then separately delineate aspects, the Ascendant and Midheaven, etc.). The reader is then to take all the different elements, read the paragraphs applicable and from those formulate a reading as a whole. Cookbooks are not inferior as a class, but rarely can delineation operate in a vacuum—each element being isolated and separately interpreted. The planets in a chart are tied to each other by aspects, by rulerships of signs and houses, and by reinforcement of indications—the astrological rule of three. If something is indicated in three different ways, then it will come to pass—probably.

There comes a point in interpretation where a cookbook just cannot go. This is where the "art" of astrology comes into play. And a living human brain is required to tie all the elements together to weigh and balance influences and use judgment about how much and in what way to pass the conclusions on to the native. Also, a good reading is ideally a dialogue—the astrologer gets a better handle on the chart by listening to the individual and seeing how the person chooses to deal with the chart, and then revising the reading accordingly. It is through such a continuing dialogue that accurate prediction becomes possible.

Evangeline Adams' famous prediction about the hotel fire in New York was made by her seeing a transit coming up. She looked back into the ephemeris and asked the client what happened to him the last times that transit had been in effect. He told her and she predicted that the same thing would happen again. And it did. This may burst bubbles about the omniscience of the astrologer, but in many ways it is as easy as that. The transits of Sun through Saturn (the ancient planets) are easier to delineate because a person will experience multiple transits in an average lifetime. The trans-Saturnian planets, Uranus, Neptune, and Pluto, will never make a full orbit in the average lifetime (a Pluto return, for example takes place every 248 years). So prediction can be trickier than it seems. Ain't astrology fun?

HOW TO START A FISTFIGHT AMONG ASTROLOGERS

There are many ways. There are quite a few topics in astrology which have many "answers," many ways of achieving various ends. There are no absolute correct answers, you can achieve your endpoint by various means. Anyhow some topics certain to cause controversy are:

House systems—which is the best (there are about 20);

Orbs allowed for aspects (from 0 to up to 17 degrees);

What gemstones signify what in the breastplate of the High Priest of Israel (where all birthstone correspondences are said to come from);

What planets (and/or asteroids) are vital for chart interpretation;

Midpoints—whether or not to use them;

Why and how exactly astrology works;

What is an absolute indicator of "true love" between two charts;

What makes a person a jerk or a nerd, astrologically speaking;

Which aspects are required for optimal chart interpretation;

Hypothetical planets (there are lots out there—maybe);

Whether computer calculated chart interpretations have "soul";

What is the correct astrological chart for the United States;

When will the Age of Aquarius begin, exactly.

If you find yourself at a dull party and know there are several astrologers present, one way to liven up things is to loudly state, "Placidus is the only house system valid for natal astrology." Or "Five degrees is the absolute orb I allow for a square." "Equal House is just for lazy people who don't want to calculate cusps." "The Ancients only used seven planets and nobody needs any more." "I don't care how accurate computers are, any astrologer who cannot hand-calculate charts is no real astrologer."

You then step back and watch the arguments. If you are lucky, violence may break out! These are hot topics, astrologically, and astrologers have cherished opinions on these subjects (or should—if they don't, they are just amateurs dabbling in a topic which is beyond their comprehension—another inflammatory statement). Just be sure nobody is able to pinpoint you as the original instigator, and don't tell anyone where you got the idea in the first place.

TRANSITS, PLANETARY STATIONS, AND ECLIPSES

Another way of blending magick and astrology is to do a working to acknowledge a transit or station or eclipse which influences your natal chart. In the summer of '92 an eclipse took place which had had powerfully catastrophic influences on me in the past. I was more than a little bit apprehensive about the eclipse repeating, so I devised an astrological circle and guided meditation based upon the Sabian Symbols of the eclipse degree and the degree of the Saros Cycle of the eclipse. I figured if I honored and respected the power and influence the eclipse was likely to have, at least I would be better prepared for what was to come, and at best, by confronting the energies head-on, so to speak, I might spare myself some grief and upset which eclipses have been known to bring. I did this, and two days before the eclipse, had my working group over for our regular meeting and we all participated in the Astrological Circle, and did the guided meditations and it was fun. I certainly worked out some worries and insecurities in the planning and execution. As it turned out, the effect of the eclipse was not as traumatic as I had feared. Now, whether it was because of the circle, or because my imagination had run amok beforehand, I will probably never know. Still, the effect was not nearly as dire as the last two times that eclipse had occurred, so I must have done something right.

The point of all this, is that Max Heindel and Co. aside (the old fatalistic, fuddy-duddy turn-of-the-century astrological crowd),you can work with the energies of the planets as they move here and there and contact stuff in your chart. You cannot negate the energies, they will occur whether you want them to or not. But you can choose the method in which you will deal with the energies. You may not totally avoid negative or upsetting transits, but in honoring and choosing to deal with these energies head on, you may lessen the negative influences. After all, this is one of the reasons we all are doing this Magick stuff. We want to work with the energies around us and make things as harmonious and easy as possible. If we see a storm coming, we are best occupied with preparation, rather than running around screaming and wailing. We cannot stop the storm, but we can do something about how and where we will meet it. That is all that this is about. Really.

Transiting planets over natal conjunctions or oppositions—three way blend, big effects, especially if the transiting planet is an outer planet—Mars to Pluto and if a modern planet—Uranus, Neptune, Pluto—may be matters which are societal and transpersonal. The longer the period of the transiting planet, the greater the effect of the transit. Or transiting conjunctions or oppositions conjunct or opposite natal placements will also be very powerful. Certain aspects between the slower planets are generational and color whole eras with their influence. Uranus conjunct Pluto from 1964 to 1967 is a good example. The 1993 Uranus-Neptune conjunction is another excellent example; it comes about every 174 years or so, and if this configuration is conjunct or opposite a planet or point in your chart, it brings inspiration and spirituality to that planet by house placement and rulership. Look also to the houses which Uranus and Neptune rule natally (mundanely they rule the 11th and 12th), and also the houses occupied natally by Uranus and Neptune. Use keywords to blend meanings, it can be really heavy stuff.

This book you are reading is a result of that Uranus-Neptune conjunction, opposite my natal Mercury-Uranus. Even the name, *Astrologickal Magick*, relates to the conjunction, Uranus ruling astrology and Neptune ruling magick.

Planetary stations are powerful times. Planets which are stationary are apparently holding still before either going retrograde or direct, and this intensifies the planet's energies. If a station is conjunct or opposite a planet or point in your chart, the stationary planet's energies will be laid on thick on that planet or point. It becomes a super conjunction or opposition. Look to the house the stationary planet rules, both in the natal chart and mundane chart, for that is where the action will come from. Also look to the planet hit and the house it rules natally and mundanely. Blend the influences from the stationary planet and the planet being contacted. Doing a ceremony, using the influence of a stationary planet contacting one of yours is like having a double conjunction or opposition, and you will double the energies and results.

Eclipses: solar and lunar, conjunct or opposite a natal planet or point stirs things up. Look to the planet hit and the house it rules natally and mundanely for the areas of life affected. A solar eclipse will be in effect for six months to a year, starting about a month before the eclipse, itself. A lunar eclipse will be in effect for a month to six months, starting about a week or two before the eclipse. Blend the energies of the planet and houses affected. I use tight orbs for these aspects from eclipses: three degrees or less.

• • •

Be aware of such influences and go with the flow. Try to channel the energies in a way you can be comfortable with. Try a ceremony to "communicate" with the planets involved, acknowledge the effects and ask for ideas and inspiration. Use the word lists of the planets to find comfortable or acceptable ways to express the energies in effect. With a Mars transit, you could experience it as cutting yourself, speeding, having an argument, working out in the gym, having an evening of hot sex, becoming ill with a fever, insisting that things be done your way for a while, wearing bright red, having an accident, beating up the neighborhood bully, having a bonfire, burning your dinner. All are expressions of Mars energy, but some are more easy to live with, some are more upsetting and catastrophic, and some merely unpleasant. However, it gives you some idea of the range of expressions available to the aware person.

SYZYGY

Syzygy is one of those wonderful scrabble words which can get you a whole bunch of points if you put it on a triple word square. But even though it is popular, few people know what it means. Syzygy is an astronomical term which has validity in astrology also. It is a conjunction or opposition of two or more planets within a five degree orb. Every month, there are two syzygys—the new and full moons. In astronomy, a syzygy is considered to be three planets in a line, as at new and full moons. In astrology we say it is two or more planets in conjunction or opposition, and as the Earth is always implied at the center of every chart, it is de facto included in these patterns. However, it is more significant when there are three or more planets, in addition to the Earth, in the pattern. The closer the conjunctions and oppositions, the more powerful the syzygy.

Generally syzygys include the Sun and/or Moon. The Moon moves so quickly that it can usually be in orb of most any major conjunction or opposition, before the orb is passed. In mundane astrology, the syzygy is used as a predictor for world events. It works like this: A chart is erected for a new or full Moon. The astrologer examines the chart and sees if any other planets are conjunct or opposite the degree of the lunation. Lunations themselves are significant, but if they are conjunct or opposite other planets, especially planets which cause change (Mars, Saturn, Uranus, Pluto, and some consider Neptune also), then the lunation becomes highly significant and sets up a sensitive point, a "trigger point," if you will. The degree of this trigger point, and the degree opposite are "sensitized" by the syzygy. These degrees become a marker for action. The timing of the triggering of the action comes when another planet moves across one of those degrees by transit. That time, within 24 hours or so, times the release of the energies built up by the syzygy. Think of the syzygy as a rubber band, stretched and ready. The transiting planet then cuts the rubber band, thereby releasing all the energy held in stasis by the stretched band, and it flies off and eventually lands on the ground, its energy spent.

The New Moon chart sets up events and is considered to be in effect for a month to three months. A Full Moon chart is considered to be a culmination of events and is in effect for two weeks to a month. If the New or Full Moon is also an eclipse, then those time periods of influence are in effect.

It is fun to look in an ephemeris and see when there are powerful configurations and when the triggers happen, and to see what happens in the world as a result of these energies being released. How does the mundane astrologer determine how and/or where these energies will manifest? There are a couple of pointers. One is that where the configuration lies across the Asc/Dsc or MC/IC axis, in the world, is where the energies will manifest.

One example of this is the Full Moon at 18 degrees of Capricorn on 8 January, 1993. This full moon was within a degree of the Asc/Dsc axis in Washington D.C. As this city is the capital of the U.S., any configurations which are across the axes of this city will affect the government (and the populace) of the U.S. This was an especially powerful lunation because there were three other planets within a degree of the lunation. Mars was at 17 degrees Cancer, conjunct the Moon and retrograde. The Sun was wedged between Uranus and Neptune, also at 18 and 19 degrees Capricorn. So added to the energies of the Full Moon (which can make people crazy anyway) are those of Uranus (sudden unexpected action), Neptune (unclear hidden things and also oil) and Mars retrograde (action energy, ego, violence, war, but all these are sublimated or directed inwardly or repeating from before due to Mars' retrograde motion). This then set up a very powerful trigger point along the 18 Capricorn/Cancer axis. Late on Tuesday, 12 January, Mercury moved to 17 Capricorn, thereby opposing the degree of Mars in this configuration. Within 12 hours, the U.S. was engaged in a U.N. sanctioned bombing of Iraq designed to destroy Iraq's nuclear capability. This timing comes uncannily close to that of the trigger of the syzygy.

Now, in retrospect it becomes pretty clear that this was the release of the energies of this lunation. Before the fact, it is possible to predict something potentially violent and dangerous will happen, but how does the mundane astrologer narrow it down? Using the charts of countries, capitals and world leaders is one way, when a pattern is conjunct or opposite a planet in the natal chart of a nation, its capital, or a world leader, then they will be affected by the energies. Where the syzygy is on the Ascendant or Midheaven axis in the world is another predictor. The mundane astrologer must also be up on world politics and geography and geology to make accurate predictions. These syzygys over earthquake areas can set up stresses and are used as possible earthquake predictors. The word possible is used, because there are many other factors which also seem to operate. Weather conditions at the time of the triggering of the syzygy are important—there seems to be a correlation between low atmospheric pressure and earthquakes. If a high pressure cell is over the affected area, an earthquake will probably not result. Then the charts of the communities involved should also be consulted, to see if there are stresses to those charts in operation. And if the area is not subject to earthquakes, then prediction of an earthquake is not really feasible. As you can see, it is an inexact and difficult art, but it can also be challenging and fun.

Conjunctions or oppositions of planets other than the Sun and Moon also are syzygys. That is one reason that conjunctions or oppositions which occur between the slower moving outer planets are so significant. They occur infrequently, due to the slow motion of the outer planets, and the planets themselves are so important in terms of influence. Sun, Moon, Mercury, Venus and Mars are considered to be personal planets. They affect the individual. Jupiter and Saturn are considered to be more societal in influence, their aspects can affect communities. Uranus, Neptune and Pluto are transpersonal planets. Their aspects affect humanity as a whole. So when you add together the infrequency and transpersonal energies of the outer planets, you can see why whole books are written on the influence and effects of major outer planet configurations. The conjunctions are considered to be most powerful, but oppositions are also powerful. The conjunctions are the beginning of a new cycle of the energies of those two planets. It is a "cosmic new moon" between those planets. The opposition is like a "cosmic full moon" between those planets. The cycles and trends which started after the conjunction come to full fruition and influence and will wane until the next conjunction, which begins another new cycle. Whether the new cycle will be better or not depends upon how well humanity learned the lessons of the previous cycle.

This is the astrology that Nostradamus used when making his predictions. There is some conjecture that he was aware of the modern planets Uranus and Neptune and possibly Pluto. Again, if you buy into the Atlantis theory, these planets have merely been rediscovered by modern astronomers, and the astrologers of Atlantis were aware of them and their influences, and this knowledge was passed down through the ages. But whether or not Nostradamus knew about these planets, he sure was good at what he did.

Because astrology was considered suspect and some of his predictions were not favorable for nations or people in power who were alive at the time of the predictions, Nostradamus chose to cloak his predictions in deliberately flowery archaic language. One has to be fluent in French, Old French and astrology to make best sense of his quatrains. Still, they have survived and usually they are proven to be correct, after the fact. One certainly needs to have a certain amount of prescience and psychic ability to correctly choose the predictions from the many possibilities presented by these planetary configurations, but an accomplished practitioner can achieve a high degree of accuracy.

This section is presented as an example of the usefulness of astrology beyond that of persons and their interrelationships on an individual level. This is the astrology of humanity as a whole, and of the Earth itself. Everyone starts with, "How will it affect me?" but the evolved person will also be interested in "How does it affect my community, my country, the Earth and humanity as a whole?" Those who try to teach the lessons presented by the major outer-planet configurations and try to offer peaceful constructive solutions which use these energies are the teachers of humanity. Their lessons may fall on deaf ears at the time, but often their message is heeded by later generations, and they are hailed as heralds of new ways of thought and living. Invariably you see how the teachers' natal charts tie into the energies of the configuration, and they become possessed by those energies and spreading their solution to the problems presented. They are considered ahead of their time, but these souls are needed for humanity to advance and move toward more pure, peaceful, and effective expression of the energies of all the planets. If humanity is to survive into the centuries beyond the 20th, it must start thinking and acting globally, putting the needs and lessons of humanity as a whole before those of individuals or communities or mere nations. This is the ultimate lesson which astrology offers.

THE URANUS-NEPTUNE CONJUNCTION
AND THE OUTER PLANET CYCLES

This section addresses specifically the Uranus-Neptune conjunctions of 1993 and the possible effects they may bring. It also ties those conjunctions in with other conjunctions and oppositions of the three outer planets which started in 1892. It is a short sojourn into mundane astrology and presented for the enlightenment and edification of all. Time will tell if it is prophetic or merely an exercise in futility.

Infrequent outer-planet conjunctions and oppositions are era-markers. They usher in new ways of thinking and offer new solutions to problems which are old, or which are becoming more persistent and pervasive in society. The Uranus-Pluto conjunction of June 30, 1966 was in orb for about five years, from late summer 1963 to fall 1968. It brought about the hippie movement, anti-war protests, broke the back of the fashion industry, started a health food revolution, accelerated the rise of the drug culture, caused one president to not seek re-election, signaled a change in parties in power in the White House which has remained with only one brief four-year respite until 1992, and other changes. This conjunction was also sextiled by Pluto at the time.

In fact, Pluto and Neptune are sextile for about sixty-some years, starting after WWII and continuing within orb into the next century. This is a moderating influence and may help us to peacefully and easily integrate the energies of the two great conjunctions which occur during its orb of influence. It at least provides the opportunity to peacefully negotiate change, rather than having it forcefully thrust upon us.

Now, in 1993, we saw three exact conjunctions between Uranus and Neptune. This has been within orb of aspect since December 1988 and continues until roughly January 1997, about eight years. This aspect will cause great change, just as the Uranus-Pluto conjunction of the 60's, but due to the more subtle and elusive quality of Neptune, the effects will not be as readily apparent for a few years. One thing is that the Democrats have re-gained the White House, which may continue for a while. There seems to be a revolution about Government, the restructuring of Government and the "get 'em out" fever which characterized the 1992 election. This fits with the imagery of Capricorn (Government) and Uranus and Neptune (sudden change and subtle effects). Uranus is the planet of the people, of freedom and democracy. There may be more governmental reform, but on a subtle level. Where the 1960's were characterized by riots and violent emotional confrontations (images of Pluto), this possible revolution will be quieter, in before you knew it was taking place, more dreamy and illusory. Health will be a number one priority, and prison reform will also be a topic we will hear a lot about. There may be a middle class revolt, but it will be quiet: non-resistance and passive means will probably be the methods used. Look for more tax-resisters, people who just quietly refuse to pay. As the late 60's brought an occult revival, look for the New Age to keep moving along, bringing more and more people into its many doctrines and disciplines. Look for a revolution in established religion; the rigid fundamentalists should have a tough time of it. Any societal structure which is established, rigid, and authoritarian will probably suffer and change, as it falls under the influence of this conjunction.

The Catholic Church is also probably in for change from within. The hierarchy of the Pope and his absolute pronouncements may end. The Catholic Church may fragment into several separate Catholic Churches, all giving nominal lip service to the Pope and his pronouncements, but in actuality, picking and choosing which doctrines they will and will not pay heed to. Look for an American Catholic Church, perhaps two separate North and South American Churches, a European (or several European) Churches, and so forth. Look at that Bishop in Southern

France who started his own brand of Catholicism based upon the older more traditional church of the past. Students of history will remember the times in the 1300's of the two Popes, one at Rome and the other in Avignon (which is near this Bishop). That schism lasted nearly 100 years. Are we in for another similar time? Both the Bishop and the Pope have mutually excommunicated each other. The Catholic Church may not survive this breakup as a unified homogeneous whole.

In the U.S. we may actually see the establishment of true democracy here. The U.S. has never been a true democracy, just a representative democracy. The electoral college determines who becomes President, which is why you can have a President who won yet who received fewer popular votes than his opponent. The electoral college was established to protect an uninformed populace from making stupid mistakes. But those days are long past and with TV and other mass media, nobody is ignorant of at least the more popular and saleable issues of a campaign.

Health and hospitalization is now a hot topic. The public feels that reliable, reasonably priced medical care is something to which every person in this country is entitled. Look for nationalization of health services in the next few years, slowly but inexorably. AIDS is a worldwide pandemic, and research is being funded at almost criminally low rates. But with the rise of AIDS, other sexually transmitted diseases are rampant. Look for attempts to combat those diseases as well. And AIDS is probably not the only killer which will be in the news; diseases which were thought to have been wiped out are returning, and in newer more virulent mutated forms. AIDS itself has mutated into several strains. The origin of AIDS has also been uncertain. Look for more revelations on that including the news that it may be a manmade biowarfare germ which either escaped or got out of control in a test population.

Chemical warfare will take new turns, or hopefully be abolished. Also chemical pollution and toxic wastes will be hot topics and hopefully receive the attention they deserve. Note the rise in oil spills and other chemical accidents in the past years. The ozone layer situation may finally turn critical.

Another effect of this conjunction will be on people born during this time. This will mark another generation of people, who when they come of age, will help implement the changes which were brought about by this conjunction in the first place. They will be unusual and some may be "lost," just as some of those born during the Uranus-Pluto conjunction in the 1960's are, due to the strong effects of this conjunction. The post baby-boom generation (people born from 1964 to roughly 1970), are called "baby-busters," "Generation X," and "the lost generation." These names all seem to be derivations of the images of the Uranus-Pluto conjunction. This generation has been overshadowed by the more numerous and highly active "baby-boomers" of the Uranus-square-Neptune generation, hence they are perceived as "lost." Not everyone is able to handle the energies involved. If an individual has a personal planet conjunct, opposite, or square this conjunction, she or he will be affected and may play a role in world events in the coming years. Also, many of the people born during that Uranus-Pluto conjunction are now coming into their own, and those that may have seemed "lost" are now becoming effective and powerful in new and unusual ways. The Uranus-Pluto conjunction is within orb of a trine to the 1993 Uranus-Neptune conjunction. That Uranus-Pluto generation will move to take their place in the world and demand something for themselves, and maybe even wrest power from the "baby boomers."

Another generation affected is the Uranus-square-Neptune generation born mid-1950 to early 1958. These people are experiencing this conjunction at the same time they are going through their midlife crisis of Uranus opposite its natal place, and also Pluto square natal Pluto, which, for these people, comes as early in life as possible, due to Pluto's highly elliptical orbit. These people are experiencing the Pluto square Pluto as early as 37. So this group is experiencing three powerful transits to birth placements almost simultaneously: Uranus opposite Uranus, Neptune square Neptune, and Pluto square Pluto. These aspects should energize this generation like no other. This group is the height of the Baby Boom; more children were born in 1954 than any other year. After the conjunction and opposition, the square is the next most powerful aspect. Squares stir up energies, cause change, though the changes may be neither quiet nor pleasant. If there is a middle class revolution, look to this group to start it. And if you factor in Chiron, which was opposite Uranus and square Neptune from 1953 to 1955, you have another planet adding to the mix, Chiron being a maverick, interested in among other things, alternative medicine, healing, and non-traditional methods of teaching and mentoring.

How do you predict where your place is in all of this? First, if you are born during one of the periods mentioned above, you are a prime candidate for getting caught up in all of this. But also if you have a personal planet in your chart near any of these sensitive degrees, within 6 degrees of 19 Cancer-Capricorn, or 19 Aries-Libra. The people with trines and sextiles to this conjunction, 3 degrees either side of 19 Taurus, Virgo, Scorpio, or Pisces, may play a role, but it will be more voluntary and less compelling.

Also if you were born between mid-1950 and early 1958, you may not be caught up in all of this unless you have a personal planet conjunct, square, or opposite one of these points. You still have the configuration in your chart, but without the personal planet to tie the energies into your psyche, you have no personal tap into what is going on in the world. This is not bad, because those with a personal tap into all of this, the "9 ampere tap into God," may be caught up in forces which are larger than they are, or beyond their control. They may feel as if they are under a geas to do things or speak out on certain topics or to get involved in causes which they do not fully understand. The personal planets are Sun, Moon, Mercury, Venus, and Mars. If you have Jupiter and / or Saturn in the mix, you can get caught up in things, but more on a societal level as a member of a larger group. You are not as personally involved, the personal stake is not as high. And especially those born with Chiron also in the mix may well end up being the ringleaders of this movement, Chiron being the bridge between the inner and outer planets,

We are living in interesting times, times of great change and upheaval. The world will not be the same after this. We just do not yet know exactly how it will be different. Add to the mix that Pluto is in its own sign, Scorpio. Pluto in Scorpio times are ones of change anyhow, afterward the world is never the same. The Protestant Reformation and the Industrial Revolution both had their first beginnings while Pluto was in Scorpio and the later leaders of these movements which spread these changes throughout the world were born when Pluto was in Scorpio.

No wonder there are so many crackpots preaching doom. The prophecies of coming world changes all seem to zone in on the last decade of this century, from Nostradamus to Edgar Cayce to Sun Bear. Astrologically it is a time of great change and new things. There are other momentous astrological portents, grand conjunctions in Capricorn, eclipses which tie into these energies, other transiting squares, oppositions, and conjunctions which serve as triggers for the energies built up by this great conjunction. Many of us have lived through one great conjunction in our lifetimes already—Uranus-Pluto.

Neptune was conjunct Pluto in Gemini in 1891-1892, and these planets will not be conjunct for another 400 some years (the conjunctions are roughly 495 years apart). If one looks to that great conjunction (the most infrequent and wide-reaching we know of at present) as the start of all of this, and these two others as the climax of the energies set into motion before this century began, it indeed looks like life will be not at all dull for the world as we head into the 21st century. Life certainly has accelerated in pace since the 1890's. Learning has increased exponentially, and technology has grown more than anyone could imagine. A person born in the 1890's was born into a rural horse-drawn world. Nowadays the world is urban and automobile driven. All within a short 100 years. Change seems to never have happened so quickly ever before in recorded history.

Also interesting that the two previous conjunctions (Neptune-Pluto and Uranus-Pluto) were triple hit conjunctions, and the transiting square between Uranus and Neptune was exact five times. This present conjunction (Uranus-Neptune) will also be exact three times due to retrograde motion. It is not unusual for an outer planet aspect to be exact more than once. Transiting conjunctions and oppositions by an outer planet to a natal chart happen most often three times, and can occur five times (or more), due to retrograde motion.

Uranus opposed Pluto five times in 1901-1902, and Uranus opposed Neptune eleven times between March 1906 and October 1910. This is an unusual number of hits. Aleister Crowley, in his book *Astrology*, said that under the opposition of Uranus and Neptune, the Grand Master of the Temple would be born. But there is another key which is necessary for the aspect to have full effect, and that is involvement with another planet in the natal chart, preferably a personal planet. If that Grand Master was born at that time, the involvement of a personal planet is more important than the exactness of the Uranus-Neptune opposition. The more personal planets involved, the more highly in-tune with the energies the person will be. And for it to be within orb of exact between eleven hits for a period of four-and-a-half years, gives ample opportunity for a whole lot of Grand Masters to be born under the opposition's influence.

Now Uranus has come around to make the last conjunction with the other outer planets. This has been a momentous century. Hopefully it will not go out with a bang, but rather a coming to terms with all which has happened to the world, and a healing and balancing of resources and opportunities. Establishment of a world government is not out of the question. The U.N. is gaining legitimacy and influence in the world. And we all need to think and act globally instead of being artificially blinded by regional or national concerns. Prayer and faith will certainly be important elements in this quiet revolution. Gatherings, such as the Harmonic Convergence, are helpful, but they have to continue. If enough people hold on to the same thought-picture of what they envision the world becoming, they can create substantial change. And maybe, in the end, this is what the nature of this change is all about. Change by prayer and creative visualization, both Neptune images. Proof of mental ability to change the world by the power of thoughts alone. If we all try it, and truly pray for peace and global unity, then we can say when the changes come, that we were agents of those changes, each in our own way. One person may not be able to do it alone, but all of us together may help to effect great change, if we only put our minds to it. Together, in unity of vision and hope.

CONSTELLATIONS VS. SIGNS

In astrology, there are twelve signs of the zodiac which sort of correspond with certain astronomical constellations in the sky. Modern astronomical almanacs show fourteen actual constellations which cross the ecliptic, yet astrology still insists that there are only twelve signs. What gives?

The ancients did not precisely demark the constellations as they are known today. The pattern of the stars in the sky suggested designs and figures which were mythologized, or the figures were imposed upon the patterns in the sky to correspond to local myths. The skies themselves became a picture book, teaching and memory tool. The constellations (literally groups of stars) roughly divided the sky. Some constellations in the past "shared" stars; that is, a star was considered part of two adjacent constellations. The star Alpheratz was shared by Pegasus and Andromeda, for example.

In the 1700s when telescopes became valid scientific tools, and astronomy was concerned with mapping the heavens, precise demarcation of constellations along lines of Right Ascension and Declination were mapped out. Nowadays the constellations have very precise boundaries which have been determined by the I.A.U. (International Astronomical Union). We now have fourteen constellations whose boundaries cross the ecliptic, and some of these constellations are more or less than 30 degrees in width across the zodiac.

There are some who call themselves astrologers who feel that because there are fourteen constellations along the zodiac and that they aren't uniform in width, that the ancient astrological signs, the twelve signs of precisely 30 degrees each are no longer valid. They also think that siderial astrology, which does count the signs from the position of the constellations, is totally wrong. This isn't true.

The signs and constellations do have a relationship, but even in siderial astrology, there is not a 100 percent correlation. Siderial astrologers still use the 0 degrees Aries point in the sky as their 0 degrees Aries point, but they then still count twelve signs of 30 degrees each. So they are about 24 degrees behind Tropical astrologers, but that's all.

The strange offshoots of a slavish devotion to constellations and I.A.U. boundaries has led to such aberrations as *Astrology 14*.[2] This book postulated that astrology was all wrong because it did not follow precisely the I.A.U. constellation boundaries and re-designed astrology to match those boundaries with the Sun's actual placement in the sky over the year. The author also introduced two new astrological

---

[2]Steven Schmidt, *Astrology 14* (New York: Bobbs-Merrill, 1970).

signs to account for the two other constellations whose boundaries cross the ecliptic. They are Ophiucus the Serpent-Bearer, and Cetus the Whale. There were revised dates for all fourteen signs and interpretations of sun-sign characteristics for all fourteen signs. It was, for what it was, a really well done work. This work supposedly invalidated all other astrology books and proved classical astrology to be invalid. Too bad it was all based upon two different and conflicting worldviews.

The astrological signs were determined thousands of years before the I.A.U. or any scientific organization determined any constellation boundaries exactly. The I.A.U., when determining those boundaries, used the constellations as a guideline, but was not at all concerned with astrological needs or wishes. So this is why we have fourteen signs which are part of the ecliptic and signs of more or less than 30 exact degrees. Astrologers (and there are some) who try to correlate the zodiac and astrology with this scientific demarcation are just wasting their time. The Siderial Zodiac, the Tropical Zodiac and the Constellation boundaries are in some ways coincident, and are certainly based upon the same root system, but are not correlated with each other today.

The precession of the equinoxes is another facet of astrology which is based upon the difference between the actual constellation positions and the actual placement of the Vernal Equinox point. The Vernal Equinox is the day when the day and night are of equal length. This is in the Spring in the Northern Hemisphere. As the Earth is more Northern Hemisphere biased, and the civilizations which developed astrology were north of the equator, it is the Springtime day, or Vernal equinox which marks this point. This vernal equinox point is where the Sun is in the sky, along the ecliptic when is it said to be at 0 degrees of the sign Aries in Tropical Astrology. That may seem like a lot of qualifying for one point, but it is important to understand that we are being very precise with this point. It is Northern

Hemisphere-Spring-Tropical Astrology oriented. So we have this 0 Aries point. It is the base for all the other zodiac signs. It is where the starting point for the Tropical Zodiac is. Without it, we can see the planets, but we have no reference as to what signs they are in.

The Earth rotates on its axis. That axis is tilted $23\frac{1}{2}$ degrees to the plane of its rotation around the Sun. This tilt accounts for the seasons and variations in the length of the days and nights as the seasons progress. That axis also rotates slowly. Currently the northern end of that axis is pointed toward Polaris, the pole star. It was not always pointed there, and it will not always be pointed there. The rotation or wobble of the Earth on its axis is slow. It takes 25,400 years (or thereabouts) for the Earth to rotate around a complete circle on its axis. As it does so, the vernal equinox point precesses (moves) backward through the zodiac. So the 0 Aries point eventually moves backward through each sign.

We are currently at the end of the Age of Pisces, or the beginning of the Age of Aquarius, depending on who you listen to. Again, there is no exact fixed scale to measure the beginning of one age and the ending of the previous one. Astrologers know the length of the full cycle, and how long each age lasts, but as to when each age begins or ends, there is no specific time marker. We can say that the end of the Age of Aries and the beginning of the Age of Pisces was near (within a couple hundred years) the birth of Jesus. Whether it was immediately before or a hundred or more years before, or even a hundred years after is not known exactly. One thing which is agreed upon is that the ages do not suddenly end and begin. There is a transition from one age to the next, a blending of influences as the old age sort of dies out and the new age is born and establishes itself.

Each age vibrates to the influences of the sign of the age and its polar opposite. So the Age of Pisces is like Pisces and Virgo. The Age of Aquarius (as celebrated in the song) will be like Aquarius and Leo. The times when the influences are changing are interesting times. There are supposedly a lot of Earth changes, climate and topological, the pace of life is supposedly accelerated and important things happen.

This whole discussion of the Great Year, as the complete cycle of the ages is called, is definitely part of esoteric astrology. Still, with all the hoopla about the Age of Aquarius and the Harmonic Convergence and all that other millenarian stuff, I decided to include it for the curious. Below is a brief list of the various ages and approximate dates and supposed events connected thereto. It is certainly food for thought.

Age of Leo 10900 B.C.E. to 8740 B.C.E.: A Golden age of triumph and self-expression. Height of Atlantis' Power and influence. With Aquarian subinfluence, there were great achievements in science and technology, use of the Great Crystals for power, development of psychic talents. Magnificent cities. People felt power was in them rather than coming from the universe through them. Spread of knowledge and learning. Air travel. Ended with first breakup of Atlantis.

Age of Cancer: 8740 B.C.E. to 6580 B.C.E.: The decline and fall of Atlantis, ending with the Great Flood. This is the age of the Sons of Belial, who experimented on humans and animals and created monsters who were combinations of both. They were supposedly living, thinking beings, but without a soul. The perversion of the great power of Atlantis for short-term ends rather than striving for betterment of humanity as a whole. Much turmoil and trouble, many Earth changes. After the final sinking of Atlantis, great leaders arose, but they were not what were needed, more tyrants than enlightened guides for their peoples. Back to sea travel.

Age of Gemini: 6580 B.C.E. to 4420 B.C.E.: Time of nomads, wandering tribes. Polarities—yin/yang—worshipped. Lots of travel, commerce, exploration. Dispersion of humanity, wandering and looking for an ideal place to settle after the disaster of Atlantis. Small groups, not great consolidated nations. Attempt to save the knowledge and science lost when Atlantis fell. Re-invention of language and writing. Time of the Tower of Babel, when different languages made communication more difficult among peoples. Astrology re-invented or remembered from Atlantis.

Age of Taurus: 4420 B.C.E. to 2260 B.C.E.: Back to the land, agriculture predominant. Bull worship. Heyday of the Great Mother Goddess. Height of the ancient empires— Egypt, Babylon, China, Central and South America, India. Matriarchal societies, fertility worshipped. Building of the Great Pyramids, ancient cities, other solid expressions of wealth, power, and authority. The coming of Buddha. Ended with explosion of Santorini (or thereabouts).

Age of Aries: 2260 B.C.E. to 100 B.C.E.: Fall of matriarchal societies to patriarchialists. Age of Great Wars, conquest by battle and bloodshed. Invasion of Europe and the Middle East by Aryan tribes. Indigenous peoples enslaved, repressed, or moved on. Height of Athens, establishment of Rome, India in its dying classical days. Bull sacrifice gave way to lamb sacrifice. Establishment of laws and courts for supposed even-handed justice for all. Monogamy came into vogue. Moses and the return to Israel. Old Testament times.

Age of Pisces: 100 B.C.E. to 2060 C.E.: The coming of Jesus, compassion for others, principles of brotherhood of man. Heyday of Christianity. Sea power became predominant. Ideals expressed, but not lived up to. Spread of religion by forcible conversion by both Christianity and Islam. Sex repressed and taboos established. Exploration and colonization by sea. Brittania rules the waves. Faith is required for salvation. Repression of magick, mysticism which is not in accord with prevailing religious beliefs. Ends with pole shift and re-emergence of Atlantis.

Age of Aquarius: 2060 C.E. **to 4420** C.E.: World government. Ideals of Brotherhood of Man lived up to. Moving out into space. Re-discovery of Atlantean scientific knowledge. Psychic and mental studies grow and become accessible to all. Global telepathy. Humanity discovers other alien races and begins to communicate with and learn from them. Exploration and colonization of space.

Age of Capricorn: 4420 C.E. **to 6380** C.E.: Supposed establishment of a Federation of Races and colonies in this arm of the Galaxy. Interstellar Government. Humanity losing ties to Earth as the Cradle of Humanity. Exploitation of interstellar resources.

Of course, all this is conjecture. Written history covers only about 5000 years. The rest is legend and fable. Still, it seems to follow a pattern and has an internal consistency. It will be interesting to see just how accurate all this is as the years and centuries progress.

FIXED STARS

In astrology, the planets are often referred to as "stars." But the planets move against the background of the real stars. "Planet" means wanderer in Greek. Other than the constellations themselves, rarely do astrologers use individual stars in astrological interpretation. Some astrologers do concern themselves with individual stars and their influence in individuals' and mundane charts. These stars are referred to as fixed stars because they do not move as the planets do. There are approximately 8,000 stars visible on a clear night. Astrology does not deal with all of them, just the most bright or notable or unusual. There are about 125 fixed stars which have been delineated and meanings researched. We will only worry about the most prominent ones, about 34 in all.

Fixed stars generally are considered to have unfortunate or upsetting influences. Some are noted for being beneficial, but most have influences which cause notoriety or misfortune. These influences are seen in individual's charts, and also in charts for accidents and disasters. This is the older interpretation. A more contemporary view is that these fixed stars, when in conjunction with prominent points in a chart, make for a high focus. They make the chart or individual a stand out, they tend to exaggerate the good and bad. They make for an interesting life, as in the saying, "May you live in interesting times." How one feels about this depends upon the outlook in general. Fixed stars make for lives which cannot be dull, either through the individual's efforts or through circumstances imposed from the outside.

This area of study is quite old, perhaps dating from the original astrology, before the influence of the zodiac or signs was codified. In horary charts, certain stars are considered significant and can change the meaning of a chart. Also there is an area of the zodiac known as the Via Combusta, from 15 Libra to 15 Scorpio, which is an area of the zodiac so heavily tenanted with malefic fixed stars, that the Moon in these degrees renders a horary chart unreadable. The exception is if the Moon is at 23 Libra; it is then conjunct Spica, which overrides the prohibition on judgment, and is considered very fortunate.

This influence has come down to us as the study of fixed stars. Some of the fixed stars are not necessarily individual stars at all, some are groups of stars, one is a nebula. But all are considered important and to have some influence in astrology.

The orb of influence for fixed stars in the natal chart is tight—1-$\frac{1}{2}$ degrees on either side only. No fudging. These fixed stars have influence and meaning. They were said to be among the influences which brought greatness to an individual. You can use them in your magickal workings. You may choose to combine a Moon sign with a particular fixed star to bring in complementary influences. It is another way of adding different planetary influences, when you cannot get them with the planets themselves. Or perhaps reinforcing influences already present. Or perhaps bringing in the influence of certain deities to your working, according to the star itself, or the constellation in which it resides.

Most constellations were named by the Greeks and are said to have the influence of the entity they were named for. The Arabs named most of the fixed stars. This is why so many stars have names beginning with "Al," which is Arabic for "the."

The four most prominent fixed stars are Aldebaran, Regulus, Antares, and Fomalhaut. All four are first magnitude. They are also roughly equidistant from each other. The Persians referred to them as the Four Royal Stars or the Four Watchers. They marked the Sun's position at the start of the seasons at about 1500 B.C.E. These stars can also be prominent in magick. Aldebaran is known as Watcher of the East; Regulus is Watcher of the North; Antares is Watcher of the West; and Fomalhaut is Watcher of the South. With a Midheaven of 4 degrees Pisces, you can have all four stars near the Midheaven-Ascendant axis. This would be interesting if you were using astrology in or as an end of your working. It works pretty well up to about 35 degrees north. Further north and the Ascendant is too far into Gemini to have Aldebaran/Antares within orb of the Ascendant-Descendant axis.

Using these stars in your workings requires you be able to figure exactly the angles of a chart, or figure backward from a particular Midheaven-Ascendant degree to find a time in your locality.

If you find this study interesting, there are a few good books which expand on this subject and number of fixed stars. This star list is arbitrary, mostly taking some of the most notorious and bright stars. There are other stars which may be considered as important, but space limitations demanded that I be choosy.

There are also usually several names for various prominent stars. Where there are other names used commonly, they are indicated.

Each star ends with a list of planets. The fixed stars were assigned influences similar to various planets, and these correlations can vary widely from author to author. You are encouraged to study and see which influences seem most accurate to you. The planetary influences may vary, but the influence of the star itself remains pretty constant, especially regarding the malefic/benefic nature. These interpretations come from an older, more fatalistic, more black and white astrology than that which is practiced today. Some of the influences are archaic, but they translate into modern terms easily. Here is a list of some of the most prominent or notorious fixed stars.

Alpheratz (Sirrah)—alpha Andromedae [14 Aries 05]. Often called Andromeda's Head. Name means The Horse's Navel. Used to be listed as a part of Pegasus. Indicates riches, honors, independence and a keen intellect. Gives a harmonious nature which makes for good personal relationships and popularity. This can extend to being well-known in public and popular with the masses. Influences: Jupiter or Venus-Mars.

Mirach—beta Andromedae [00 Taurus 15]. The side of Andromeda. Indicates beauty, love of home, brilliant mind, fortunate marriage, renowned for benevolence. Altruism and a tendency to inspiration and mediumship as a basis for artistic inspiration. Makes friends easily and has a stimulating effect upon others. Influences: Venus, Venus and Neptune, or Mars and Moon.

Almach (Alamak)—gamma Andromedae [14 Taurus 20]. The feet of Andromeda. Indicates eminence, artistic ability. A cheerful nature and a liking for amusements. Popularity which brings benefits from others. Influence: Venus, with a lesser influence of Jupiter.

Algol—beta Persei [26 Taurus 11]. From Arabic "Al Ghoul," meaning "demon," or "evil spirit." A variable star, which is said to represent the Medusa's head in Perseus' hand. Considered to be the most malefic star. The variability is caused by a rotating binary pair, one of which partially eclipses the other for nine hours and has a 69 hour period. The times when Algol is darkest are the times when it is most malefic. Indicates one of a violent nature, can bring mob violence and murderous tendencies which may cause a tragic end. Can also cause one to be accident-prone. Conjunct Sun, Moon, or Jupiter it can bring victory in war. Much study has been done which links Algol with accidents and disasters which result in great loss of life. Influence: Saturn and Mars, or Saturn, Mars, Uranus and Pluto together.

Alcyone—eta Tauri [29 Taurus 54]. The brightest of the **Pleiades**, the Seven sisters or doves/pigeons sacred to the Goddess. The root word indicates they rose at the time of year when sailing was best. They are also referred to as The Weeping Sisters because they rise when the rainy season comes to Mediterranean climes. They were daughters of Atlas, and were considered to be the center of the universe in ancient times. Indicates eminence, a strong love of nature, ambition, can cause injury to face or blindness. Many cases of eyesight problems connected to Alcyone are recorded. Can indicate that the native will have something to weep about in the life. Influence: Mars and Moon.

Hyades—gamma Tauri [5 Gemini 38]. First of another group of seven stars, considered to be a group of piglets, sacred to the Goddess. Also called Weepers because when they rose or set with the Sun, they were supposed to bring rain. Indicates a contradiction of fortunes, injuries to the head, impaired eyesight. Increased energy, overabundant sexual energy and appetites. Can cause one to be exploitative of others. Can give military aptitude. Influence: Saturn and Mercury, Mercury and Mars, or Mars, Neptune and Uranus together.

Aldebaran—alpha Tauri [9 Gemini 37]. The Watcher of the East, the Bull's Eye. "One who follows the Pleiades." Brightest of the Hyades. Said to rule the hands and fingers. Can indicate a disposition to pneumonia, may presage a violent death. Great energy and drive, ambition can make great enemies. More malefic due to its exact opposition to Antares. Influence: Mars, or Mercury, Mars and Jupiter together.

Rigel—beta Orionis [16 Gemini 32]. Left foot/knee of Orion. Indicates preferment, riches, great and lasting honors. Can also indicate great military or ecclesiastical preferment if on MC. Can stay on top as long as effort is maintained. Influence: Jupiter and Mars.

Bellatrix—gamma Orionis [20 Gemini 46]. Left shoulder of Orion. "The Amazon." Indicates military and other honors which end in disaster. Can bring blindness. Quick decisive decision-making, bold ideas, can become belligerent or a dare-devil. If on MC, a forger or swindler. Influence: Mars and Mercury.

Capella—alpha Aurigae [21 Gemini 40]. Hircus, the goat. Indicates martial or ecclesiastical honors and riches, followed by waste and dissipation. Persistent curiosity, sharp mind, love of learning studiousness and research. Also inclines to an eccentric personality. Influence: Mercury and Mars.

Alnilam—epsilon Orionis [23 Gemini 15]. Middle of three stars in Orion's belt or girdle. These stars are said to confer signal honors when on the MC. Influence: Jupiter and Saturn or Mercury and Saturn.

Polaris—alpha Ursae Minoris [28 Gemini 25]. The Pole Star, tail of the little bear. Indicates sickness and affliction, legacies with unfortunate effects. Bestows spiritual powers and gains respect therefrom. Gives good instincts and ability to find one's way. Influence: Saturn and Venus or Saturn, Sun and Venus together.

The Pole Star has changed over the millennia due to precession of the equinox. The North Pole has moved from alpha Lyra (Wega) c. 12,200 B.C.E.; iota Draconis (Ed Asich) c. 4500 B.C.E.; alpha Draconis (Thuban) c. 2700 B.C.E. to Polaris from about 1000 B.C.E. and will move to gamma Cephi (Er Rai) c. 4500 C.E.; alpha Cephi (Alderamin) c. 7500 C.E.; delta Cygni c. 11,300 C.E.; and again Wega c. 13,500 C.E.

Betelgeuse—alpha Orionis [28 Gemini 34]. Right shoulder of Orion. A military star. Indicates honors but can also bring accidents. Preferment, luck, success, and fame. Influence: Mars and Mercury, or Mercury, Saturn and Jupiter together.

Sirius—alpha Canis Minoris [13 Cancer 54]. Orion's great dog-the Dog star. Also associated with Hecate in her "Bitch Goddess" aspect. Loki's Brand (fire of Loki) "The Royal One" (not to be confused with the four royal stars of the Persians). Brightest star in the Northern Hemisphere. Indicates honor, renown, custodians, guardians, curators, high offices in government, can confer great dignity, also associated with dog bites. Brings fame, but also danger and violence. Important in mythology and conjuring magic. Influence: Jupiter and Mars or Moon, Jupiter and Mars together.

Castor—alpha Geminorum [20 Cancer 50]. Mortal twin—associated with Apollo. Indicates violence, sudden fame, honors followed by disgrace or imprisonment, weakness, sometimes blindness, injuries to the face. Good nature, strong morals, refined manners, champion of causes. Influence: Mercury, or Mercury and Jupiter, or Mars, Venus and Saturn, or Moon, Mars and Uranus.

Pollux—beta Geminorum [23 Cancer 03]. Immortal twin—associated with Heracles. "The Wicked Boy." Indicates connection with poisons, art of self-defense, subtle, crafty, rash, cruel, honor and preferment followed by disgrace, can cause eye weakness, blindness, injuries to face, wounds, imprisonment. Influence: Mars, or Moon, Mars and Uranus.

Castor and Pollux together were considered important as "Herdsman and Warrior" (Babylonian), Thiassis' Eyes (Old German), helpers if in peril on voyages at sea (Phonecian), brother and sister.

Procyon—alpha Canis Minoris [25 Cancer 35]. Orion's small dog. The dog in front. Indicates sudden preferment which is the result of individual exertion, eventually the activity it promotes brings sudden misfortune, also trouble and danger through liquids, gas, poisons and dog bites, can inspire admiration for dogs. Will power, able to put thoughts and plans into action, can become jealous and belligerent. Influence: Mercury and Mars, or Moon, Jupiter and Uranus.

Praesepe—44M Cancri [7 Leo 07]. A nebulous cluster. Manger of the Ascelli—the asses ridden by Bacchus and Vulcan in the war between the Gods and the Titans. Faint, but very important fixed star. Indicates adventure, wantonness, brutality, can be fortunate, but liable to losses through others, industry, order, fertility, big business, possible blindness, weak eyes, facial injuries, fevers, wounds, violent death possible, disgrace. An addictive personality. Conjunct

Moon can give ability to communicate with ancestors and be spiritualistic. Influence: Mars and Moon, or Moon, Mars and Neptune.

Alphard—alpha Hydrae [27 Leo 01]. Heart of the Hydra. Arabic El Ferd-One who stands alone. Indicates wisdom, artistic appreciation, knowledge of human nature, immoral, uncontrolled, subject to tragedy. Connection with poisons/toxins, can give enlightenment through hard work. Influence: Saturn and Venus, or Sun sextile Jupiter, or Saturn, Venus and Neptune.

Regulus—alpha Leonis [29 Leo 40]. Heart of the Lion. Watcher of the North. Marked summer solstice about 3000 B.C.E. Indicates destructiveness, military honors with ultimate failure, magnanimity, liberality, generosity, independent and high-spirited, honor and wealth but subject to ill health, high office in government. Causes exciting world events when conjunct outer planets. Influence: Mars and Jupiter, or Mars, or Sun trine Uranus.

Denebola—beta Leonis [21 Virgo 23]. The Lion's Tail. Indicates honors and wealth but leads eventually to disgrace; swift judgments, despair, regrets, misfortunes through natural forces; good fortune attended by dangers and anxieties because of folly. Influences: Saturn and Venus, or Mercury, Uranus and Mars.

Algorab—delta Corvi [13 Libra 14]. The Crow or Raven. Indicates one who is destructive, malevolent, a scavenger, fiendish and lying; high business and/or government preferment, one who is self-seeking, charming and clever, can be destructive and misrepresenting. Influences: Mars and Saturn, or Saturn and Mars.

Spica—alpha Virginis [23 Libra 38]. The Wheat Sheaf. The most fortunate of the fixed stars. Indicates riches and renown, a sweet disposition; honor and fame, good influence for scientists, artists, writers, musicians, those who create; brings sociability. Benefits any planet or point in conjunction. Influences: Venus and Mars, or Venus, Jupiter and Mercury.

Arcturus—alpha Bootis [23 Libra 56]. Arctophilax, the bear-watcher. Mentioned in the Book of Job (38:32). Indicates renown through self-determination, prosperity by navigation and voyages; ability to achieve justice through power, enterprising spirit, can give lasting success, can be overbearing and quarrelsome. Influence: Mars and Jupiter, or Venus conjunct Mercury.

Both these stars are considered to be fortunate. They are also conjunct, so anyone with one generally has the other also. Spica relates to Virgo and the Great Goddess. Arcturus relates to Ursa Major and Minor (hence the Bear-watcher), and has a connection to Artemis. Arcturus may be better for men to relate to, and Spica women.

Alphecca (Gemma)—alpha Corona Borealis [11 Scorpio 54]. Jewel of the Northern Crown. Indicates dignity, artistic sensibilities, inclination to poetry; success in trade and commerce; gives occult abilities, healing talents, leadership qualities, tendency to being a loner; can indicate dishonor. Influence: Venus and Mercury, or Moon and Neptune, or Mars and Mercury.

Antares—alpha Scorpii [9 Sagittarius 41]. Heart of the Scorpion, Watcher of the West, Mars' Deputy, Rival of Mars. Indicates malevolence, destructive, generous, subject to flashes of impending tragedy, rash impulses, headstrong obstinacy, can bring honor, preferment, and good fortune; keen mentality, courage, unpredictable events, self-destructive, turbulent life; good for military persons. Influence: Mars and Jupiter, or Mars, Mercury, Jupiter and Saturn.

Wega (Vega)—alpha Lyrae [15 Capricorn 10]. The Falling Eagle, Star of the Queen of Life. Indicates one who is beneficent, idealistic, hopeful, refined, changeable, grave, outwardly pretentious but usually lascivious; artistic talents, sensuality, can give occult abilities, possible riches and fame; leadership ability, social responsibility, idealism. Influence: Venus and Mercury, or Jupiter trine Saturn in earth.

Deneb—zeta Aquilae [19 Capricorn 39]. Tail of the Eagle. Indicates benevolence, liberality, ability for command, a successful warrior; success beneficial. Influence: Mars and Jupiter.

Altair—alpha Aquilae [1 Aquarius 35]. The Flying Eagle. Indicates one who is bold, confident, unyielding, liberal, valiant, sudden but ephemeral wealth, a position of command, danger from reptiles; hardiness, courage and generosity, one who "goes for it." Influence: Mars and Jupiter, or Uranus and Mercury sextile Sun.

Deneb Algedi (Nashira I)—delta Capricorni [23 Aquarius 23]. Back of the Goat. Indicates sorrow and joy, life and death, always hanging in the balance; brings a life of change, ability to hold a position of trust, integrity and justice, knowledge of human nature. Influence: Saturn and Jupiter.

Deneb means "tail" in Arabic and as many of the constellations represent animals, there are quite a few tails represented in the lists of fixed stars, hence the need to distinguish between various Denebs.

Fomalhaut—alpha Pisces Austrinus [3 Pisces 42]. Watcher of the South, The Whale's Mouth. Indicates a sublime malevolence which fluctuates between material and spiritual expression, also fortunate and powerful, great learning and an immortal name; variable effect for good and/or bad, makes for "more" of whatever it conjuncts. Influence: Venus and Mercury, or Jupiter square in Pisces or Sagittarius.

Deneb Adige—alpha Cygni [4 Pisces 49]. Tail of the Swan. Indicates a facile and ingenious mind; good for artistic or scientific matters and can make for financial gain through those pursuits, psychic and idealistic, likeable person. Influence: Venus and Mercury.

Achernar—alpha Eridani [15 Pisces 04]. The Cherub and Sword, End of the River Eridanus. Indicates royal honors, success in public office; philosophical, patient, religiously inclined, good morals, adherence to one's personal beliefs. Influence: Jupiter or Jupiter, Mars and Uranus.

Markab—alpha Pegasi [23 Pisces 14]. The Saddle of Pegasus. Indicates honors but danger from fire, fever, cuts and blows; good fortune, possible unluck and ambitions not realized, aids spiritual and mental nature, good with propaganda. Influence: Mars and Mercury

ASTEROIDS

The Asteroids are a relatively new field of study in astrology. The first and largest asteroid, Ceres, was discovered in 1801. Subsequent asteroids were discovered as time went by. Nowadays, it is common practice for astronomy grad students to discover and track new asteroids as a part of their studies. There are several thousand bodies which have been tracked and ephemerides of their movements compiled.

Contrary to earlier belief, the asteroids are not a broken-up former planet, but rather a planet which never fully formed. The gravitational effect of Jupiter is so strong that it caused tidal effects which allowed the asteroids to form, but never allowed those asteroids to coalesce into a larger planet. There are groups or families of asteroids which orbit in bunches at various gravitational points projected by Jupiter.

There are many methods for naming asteroids. The discoverers are allowed to name the asteroid, but cannot name it after themselves. Otherwise they can name it what they will, not duplicating any other named asteroid or celestial body. There are asteroids named after most every entity in classical Greek and Roman mythology. There are asteroids named after deities in other pantheons—Norse, Hindu, Chinese, Aztec, Incan, and Maya. One group of asteroids is named after the principle characters of Arthurian Legend. There are a number of asteroids named after cities on Earth. There are asteroids named after people (usually the significant others of the discoverers). There are even a group of asteroids named after Star Trek characters. All these asteroids are known and tracked. There are services where a person can send away and for a small fee get a listing of the placement of various asteroids in one's natal chart. This can be fun. I happen to have the Asteroid Mr. Spock on my Ascendant, and have been compared to the Vulcan in physical appearance for many years, even before I found out I had that asteroid on my ascendant. Spooky, huh?

All these possibilities notwithstanding, the asteroids which are encountered most in mainstream astrology are the big four—Ceres, Pallas, Juno, and Vesta. They are the four largest asteroids; they are the first four discovered, and also are named after major Goddesses in the classical pantheon.

Mainstream astrology has "ten" planets and seems to operate quite well with these. However, except for the Moon and Venus (and possibly Pluto), the planets are named after male deities. Modern women are addressing feminist and women's issues and feel that the standard planets do not all adequately address these modern issues, pertaining to women. So the asteroids were resurrected, new ephemerides compiled and they are now available for general use in natal charts.

When the asteroids were originally discovered in the early 1800's, ephemerides were compiled and there was a small group of astrologers who experimented with placing them in charts, and seeing what influence they might have. This is standard astrological practice. A new celestial body is discovered, and ephemerides are compiled, and astrologers place it in charts and see what influences it may exert natally, and by transit or progression. When enough charts are compiled and the influences seem to be standardized, someone writes a book and then everyone can begin to use the new body in charts. But that research never went very far, and the asteroids were forgotten in mainstream astrology. Then in the 1970's, with the rise of the women's movement, Zipporah Dobyns decided to look into the big four asteroids and try to resurrect their use. Her *Asteroid Ephemeris* is the best and most complete ephemeris for the asteroids. And then, in the 1980's, Demetra George wrote the book *Asteroid Goddesses*, which is still the main work which deals with the Big Four asteroids and their influence, and rulerships in astrology.[3]

I have been placing the asteroids in natal charts since about 1983, and been actively using them in natal interpretations since about 1987. It takes a while to get used to them, see how they work, and become fluent in their energies in order to be able to add them to your astrological vocabulary. I have found that not only do the asteroids address feminist and women's issues, but they also address craft and pagan issues which are not necessarily covered by the "regular" planets, or they refine and elaborate on those issues in addition to those which are brought out by the

---

[3]Emma Bell Donath, Eleanor Bach, and Lee Lehman have also written books on asteroids. Donath's book, *Asteroids in the Birth Chart* (Tempe, AZ: American Federation of Astrologers, 1979), deals with the Big Four, as does Bach's book, *A Graphic Ephemeris of Sensitive Degrees* (New York: Planet Watch Publications, 1987). Lee Lehman includes many other asteroids in *The Ultimate Asteroid Book* (West Chester, PA: Whitford Press, 1988).

regular planets. They tend to complete planetary patterns, and when prominent, can indicate a propensity for interest in pagan, craft, and possibly magickal studies. They offer alternative ways to express energies which may not be as acceptable in mainstream society, but which may operate in the craft/pagan world. Issues of sexuality, partnering, and parenting are usually the areas where the asteroids offer alternatives to a mainstream lifestyle.

This section will introduce the reader to the big four asteroids—their areas of influence and rulerships. Also included will be the areas where they seem to operate well in craft/pagan life. These influences may not be accessible to all people, as all may not be in an environment where a person may easily or comfortably express these energies, but the potentials are still there. I have found that the people who seem to resonate to these asteroids in their charts are people who are already very in touch with their spirituality, and open to non-mainstream ideas and lifestyles. People in the feminist movement find these archetypes speak to them also.

Each of the four asteroid Goddesses started as a Great Goddess in her own right. With the fall of the matriarchal societies, each was subordinated to various male gods and her powers diluted. Some of the original attributes remained, but they were lessened or distorted by the subjugation to the male "Gods" ruling over each.

Ceres ?

Ceres is the name given by the Romans to the Greek Earth Goddess Demeter. They were similar in powers and scope and had similar myths.

The standard myth concerning Persephone, Demeter, and Pluto goes like this: Demeter was the Earth Goddess, she caused Earth and all living off of it to be fertile and fruitful. She also ruled the harvest and plenty. Persephone was her daughter. Mother and daughter were devoted to each other and they felt they were complete in themselves, neither needed anyone else to be happy. They roamed Earth together and there was a perpetual spring/summer, crops were growing and fruitful and plants and animals were always bearing fruit. It was a permanent time of fertility, harvest and plenty. Pluto had spied Persephone, and desired to make her his wife. He went to Zeus and Zeus agreed to allow Pluto to have her as his wife, even though Persephone herself did not desire to marry. One day, when Persephone was strolling in a meadow, she spied a narcissus and, inhaling its fragrance, was overcome by the scent. Pluto had placed the flower there and when she was overcome, he caused Earth to split open and he emerged into the light, ravished and abducted Persephone, carrying her back to Hades/Tartarus in his chariot drawn by four black screaming horses. Earth then healed up and no trace of what happened remained.

Demeter came searching for her beloved daughter, and could not find her. Demeter searched all the Earth, but Persephone was not on Earth, so she was not found. She went to Olympus, but nobody claimed any knowledge of her location. She returned to Earth and went into mourning for the loss of her daughter. Demeter eventually went to Hecate, a Crone goddess and asked her about Persephone. Hecate suggested Demeter go to Helios, whose unblinking eye saw all which happened on Earth. Helios reported to Demeter all he had seen, and Demeter went to Zeus and demanded her daughter back. Zeus refused. Demeter then decided that if she could not have her daughter with her, she would not perform her duties, and she withheld her fertility from Earth. Soon the plants withered and died, animals ceased to bear and even humans became barren. Zeus sent various Gods to Demeter with presents and admonitions, but she refused to restore fertility to Earth unless her daughter was returned to her. Zeus saw that if humanity was to perish, there would be nobody left to worship the Gods, and relented, but with a condition. Persephone could return to her mother, but only if she had neither eaten nor drunk anything while she was in Tartarus.

While Persephone was in Tartarus, she also went into mourning for the loss of her mother. She abstained from food or drink. After Zeus' decision, Pluto came to her and informed her she was to be returned to her mother. He offered her a pomegranate, and in her relief and hunger and thirst, she ate some of the seeds. Of course, this nullified the agreement, and Pluto refused to return Persephone. Zeus was desperate and a compromise was negotiated. Persephone was allowed to spend part of the year with her mother, and then because she had eaten the pomegranate seeds, she was also to spend part of the year as Pluto's bride in Tartarus. So while Demeter and Persephone were together, the Earth bloomed and was fertile. But when she was forced to return to Tartarus, the fertility was withdrawn and Earth became cold and barren and dormant, until it would bloom again the next spring when Persephone once again was returned to her mother, Demeter.

This is the classic myth, but there is another interpretation based upon older, pre-patriarchal myths. It changes the focus of the story substantially.

Pluto was originally a female deity, but when the matriarchialists were subjugated, was changed to a male, although the powers and attributes remained pretty well intact. Pluto as a female deity was a Crone aspect of a chthonian, deep-earth Mother Goddess. She ruled underground wealth, mines, magick, deep mysteries, death and spirits of the dead, initiation and transformation. Persephone was a Maiden Goddess, daughter of Demeter the Earth-Mother, who ruled fertility, the fields, crops, and agriculture. Now consider that when Persephone left her mother to go down to Hades/Tartarus, the underworld, it was of her own free will. She voluntarily left her Mother to study with the Crone the things which were in her sphere of influence. She went to study, in brief, magick. And she was initiated into the Mysteries and underwent a transformation. This was symbolized by the eating of the pomegranate and her need to spend a portion of each year in Hades/Tartarus. Once she was an initiate, she was bound to pay homage for all she had learned, and to presumably spend a certain amount of time studying and broadening her knowledge, and hopefully attaining higher levels of initiation, eventually becoming One with the Crone in knowledge and understanding. Yes, Demeter suffered from loneliness because of the loss of her daughter, but both benefitted from the transformation and knowledge gained. And this may be a myth explaining the true reason for winter—a time to study, to go within and explore the mysteries of life, death, the cycle of the seasons, and renewal. The Maiden returns each spring and life renews itself, but the Maiden is more wise and tempered by her sojourn into the underworld, and the secret knowledge she has gained. Eventually there is little difference between Maiden, Mother, and Crone—all are aspects of the same Great Goddess. And that is the deepest Mystery of all.

The exact rites and teachings of the Eleusinian Mysteries are lost. They were verbally transmitted, and initiates were bound by oaths of secrecy not to reveal what they had experienced. Yet by going back to the original myths, we may try to deduce parts of the Great Teachings. And if what is discovered works for us, then does it really matter if these were actually the Eleusinian Mysteries, or just what we have deduced them to be? The proof of the magick is in the results. If we are transformed or gain deeper understanding through these deductions, then they are Mysteries, for us in our own times.

Pallas ⚢

Pallas was supposedly a Sky Goddess in her own right, but very early her attributes and worship were subsumed in the worship of Athena. Athena then took Pallas' name as her own in tribute to her. Pallas Athena was also a Sky Goddess and Great Goddess. She was originally virgin in the sense of being sexually autonomous and there are old myths of Athena of giving birth to a Snake deity, symbolizing wisdom. When her worship was co-opted by the Patriarchal invaders, her attributes were altered, but only slightly. She became the daughter of Zeus and Metis (wisdom). But she was not born in the usual way. Zeus lusted after Metis, a Titan, and lay with her, and she conceived a child. When Zeus was informed by a prophecy that any son of Metis' would be greater than his father, Zeus contrived to swallow Metis, and thereby prevent her from coming to term. The child in Metis' womb did mature however, and one day Zeus was gripped with a headache so painful that he asked Haephastos to strike him on the forehead and let the pain escape. Haephastos did so, and from Zeus' skull Athena sprang, adult and fully armed.

This myth again symbolizes the takeover of a Goddesses worship by patriarchal invaders. However, this time the takeover was less traumatic and Athena was allowed to keep most of her original attributes, all but the sexual autonomy and fertility. She was a virgin Goddess of war, but not the war of Ares. She ruled the kind of war which must be waged to gain a lasting peace, or which is waged to defend a homeland. She was the Goddess of "calculated war," or strategic war. She also ruled law, wisdom, logic, and learning. She ruled weaving and handicrafts, and was the patroness of all artisans, as well as of arts and crafts. She was the deity of Athens, and protectress of the State. She also parenthetically ruled the home, hearth, women, and childbirth. In her aspect of Hygeia, she was also the Goddess of miraculous healing.

Juno ⚹

Juno had three aspects—Virgin/bride, Mother/wife, Crone/lawgiver/judge. The lawgiver aspect stayed with Juno as well as the Mother/wife aspect. She also retained the ability to bestow the gift of prophecy, which had been stripped from the Goddess in most of her aspects when the patriarchy took power from the matriarchies. In her functions in Roman society she ruled each woman's inward conceiving and reproductive power, the feminine version of the male "genius." She had several aspects; as Juno Lucretia she was the feminine principle of celestial light, and as Juno Lucina, she was the birth Goddess who leads each child out of the womb into the light. She was also patroness of brides, marriage, and married women. Even nowadays, many brides wish to be married in June and thereby receive Juno's blessing. She also ruled the calendar and the passage of time, the cycle of fertility, and menstruation in women. As a sky Goddess, Juno ruled the weather, and as Juno Moneta, she ruled coinage, money, and the minting and safekeeping thereof.

Juno's sacred marriage to Jupiter was a symbol of the forced monogamy brought by the patriarchialists to the polyandrous matriarchal cultures. At first Jupiter and Juno were happy, but soon their marriage degenerated into bitterness, bickering and sniping, with Jupiter reigning supreme and Juno forced to work her schemes against Jupiter secretly and with the help of other Gods. One account has their marriage barren, though each were fertile and had offspring, they had none together. Another account has Vulcan as their ugly and maimed son. Either way, it can be said that the marriage was not blessed. Juno was demoted from a Great Goddess in her own right to a subordinate to her mate with only a few of the powers and attributes she had exhibited before her "marriage." She was clearly the least happy of the Gods of Olympus.

Vesta ⚵

Vesta started as a great Goddess who was worshipped by women pledging themselves to her temple to become "sacred harlots" for a period of time. Vesta ruled all virgins—that is, women who were not necessarily sexually chaste, but rather women who were in charge of their own lives and not accountable to any man. In some societies women were required to serve in the temples as sacred harlots, giving favors to any man who was traveling and away from his home and the "comfort" of the women of his home town. This service lasted until the woman had borne a child "for the temple" and proven her fertility, as well as learning sexual prowess and how best to please herself and her partner. Only then was she considered to be qualified to marry, or if she chose to remain virgin, take partners as she wanted and to conceive children. With this in mind the three ancient aspects of Vesta are:

Maiden—learning sexual arts in the temple;

Mother—having borne a child for the temple and proven fertility;

Crone—the wise grandmother, hearthkeeper and temple elder.

When the patriarchialists took over, Vesta's powers and rites were altered. Virginity became sexual chastity, and the concept of "sacred harlots" was out of the question. Women were subject to the control of their male relatives, and could escape that control only at the expense of their sexuality. In Roman times, the Vestal Virgins were considered to be exceptionally holy; they were the keepers of the sacred hearth of the city, and thereby the spiritual livelihood. They were called upon to mediate disputes between cities when war was to be avoided. They became the keepers of wills and other sacred contracts which needed to be kept safe, and away from prying eyes. Their persons were inviolate, and any man who violated a Vestal Virgin was condemned to death by fire, as was the unfortunate Virgin who was violated, whether it was of her own volition or by forced rape.

Girls were selected for service in the Vestal Temple before menarche and served for thirty years. After her service, a Vestal retired to private life, and was given a pension at the expense of the state. She could then marry if she so wished, but generally the ex-Vestal had passed menopause and so was no longer able to bear children and raise a family.

Using the Asteroids

These myths serve as an introduction to the four Asteroid Goddesses and their attributes and areas of rulership. Certainly each has changed and evolved over the centuries, and where all started as similar Great Goddesses of fertility and life and death in general, each ended up with different aspects and attributes, through the passage of time and cultural changes.

Nowadays each of the big four asteroids is seen to govern an area of feminine life—not necessarily female, but rather the passive, magnetic, yin qualities in all of us. How we deal with these energies is shown by the aspect of each Goddess we manifest in our lives. If we accept wholly the societal roles cast for us before our birth solely because of gender, we resonate to the more rigid, repressed patriarchical versions of these Goddesses. If we honor the alternative lifestyles which are more available and accepted nowadays, we are given more choices in how we express these energies, which include, but are not restricted to, the patriarchial roles cast for us by society.

The lists below present ideas of how each asteroid operates. Rulerships are shared, as these bodies are not meant to supplant any of the "standard" planets, but are meant to augment their expressions and add another layer of interpretation to the natal chart. They are not used in horary or electional astrology, only in natal astrology and synastry. Each does have certain magickal attributes and can add more expressions of magickal abilities when considered by sign and house and aspect. Pay close attention also to how they may complete an aspect pattern, for with these asteroids the person in question may tie together planets and expressions unexplained by mainstream astrology.

There are two schools of thought when it comes to rulerships. One school thinks that the asteroids (the big four) together rule Virgo. This, in itself, is not outside the realm of possibility. All four asteroids deal with issues of work and service and also sexuality. Virgo is still an earth sign and therefore can be earthy and sensual. Virgo is just discriminating as to how that earthiness is expressed. And the constellation Virgo was supposedly a personification of the Great Goddess in the sky. All four asteroids are Great Goddesses in their own right. They all create, are fertile, and deal with other people, each in their own way.

The other school has rulerships which correspond to signs whose energies fit well with the expression of the energies of each. The rulerships are Ceres-Cancer, Taurus-Scorpio axis, Virgo; Pallas-Libra, Leo, Aquarius; Juno-Libra, Scorpio; Vesta-Virgo, Scorpio. There is also a logical rationalization for each of these co-rulerships.

The point may not necessarily be about rulerships, but the basic energies expressed by each asteroid and how each of us deals with that in our natal charts. So the various rulerships are outlined here, but for the rest, the attributes will be detailed, and readers will be free to define whatever rulerships they feel are correct for them. What is important is that they bring a dimension of yin energy and life alternatives which are expressed fairly purely. Pay attention to these and how they fit (or do not fit) into your chart and lifestyle, and they will be doing their jobs.

⚵ **Ceres**—Mother, Earth, Principle of Unconditional Love; abandonment, nurturance, growing and fertility, barrenness and waste, harvest, socialization of young people, birth, life, death and rebirth, letting go, alternative parenting, single parenting, foster parenting, nanny/governess, providing, productiveness, sharing/selfishness, powerful, civilizing, domesticating, ecological, Earth-honoring, miscarriage and abortion, menarche and menopause, Women's Mysteries, children, adaptation and survival, agriculture, animal husbandry, compassion and anger.

⚲ **Pallas**—Daughter, Air, Creative Intellect; intellectual, crafts, mental rapport, intellectual compatibility, calculated war and peace, learning, healing, perceptual difficulties, arts and crafts, working with hands, justice, political activism and social concerns, diplomacy and mediation, vocation, feminism, wisdom, skillful, strategy, rational, literate, professional soldier, martial arts, competitive, technical, police and firefighters (as protectors of the city), militia.

⚵ **Juno**—Wife, Water, Partnerships—equal or unequal and a merging with a committed partner; Queen of Heaven, lawgiver and judge, compatibility and trust, ceremony and rituals, those who are powerless and/or oppressed, receptivity to others, social interactions and propriety, women's issues, support from a partner, compromising, trust, sexuality in relationships, weather, money, shared resources, alternative relationships, seduction and rape, sex as a weapon, abused persons.

⚶ **Vesta**—Sister, Fire, Sexuality and Service as sacraments; sacred harlot, sacred chastity, sex as a sacrament, service to God/dess, workaholic, sex sublimated to work, home and hearth, childbearing, sacred fire, altar, virgin (in old and modern senses), commitment to a path, disciplined routines, health, exercise, meditation, sanctuaries, rituals, secret societies, safekeeping, hospitality, tradition, prostitution, dedication to a cause, sacred warrior, civil service.

Ceres and Pallas represent a polarity of fertility; Ceres represents physical fertility and Pallas deals with fertility of ideas and creations. Juno and Vesta represent a polarity of sexual expression; Juno represents sexuality expressed with and for a partner, and Vesta represents sexual self-expression in whatever way the individual chooses.

Magickal Applications of the Asteroids

In magick each asteroid corresponds to certain practices which use its energies.

⚳ **Ceres**—Rituals for transformation, death and rebirth; women's blood mysteries, menarche, menstruation, menopause; parenting and children's ceremonies; letting go of children as they grow; loss of children through death, miscarriage or abortion; fertility and conception; planting and harvest; abundance of the Earth; ecology; Earth-Mother; healing anger through compromise.

⚴ **Pallas**—Creative visualization; ceremony and ritual; protective rituals; shields and barriers; psychic warriors; psychic development; creating, writing and performing rituals; women as community leaders; guardians of the community; making ritual tools and other implements and accessories; rituals for warriors and soldiers and community protectors; religious freedom of expression; peace rituals; rituals for miraculous healings.

⚵ **Juno**—Tantric rites; the Great Rite as union of Goddess and God; handfasting and handparting; High Priest and Priestess as surrogates of the Divine couple; healing victims of abuse; weather magick; money magick; cutting away rituals; empowerment rituals; rituals performed by alternative lifestyle partners (homosexual, lesbian, polygamous, polyandrous).

⚶ **Vesta**—Sex used as an energy source; sacred hearth; spiritual center of a community; psychic sanctuary; dedication to the Goddess/God; service to the Goddess/God; psychic development; creative visualization; service and work for the magickal community; chastity as a sacrament; internalizing sexual energy to attain inner spiritual union; meditation; secret magickal societies; cloistered communities; rituals and ceremonies; adherence to a doctrine; following of rules or changing a lifestyle for ritual/magickal ends; ritual routines and daily practices; sacred fires; altar dedication.

CHIRON ⚷

What type of celestial body Chiron is is still being debated. It is smallish, in the range of Moon-sized. It has an irregular orbit, the furthest point being nearly to the orbit of Uranus and the nearest point being within the orbit of Saturn. It has a period of 49 years or so. But scientists are still arguing about whether it is a burned-out comet, an asteroid, or a planetoid. Whatever it is, scientists do agree that it did not originate in this solar system; it was captured some hundreds of millions of years ago, and it will eventually leave the solar system again in hundreds of millions of years from now. This may seem like a long time, but in stellar time, it is like the blink of an eye.

This property of being from and going back to elsewhere makes Chiron a maverick, an outsider. Because of its orbit, it is considered to be a key to bridging the energies between Saturn, the limit of the classical universe, and Uranus, the first of the transpersonal modern planets.

In mythology, Chiron was the most noble of the Centaurs. He was highly educated, civilized and refined. He was a teacher of young heroes, schooling them in the arts of peace and war, giving them a well-rounded classical education. He was an astrologer, philosopher, physician, poet, all-around renaissance person. As a physician, he was a gifted healer, but lacked empathy with his patients. One day Heracles was practicing with bow and arrow, and taking an arrow dipped in Hydra's blood, accidentally wounded Chiron in the knee. As Chiron was an immortal, he could not die, but the poison kept him in agony, with tremendous pain and suffering. Also, because of the poison, the wound could not heal, so his suffering was unceasing. He tried to heal himself by various methods, but the magick in the Hydra's blood was too strong for even Chiron's healing abilities. This wound made him an even better healer, for now with the continual reminder of his own pain, he could empathize with those who came to him for treatment. Aesclepius was one of his most famous pupils in the healing arts.

Chiron continued to train and educate students in various arts and eventually he became weary of the constant pain his incurable wound gave him. He asked to be allowed to die. Zeus was reluctant to withdraw the gift of immortality, so he refused. Later, through Heracles' intervention, Prometheus petitioned Zeus to end his eternal torment. Prometheus gave humanity fire against Zeus' wishes and was punished for his deed by being chained to a rock, and every day a vulture came and tore out his liver, which miraculously grew back each night. Zeus promised to end Prometheus' torment if one of the Gods would give up their immortality. He had forgotten about Chiron's request, for Chiron came forward and offered to die so as to end his own unceasing torment. The exchange was made, Chiron died of the poison, and finally achieved eternal peace. In tribute, Chiron was transported into the sky as Sagittarius or Centaurus so all would remember his deeds. (Sources credit both constellations to Chiron.)

In modern astrology Chiron has an interesting place. The object was discovered in 1977 and at first thought to be a comet. When the orbit was established, it proved to be unique. No other body has a similar orbit and eventually it was determined that Chiron was an interstellar visitor. As soon as it was discovered and named, astrologers started putting it into charts and seeing what influence it had. Then the issue of how to treat this body came up. Should it be treated like another planet, should it be treated like an asteroid, should it be ignored? (There is actually a moderate body of astrologers who are in this camp.)

A number of books have been written about Chiron. Personally, I have put Chiron in charts since about 1982, and have been using it in natal interpretations since about 1986. I like Chiron. It addresses a number of issues which are not dealt with by other planets, and observing the transits of Chiron over the years, it does indeed operate as another planet. Hooray! Unfortunately there is still quite a bit of controversy as to which sign (if any) is ruled by Chiron.

One group assigns Chiron co-rulership of Sagittarius, for obvious reasons. Another group says that Chiron rules Virgo. Personally I like the Virgo rulership. So many of the issues addressed by Chiron relate to Virgo, and Virgo is in need of a planet to rule it all by itself. There is another school of thought which says Chiron should have no specific rulership, as it isn't of this solar system and therefore being just a visitor, will go away someday. Why give Chiron rulership of some sign if it won't bother to stick around and stay the sign's ruler? That is a romantic notion, but elegant also. Again, as with the asteroids, the question of rulership is not the main point. Chiron does address specific issues which are very pertinent to modern society. And this is what we want to concentrate upon. See where Chiron is in your chart—by sign, house, and how it ties in by aspect to the other planets. It may complete planetary patterns. And when it aspects both classical and modern planets, it then can operate as a key to blending personal and transpersonal effects in one's life.

⚷ **Chiron**—is a key, to understanding, to unlocking doors, to blending personal and transpersonal energies. It deals with issues of teaching and mentoring; being a student/ apprentice; medicine and healing, both by traditional and alternative methods; it is an inconvenient benefic, it closes old doors so it can open new doors and offer new opportunities; it shows the individual's point of wounding and healing; it deals with ecology and recycling; it deals with issues of euthanasia and death with dignity, the right to die; it deals with extraordinary measures used to save lives; it also deals with the realization of when to acknowledge something is unable to be treated anymore and to start to learn how to live with it as opposed to how to defeat it; it has a strong correlation with people who are alternative healers; it is a rebel, a maverick; it rules holistic medicine, herbology, Bach flower remedies, homeopathy, chiropractic; Chiron transits cause people to take their health in their own hands and often achieve miraculous healings; Shamanism is a Chirotic discipline; people who are "natural" healers have prominent Chirons; strong Chiron can give chronic pain and the means to be transformed and overcome it; if Chiron brings disease, it is best to work with others who are ill or hurting, and through compassion for others transform the self; Chiron offers a well-rounded education either formally or by self-learning; Chiron also probably deals with organ donation, those who die can still help the living; Chiron may also herald contact with alien races from outside our solar system; it may help legitimize astrology; it gives crazy ideas and inventions which actually work, even though they aren't mainstream or logical; it deals with health and disease prevention through diet, exercise and a healthy lifestyle; it rules the ecological warriors; it probably has a lot to do with AIDS and how a person deals with it, in themselves or others.

EIGHT MOON PHASES

The Moon is important in the craft and paganism. The Full Moons define the Esbats, the monthly celebrations of the Goddess and the cycles of daily life. The eight Sabbats are determined by the Sun, regardless of the Moon's position. At first the two cycles do not seem to interrelate. We also celebrate the Goddess in her three forms, Maiden, Mother and Crone. This tripartite division of the Goddess is ancient and prevailed widely throughout the world.

The eight Sabbats are a depiction of the relationship of the Goddess to the God, compressing their relationship cycle into a single year which repeats endlessly. It is a cycle of birth, marriage and procreation and death leading to resurrection with each subsequent rebirth. This is a solar cycle celebrated at the solstices, equinoxes, and cross-quarters of the year.

So in the craft we have a solar cycle and a lunar cycle, which do not seem to coincide.

In astrology there is a new field of study which analyzes character and action in a monthly cycle, from New Moon to New Moon, which mirrors the cycle depicted in the twelve houses in the birthchart, but this cycle is eightfold. This cycle is referred to as the Eight Moon Phases, and defining which phase the moon was in at your birth can give insight as to the soul's mission in this life. See figure 8. This cycle can also be used to chart the ebb and flow of daily life as the days pass. It postulates that at the New Moon each month is a new beginning, the slate is wiped clean from the month before and work and commerce start a new monthly cycle. As the Moon waxes and then wanes through the month, projects begin, come to fruition, are implemented and are ended, wiping the slate clean for the next monthly cycle to begin. This is but one of many cycles which operate concurrently, so it may take a bit to see it, but track it over the next year or so. See if things tend to start over each month around the New Moon, become organized and are ready for implementation around the Full Moon and end just before the next New Moon with analysis and lessons learned which are brought to the next project.

The reason that all of this is here is that this cycle coincides well with the yearly Sabbat Cycle, yet is lunar and

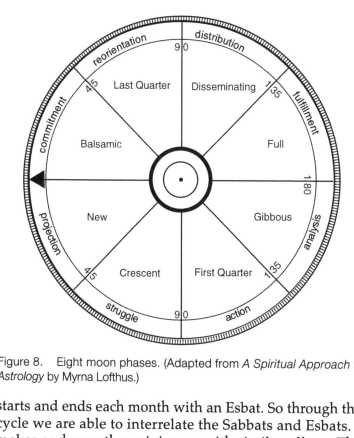

Figure 8. Eight moon phases. (Adapted from *A Spiritual Approach to Astrology* by Myrna Lofthus.)

starts and ends each month with an Esbat. So through this cycle we are able to interrelate the Sabbats and Esbats. It makes each month a mini-year, with similar effects. This Sabbat/Esbat overlay is new and probably will generate a bit of discussion, but it is another way to interrelate the cycles we live with. It is also a way to celebrate each Sabbat each month, thereby providing another way to experience Samhain in July.

There are two yearly wheel cycles based upon this. One starts with Oestarra at the New Moon and the other starts with Yule at the New Moon. Both cycles seem valid and can be justified. This may drive some people crazy— which cycle to use?—but as both seem to work, the answer can be either. The Oestarra Cycle is more oriented to the

Goddess and her life cycle, and the Yule Cycle is more oriented to the God and his life cycle. As each relates to the other, there is Goddess in the God Cycle and God in the Goddess Cycle. Women could try using the Oestarra Cycle and men could use the Yule Cycle. Whatever works. There are other ways of dividing the year which also work.

The close relationship between the four great Sabbats—Imbolc, Beltane, Lughnasadh and Samhain—and the 15 degree point of the four fixed signs is significant. The 15 degree fixed points are considered powerful degrees. They are exactly between (on the midpoints) the 0 degree cardinal points—solstices and equinoxes. Whether there is also a correlation between the 15 degrees of the fixed signs and the Great Year of Precession is not known but the 0 Aries point was at what we call 15 Taurus back in the time of the dawn of "history," at the rise of the Mesopotamians, when the Chaldeans practiced what was to evolve into modern astrology. The dates of the sabbats have stayed the same over the centuries—1 February, 1 May, 1 August, 31 October—but the actual 15 degree points are later—5 February, 6 May, 8 August, 8 November. Shakespeare's *Midsummer Night's Dream* has Midsummer at 24 June, now it is 20 or 21 June depending. It has moved back (precessed) 3 or 4 days in 400 years.

The eight phases of the Moon involve 360 degrees of the ecliptic that are divided into eight segments of 45 degrees each. The 0, 90, 180 and 270 degree points correspond to the solstices and equinoxes. The intermediate points correspond to the 15 degree points of the fixed signs. Remembering what was said earlier, divisions of the circle by 2, and multiples thereof, creates aspects of crisis, strife, incitement to action. They are not comfortable aspects, but they stir things up and get things going. Each sabbat is a "crisis point" in the lives of the Goddess and God. Each symbolizes a specific time in the life cycle of the God and the year, and certain actions are dictated by the yearly cycle.

Each sabbat indicates a change in focus in issues of daily life. They are based upon the agricultural year cycle. At any rate, assuming the cross-quarters are on the exact midpoints of the solstices and equinoxes, then placing the cycle of the year on the eight Moon phases makes a lot of sense.

The Cycle Based upon Yule and the God

At *Yule*, the God is born, into the darkest time of the year, which corresponds to the darkest phase of the Moon. He is young and lusty and full of potential, yet unable to really act on his own yet. He is here, but as with many young, he may not survive. So also are we still waiting to see if the light will return to the world. Everything is full of potential, yet nothing is possible yet. We throw out ideas and possibilities and plans but have not decided exactly how to proceed yet.

At *Imbolc*, the God is a child, and as he grows so can we see the light growing day by day. Now can we see if we have lain enough away to survive until Spring. So also can we see if the God is strong enough to survive infancy. As Imbolc is a Goddess celebration in the middle of the "God Time," we see how there is a chance of the Earth blooming once more, we are aware of the dormancy of the Earth, rather than its mere barrenness. We can see how the potentials born at Yule are able to be implemented to best effect. We choose the plan to implement, and decide how to go about it, using other ideas to support the plan or putting them away, perhaps to be resurrected at the next cycle.

At *Oestarra*, the Earth awakens from her winter sleep once again. The God is now a youth on the threshold of manhood, full of potential and life. As the new plants show, the migratory animals return and stake out territories in preparation for mating and creating new life. Our plans are in effect and we can see how they may manifest. We may encounter obstacles to implementation, but we persevere as we are committed to this path at least for this cycle.

Beltane is the marriage of the Goddess and God. The Earth is in full bloom and plants and animals are fertile and busy mating and providing for future generations. Now is the season of the Goddess, when the light is still increasing, and life is easy and good after the privations of Winter. In mating with the Goddess, the God performs his procreative function. The plans which were started at Yule are maturing and we may make any changes we need, due to changing circumstances.

Midsummer is the brightest time of the year; the Goddess is in her glory. She is with child by the God and the Earth reflects her fertility. Our plans are brought out into the world, fully implemented having been nurtured and altered as needed. Now we can see how others will respond to our actions. We are placing ourselves in the spotlight.

At *Lughnasadh* comes the first harvest, a God celebration in the midst of the Goddess time. Though the Earth still blooms, in the first harvest we are reminded that this plenty will not last forever, and we need to put a part of the harvests away to sustain us during the dark times of Winter. When our plans were presented to the world, we received feedback to our ideas and implementations and now we may make last minute adjustments if necessary.

Mabon is the second harvest, the main harvest. The Goddess has performed her miracle and shown her fertility once again. Now is the God sacrificed so the people can continue, nourished by the blood of the God, manifest in the Harvest. We are aware Winter is coming. The nights now become longer than the days, and plants begin to wither and die, preparing for the long sleep of winter. Our plans bring fruit, we can see how well or badly we did with our resources and actions. We bear the responsibility for our success or failure.

At *Samhain*, the first frosts of Winter are upon us. The dark is definitely coming, day is receding. The Goddess mourns her fallen consort, and the gates between the worlds open to allow all who have passed over in the last year to pass beyond into the Summerlands. The long sleep of Winter starts and the wild hunt is abroad. The Goddess retires until the birth of her child/consort, the God resurrected and renewed by his continual sacrifice. Now is the time of year for contemplation and planning for the next Spring. These are the darkest days, as night seems to become longer and longer, until it seems it might never be day again. After reaping our harvest from our plans and ideas, we may look back and analyze just what we did right or wrong, and use these lessons learned in the next project. As we look to the past, we are also looking to the future, to make the future better based upon the mistakes and successes of the past.

And then the cycle begins again at Yule.

The Cycle Based upon Oestarra and the Goddess

At *Oestarra*, the Earth blooms and Spring is upon us, full of potential. We are reborn with the Earth and begin to make new plans for the next year. The Goddess gives birth to the God and we look forward to his life and maturity.

Beltane brings the marriage of the Goddess and God. Full fertility is at its peak and we have decided upon a plan for the next year. Our crops are being planted, new life needs to be nurtured and fed.

Midsummer is a time of quiet between planting and harvest. The Goddess is in her glory, she is with child. Our crops are in and we are committed to a plan, yet we can rest while the new life grows and matures.

Lughnasadh is first harvest, we have some idea of how well our plans will turn out based upon the fruit of first harvest. We can decide how much to put aside based upon this time. We are aware winter is coming which casts a shadow over the plenty as the days become shorter.

Mabon is the main harvest. We reap the fruits of our labors, for good or ill. It is a time of plenty, yet we have to remember Winter is coming and so put a portion aside to sustain us during the cold dark times of Winter. The God is sacrificed in his prime that we may live to the next Spring and we honor him and await his rebirth.

Samhain is the time of first frost. We have finished putting away our stores and now must decide how many of our animals will be allowed to live to be breeding stock in the Spring. Save too many and we cannot feed them all. Save too few and we will not have enough new young in the Spring for next year. The Goddess mourns the God, as we mourn our dead. The Earth begins its long sleep until Spring comes again.

Yule is the darkest time of the year. We are starting to run out of stores, and may have to sacrifice more livestock if we misjudged at Samhain. It is a time of rest and contemplation of the past year and we must take responsibility for the wisdom or folly of our choices. The Goddess is alone, yet she anticipates the birth of her son/consort.

Imbolc is the time of year when stores are dwindling and we know if we can survive until Spring. We can see the light returning and are filled with hope and begin to make plans to be implemented at the start of the next cycle. We acknowledge our mistakes and successes and use these as a basis upon which to plan the future. It is a time of waiting and of hope. The Goddess begins her confinement awaiting the rebirth of the God.

With Oestarra we have survived another cycle and begin again.

• • •

This year cycle works well starting at either Yule or Oestarra. With a little thought it can be manipulated to work starting at any of the Sabbats. The point is not so much at which Sabbat you start the cycle, but that you do view it as a cycle, repeating endlessly, time after time. We may react differently each cycle, but we cannot stop the cycle nor can we turn back to a previous time. We have to follow along with the cycle, easily or with difficulty depending on how in tune with the cycle we are. If we use the cycle as a learning process, growing in knowledge and experience and maturity each turn of the wheel, we can make life more secure and comfortable for ourselves. If we keep repeating the same mistakes and refuse to take responsibility for our actions, we will repeat the same cycle endlessly until we do learn the lessons and then can move on. We may wonder why things keep turning to mush and until we realize that it is up to us to change things for ourselves, we will stay in the same rut.

The eight Moon phases and how they operate in a natal chart are shown in Table 6 on page 290. What phase the moon was in at your birth puts a stamp of those energies on your life. With reincarnation you can see where you might be in a longer cycle of lives; starting, culminating or wrapping up a cycle of action and behavior expressions. It is another theory which cannot be concretely proved, but is nonetheless interesting and certainly a springboard for meditation and thought.

To find the phase of the Moon at your birth, take the degree of your Sun and subtract from 30 (the number of degrees left in your Sun's sign), then add 30 degrees for each intervening sign (30 degrees equals one sign), then add the number of degrees of your Moon. The total of those sums is the degree of your Moon phase, and you then look it up on the chart to determine your Moon phase. For example, say your Sun is at 17 degrees Capricorn and your Moon is 12 degrees Virgo. See figure 9 on page 291. You add 13 (the number of degrees left in Capricorn 30 − 17 = 13) and 7 times 30 = 210 (30 degrees for each of seven signs—Aquarius, Pisces, Aries, Taurus, Gemini, Cancer and Leo) and 12 (the number of degrees in Virgo). That total is 13 + 210 + 12 = 235, which works out to a Disseminating Moon phase. Remember the signs are an end-

Table 6.   Eight Moon Phases.

0-44—New Moon phase: beginning of cycle, just starting out, charm, spontaneous, initiating a new cycle, forming a personality, can be insensitive to others in expression of selfhood, acts instinctively, plunges into new experiences, good at starting projects, can be easily distracted by new projects or ideas.
45-89—Crescent Moon phase: karmic stuff from the past, struggling to break out of past life patterns and make their own way, can feel inertia and dependencies from past conditions, mobilizes resources to assert self in a new direction, has chosen the path to take during this cycle.
90-134—First Quarter Moon phase: good managing ability, cardinal tendencies, reforming old structures, discarding things which are no longer needed, desire to change people, active and moving, managing energy released from crisis situations, can create crises in order to incite change, building new structures.
135-179—Gibbous Moon phase: searching for a goal through study and analysis, desire for soul growth, relating one experience with another, prophetic abilities, perfecting techniques and forms, introspective, questing for revelation, preparation for emergence into public arena.
180-224—Full Moon phase: culmination of cycle, personal magnetism, people bring problems for solution, difficulties with relationships, looking for perfect partner, can be reclusive or celibate, infusing meaning and content into life structures, emergence into public arena, objectivity, illumination.
225-269—Disseminating Moon phase: share with others what they have found to be meaningful themselves, talent for promoting others or their ideas, need to tell all they have learned so their experiences may have value, crusaders in religions/philosophies/concepts/ideas, distribution of ideas and resources.
270-314—Last Quarter Moon phase: going through crises and changes in order to reorient thinking, crisis of consciousness, strong principles, strongly affected by Mercury phases—especially retrogrades, looking outward or inward depending on natal Mercury direct or retrograde motion, turning away from old expressions and looking toward new ideas, owning up to actions and choices for good or ill.
315-359—Balsamic Moon phase: end of cycle, changing from personal to group consciousness, something new will emerge which will help others, being possessed by destiny, involvement with causes/humanitarians/metaphysicians, looking to the past and the meaning of life, prophetic abilities, commitment to the future, distilling wisdom of cycle completed and passing it along as a legacy for others, completion of Karma, making ready for new cycle, looking to the past with eye to benefitting the future by learning from mistakes and triumphs.

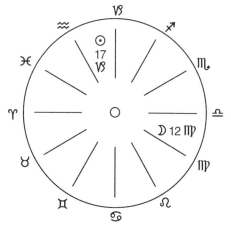

Figure 9.   Disseminating Moon phase.

lessly repeating cycle, so after Pisces comes Aries and so on.

Another Example: The Sun is 2 degrees Sagittarius and the Moon is 25 degrees Gemini (see figure 10). You add 28 (30 –2 = 28) and 5 times 30 = 150 (30 degrees each for Capricorn, Aquarius, Pisces, Aries and Taurus) and 25 (for 25 degrees of Gemini). The total is: 28 + 150 + 25 = 203, which is a Full Moon phase.

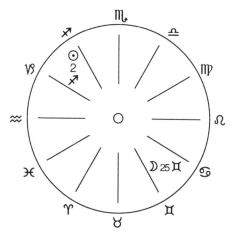

Figure 10.   Full Moon phase.

Another example: The Sun is 0 degrees Cancer and the Moon is 28 degrees Leo. (See figure 11.) You add 30 (30 – 0 = 30) and 0 times 30 (no intervening signs) and 28 (for 28 degrees of Leo). The total is: 30 + 0 + 28 = 58, which is a Crescent Moon phase.

If the Moon is ahead of the Sun in the same sign—Sun at 3 degrees Libra and Moon at 21 degrees Libra—(as shown in figure 12), just subtract the larger amount from the smaller—21 – 3 = 18, which is a New Moon phase. Or you can just assume New Moon phase since it always is anyhow.

If the Moon is behind the Sun in the same sign (figure 13), you have to add all around to get the degrees, but it is always Balsamic Moon phase, so you don't even have to do the arithmetic if you don't want to. For example, Moon at 5 degrees Taurus and Sun at 28 degrees Taurus—2 (30 – 28 = 2) and 11 times 30 = 330 (30 degrees each for Gemini, Cancer, Leo, Virgo, Libra, Scorpio, Sagittarius, Capricorn, Aquarius, Pisces and Aries) and 5 (for 5 degrees of Taurus). The total is: 2 + 330 + 5 = 337, which is Balsamic Moon phase.

Now that you know how to calculate Moon phase, go to Table 6 (page 290) for the meanings.

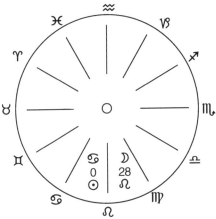

Figure 11.   Crescent Moon phase.

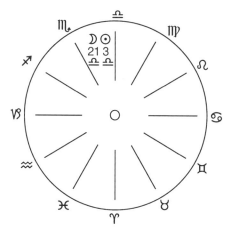

Figure 12.   New Moon phase.

Relating the Moon phases to the Goddess, you get new Moon to first trine, Maiden; first trine through full to second trine, Mother; second trine to new Moon, Crone. Another Goddess Moon cycle (said to derive from old Celtic sources) is the Maiden phase, which starts at first visible crescent, about a day-and-a-half after the true new Moon. Maiden lasts until after the first quarter, when the Mother phase starts and lasts through full to before last

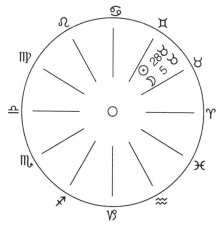

Figure 13.   Balsamic Moon phase.

quarter. Crone starts before last quarter and lasts until the last visible crescent, about a day-and-a-half before true new Moon. The Fourth Goddess, the Dark Goddess, rules over the "dark of the Moon," the time when it is not visible, about three days long, which includes the actual true new Moon. In ancient times, the new Moon was deduced, but not visible, so some cultures started the new Moon cycle with the first crescent, rather than the actual astronomical new Moon. This Dark-Goddess-fourth-phase was symbolic of the Dark Goddess of death, decay, regeneration, all things hidden and not readily discernible, and also magick (attributes also of Pluto—who may have originated as a Dark Goddess). Other cultures blended these attributes with those of the Crone to give the more commonly known attributes of the Crone in a three-fold Goddess cycle. With this four-fold Goddess cycle, you could relate it to Persephone as Maiden, Demeter as Mother, Hecate as Crone, and Pluto as Dark Goddess. Some sources also relate this dark of the Moon with the God energies within the Goddess.

RULERSHIP IN ASTROLOGY AND MAGICK

Rulership lists are a permanent fixture in astrology, especially in horary and electional astrology. A person has a chart and needs to know what to concentrate upon to get an answer or result from the chart. You find articles written which concern various rulerships of things, and often these are broken down to extreme specifics. What rules a "dry waterfall" was discussed in an article that I read (the 3rd house). As was said before, astrology uses only 52 words to express all of life and experience, so each "word" needs to have innumerable "meanings." Specialized word lists and rulerships for various subjects are common. *The Encyclopaedia of Medical Astrology* by Cornell is a classic, and has a main focus of medical and anatomical matters, but it also includes a lot of other neat and interesting information which is not medical.[4] Rex E. Bills wrote *The Rulership Book*, a general reference that lists nothing but words and what correspondences they have by sign, house, and/or planet.[5] As this book is about astrology and magick, here is a word list geared to magickal things and their astrological correspondences. Again, this is a new area of astrological study, so many of these meanings are conjectural. Rather than being extremely specific, the list is more broad, to be more inclusive. Fine detail of meaning may be lost, but accessibility to energies and ease of use are enhanced. Again, I have slanted it for use by magicians who may or may not be astrologers, rather than for astrologers only.

There are many ways to use this list. For example, say you want to make or magically activate a poppet. You look in the list and see that under "poppet" is listed: Libra, 7th, Venus, Gemini, 3rd, Mercury. You then look in your almanac and plan to energize that poppet when the transiting Moon is in Libra or Gemini, or when the Moon is transiting your natal 7th or 3rd house, or when the transiting Moon is in the transiting 7th or 3rd house, or when the Moon applies to an aspect with Venus or Mercury (making sure the nature of the aspect matches the intended use of the poppet). Or you could have the transiting Moon aspect your natal Venus or Mercury, or transiting Venus or Mercury aspect your natal Moon. Or you could have transiting Venus or Mercury in Libra or Gemini and coordinate with a Moon which deals with the use for the poppet and arrange for a compatible final aspect.

As you can see, there are lots of ways to use the correspondences. How you choose to do so will depend upon time constraints, your mathematical skill, and how well the planets cooperate. Again, the more factors you can arrange

---

[4]Dr. H. L. Cornell, *The Encyclopaedia of Medical Astrology* (York Beach, ME: Samuel Weiser, 1972).
[5]Rex E. Bills, *The Rulership Book* (Tempe, AZ: American Federation of Astrologers, 1993).

to coordinate, the more energy you are harnessing for your use. The KISS rule applies here, also. This is where you can quickly get in over your head, planning for everything to be as interconnected as possible. Do as well as you can, and then let it go and let the energies do their work for you.

Some things are included which may seem "bad" or "negative." There are reasons. Firstly, if a person wishes to combat these influences, the correspondences become important. (Use an opposition and a Pisces Moon to break the influence of a Black Magick spell.) Also these are topics which are part of magick. Calling some of them icky or bad or ignoring them will not make them go away. The Wiccan Rede and Law of Three should take care of those who choose to try to harm others. But I am not sweetness and light. I acknowledge the dark side and deal with it in my own way. One way of acknowledging the dark side is to treat it honestly and openly. And when you expose dark things to light they lose a lot of their power, for they work best in the shadows and thrive on secrecy and fear.

The order of the correspondences is somewhat important. I have tried to list the correspondences in order of strength. Use the first thing (or things if a planet, sign, and house) if possible, and later things if needed, or if the first things are not feasible or are detrimental to you. Influences in italics are somewhat applicable, but are definitely secondary influences. When breaking negative influences, try to have the Moon correspond to one of your secret power times (being in the same sign as your natal Ascendant, Sun, or Moon). You need to add that extra power to help you break the negative influences. If not possible, at least do not have the Moon working against you by being in a sign opposite that of your natal Ascendant, Moon, or Sun. Generally having your secret power times working for you is a good thing. Otherwise avoid the times when the power is against you. Unless you want to empower the other person. Then it would work well.

Think about what exactly you want to accomplish. Be as specific as possible. Make a list, if necessary, and then go to the word list and see if you can coordinate influences. Again, it becomes a matter of how important is it to you? The more important the more time and energy you will want to expend.

A

Abortion: Mars, Pluto, 8th, Scorpio, Uranus, opposition, square.

Air: Gemini, Libra, Aquarius, Mercury, *Venus*, Uranus, Pallas, 3rd, 7th, 11th.

Alchemy: Scorpio, 8th, Pluto, Pisces, 12th, Neptune, Aquarius, 11th, Uranus, inconjunct, *Mars, Saturn, Jupiter*, Ceres, Chiron.

Altar Consecration: Cancer, 4th, Moon, Vesta, Jupiter, 9th, Sagittarius, conjunction.

Altered States: Pisces, 12th, Neptune, Scorpio, 8th, Pluto, Sagittarius, 9th, Jupiter, Aquarius, 11th, Uranus, *Mars, Saturn*, Void Moon, Retrograde Mercury.

Animals: Small and domestic—Virgo, 6th, Mercury. Large—Pisces, 12th, Jupiter, Neptune, Chiron.

Astral Travel: Sagittarius, 9th, Jupiter, Aquarius, 11th, Uranus, Gemini, 3rd, Mercury, Pisces, 12th, Neptune, *Saturn*, Pallas.

Attracting: Conjunction, Jupiter, Venus, 1st, 2nd, Taurus, waxing Moon.

B

Bad Luck: Saturn, Mars, Uranus, Pluto, 12th, Pisces, Neptune, opposition, square.

Banishing: opposition, Saturn, Capricorn, 10th, Waning Moon, Retrograde Mercury, 8th, Scorpio, Pluto.

Beauty: Venus, Libra, 7th, Taurus, 2nd, Ceres, Pallas, Juno, Vesta, *Jupiter*.

Beginnings: Aries, Mars, 1st, Uranus, conjunction, New Moon, Waxing Moon.

Bi-Polar (Hermaphroditic): Mercury, Gemini, Uranus, Pisces, mutable.

Black Magick: 12th, Pisces, Neptune, Pluto, Scorpio, 8th, Saturn, Capricorn.

Brimstone: Aries, Mars, Pluto, *Capricorn.*

Bringing Out into the Open: Waxing Moon, 1st, Aries, opposition, Mars, Sun, Jupiter.

C

Career: 10th, Capricorn, Saturn, Sun, Chiron, 6th, Virgo, Mercury.

Celebrations and Parties: Leo, 5th, Sun, Sagittarius, 9th, Jupiter, Venus, *11th,* Void Moon, Retrograde Mercury, trine, sextile.

Chakras: Neptune, Scorpio, 8th, Pluto, Aquarius, 11th, Uranus, Mercury, *Mars, Saturn,* Juno, Vesta, Chiron.

Change: Moon, Pluto, Mercury, Chiron, Uranus, Mars, mutable, Ceres, square.

Chaos: Uranus, Neptune, Pluto, Mars, Aquarius, Pisces, Scorpio, Chiron, square, *semi-square, sesquiquadrate.*

Children, In General: Leo, 5th, Sun, Gemini, 3rd, Mercury, Ceres, Chiron, Pallas.

Children, Specific: Infants: Moon, Cancer. Toddlers: Gemini, 3rd, Mercury. Adolescents: Venus, Mars, Sun, Leo, 5th. Adopted or other peoples' children: Aquarius, 11th, Uranus.

Circle of Equals/Peers: Virgo, 6th, Mercury, Aquarius, 11th, Uranus, sextile, Juno.

Cleansing: Virgo, Mercury, 6th, Moon, Chiron, Vesta.

Consecration of Tools: Virgo, 6th, Mercury, *+Mars for athame,* Pallas, Vesta, conjunction.

Construction: Saturn, Earth, Taurus, Virgo, Capricorn, 2nd, 6th, 10th, Mars, *Venus, Mercury,* Ceres.

Contests and Lotteries: 5th, Leo, Sun, Uranus, Mercury, 7th, Mars, *11th, Aquarius.*

Control: Scorpio, Pluto, Capricorn, Saturn, conjunction.

Councils and Tribunals: Sagittarius, 9th, Jupiter, Libra, 7th, Venus, Aquarius, 11th, Uranus, Virgo, 6th, Mercury, Pallas, Juno.

Covens: Virgo, 6th, Mercury, Aquarius, 11th, Uranus, *Saturn*.

Cults: 12th, Pisces, Neptune, Saturn, Pluto, 6th, Virgo, Mercury, Jupiter, conjunction.

Cutting Away: Aries, 1st, Mars, opposition, Libra, 7th, Venus, Juno, Vesta.

D

Dance: Pisces, Neptune, 12th, *Jupiter*, Venus, Moon in Taurus, Moon in Libra.

Darkness and the Depths: Scorpio, 8th, Pluto, Capricorn, Saturn, 10th, 4th, *Cancer, Moon*, opposition, Ceres.

Death and Dying: 8th, Scorpio, Pluto, Mars, 4th, Chiron, *Cancer, Moon, 12th, Pisces, Neptune*.

Dedication: Cancer, 4th, Moon, Pisces, 12th, Neptune, *Jupiter, Saturn*, Ceres, Vesta, conjunction.

Deities: 9th, Sagittarius, 12th, Pisces, Jupiter, Sun, Moon, Neptune, *Uranus, Juno*.

Demons: Pluto, Uranus, Mercury, Saturn, Mars, 6th, Virgo, 12th, Pisces.

Destruction: Uranus, Pluto, Saturn, Mars, 8th, Scorpio, *12th, Pisces, Neptune*, square, opposition, *semi-square, sesquiquadrate*.

Divination: Cancer, 4th, Moon, Sagittarius, 9th, Jupiter, Pluto, Aquarius, 11th, Uranus, *Saturn*, Juno, Pallas, sextile, trine, semi-square, sesquiquadrate.

Divorce: Libra, 7th, Venus, Aries, 1st, Mars, opposition, square, Moon in Scorpio, Moon in Capricorn, Waning Moon, Juno, *semi-square, sesquiquadrate*.

Dream Work: Sagittarius, 9th, Jupiter, Neptune, Aquarius, 11th, Uranus, *Saturn*, Void Moon, Retrograde Mercury, Pallas, Chiron.

Drugs: Neptune, 12th, Pisces, *Jupiter*, Pluto, Uranus.

Drums and Drumming: Capricorn, 10th, Saturn, Virgo, 6th, Mercury, Mars.

Dualities: Gemini, Mercury, 3rd, Sagittarius, 9th, Pisces, 12th, Virgo, 6th, Chiron, mutable, *Uranus*.

E

Earth (element): Taurus, Virgo, Capricorn, Venus, *Mercury*, Saturn, Ceres, 2nd, 6th, 10th.

Edged Tools: Mars, Aries, 1st, Scorpio, 8th, Pallas.

Employment: 6th, Virgo, Mercury, 10th, Capricorn, Saturn, Pallas, Chiron.

Endings: Saturn, 4th, Pisces, 12th, Neptune, Scorpio, 8th, Pluto, Waning Moon, Balsamic Moon, oppositions.

Energy Work: Chiron, Mars, Uranus, Mercury, conjunction, *square, semi-square, sesquiquadrate.*

Ethics: Jupiter, Sagittarius, 9th, Venus, Sun, trine, sextile.

Euthanasia: Chiron, Scorpio, Pluto, 8th, Mars, Cancer, 4th, Moon, Waning Moon.

Everyday Magick: 6th, Virgo, Mercury, *3rd, Gemini*, Moon.

Evil: Pluto, Saturn, *Mars*, square, opposition.

Evil Eye: 12th, Pisces, Neptune, Pluto, Scorpio, 8th, Mars, square, opposition.

Evocation: 6th, Virgo, Mercury, sextile, trine.

F

Fairies: Neptune, 12th, Pisces, Mercury, Gemini, 3rd.

Fame: 11th, Aquarius, Uranus, Sun, Leo, 5th, 9th, Sagittarius, Jupiter, Full Moon.

Familiars: 6th, Virgo, Mercury, Vesta.

Father: 10th, Capricorn, Saturn, *4th, Cancer*, Sun, Uranus.

Female: Moon, Venus, Ceres, Pallas, Juno, Vesta, *Pluto*, Earth, Water.

Fertility (in general): Taurus, 2nd, Venus, Cancer, 4th, Moon, Scorpio, 8th, Pluto, Pisces, 12th, Neptune, *Mars, Libra, 7th, 4th*, Ceres, Vesta.

Fire: Mars, Sun, Aries, Leo, Sagittarius, 1st, 5th, 9th, Vesta, Jupiter.

Food: Moon, Cancer, 4th, Virgo, 6th, Mercury.

Freedom: 11th, Aquarius, Uranus, Jupiter.

Friendship and Friends: 11th, Aquarius, Uranus, *Saturn*, Mercury, sextile.

Funerals/Memorials: Scorpio, 8th, Pluto, Cancer, 4th, Moon, *Mars*.

G

Gambling: 5th, Sun, Leo, Jupiter, Venus, Uranus, *Mercury*, *Moon, Pluto*.

Gems in General: Venus, Taurus, 2nd.

Glamors and Illusion: Pisces, 12th, Neptune, Mercury, Gemini, 3rd, *Jupiter*, sextile, trine.

Goddesses in General: Moon, Venus, 4th, Cancer, Taurus, Ceres, Pallas, Juno, Vesta.

Gods in General: 9th, Jupiter, Sagittarius, Sun, Saturn, Uranus, Mars.

Good: Jupiter, Sun, Venus, trine, sextile, *conjunction*.

Good Luck: Jupiter, Venus, 9th, Sagittarius, 11th, Aquarius, Uranus, Sun, Leo, 5th, trine, sextile.

Grounding and Centering: Taurus, 2nd, Venus, Virgo, 6th, Mercury, Capricorn, 10th, Saturn (very effective), Cancer, 4th, Moon, *nadir* (*home base, and roots*), Ceres, Chiron.

Group Work: Virgo, 6th, Mercury, Aquarius, 11th, Uranus, Gemini, 3rd, Sagittarius, 9th, Jupiter, sextile.

H

Handfasting (and Marriage): Libra, 7th, Venus, Moon in Taurus, Moon in Cancer, Moon in 7th, Waxing Moon, conjunction, trine, sextile, Juno.

Handparting (and Divorce): Libra, 7th, Venus, Aries, 1st, Mars, opposition, square, Moon in Scorpio, Moon in Capricorn, Waning Moon, Juno, *semi-square, sesquiquadrate*.

Healing: Virgo, Mercury, 6th, Chiron, Pisces, 12th, Neptune, Pallas, Vesta, *4th, 9th, Sagittarius, Jupiter*.

Herbs and Plants: Virgo, 6th, Mercury, Taurus, 2nd, Venus, Libra, 7th, Waxing Moon, Ceres.

Hermaphroditic: Mercury, Gemini, Uranus, Pisces, mutable.
High Magick: Pisces, 12th, Neptune, Jupiter, *9th, Sagittarius,*
Vesta.
High Priest/ess: Capricorn, 10th, Saturn, Sagittarius, 9th,
Jupiter, Leo, 5th, Sun, Vesta.
High Ritual: Sagittarius, 9th, Jupiter, Scorpio, 8th, Pluto,
Capricorn, 10th, Saturn, *Mars,* Juno, Vesta.
History: Cancer, 4th, Moon, Saturn, Mercury.

I
Incense: Neptune, Mercury, Pisces, Virgo, 12th, 6th, Vesta,
Mars.
Initiation: Scorpio, 8th, Pluto, Capricorn, 10th, Saturn,
Pisces, 12th, Neptune, *Mars, Jupiter,* Ceres.
Intelligence: 3rd, Gemini, Mercury, 9th, Sagittarius, Jupiter,
Uranus, Moon.
Invocation: 12th, Pisces, Neptune, *4th,* conjunction.

J
Jewelry: Venus, Taurus, 2nd, 7th, Libra.
Jobs and Work: Capricorn, 10th, Saturn, Virgo, 6th, Mer-
cury, Vesta, Pallas, Chiron.

K
Karma: Saturn, 12th, Pisces, Neptune, Moon's Nodes.
Keeping Secret: 12th, Pisces, Neptune, Waning Moon,
Pluto, Scorpio, *8th.*
Keys: Chiron, Mercury, Gemini, 3rd.

L
Law: Saturn, Sagittarius, 9th, Jupiter, Libra, 7th, Venus,
Juno.
Learning: 3rd, Gemini, Mercury, 9th, Sagittarius, Jupiter,
6th, Virgo, Pallas, *Chiron.*
Life: Sun, Leo, 5th, 1st, Aries, Mars, Jupiter, Venus, Chiron.
Light: Sun, Moon, 10th, 1st, Jupiter, Venus, 9th, Sagittarius,
Aries, Libra, Vesta, trine, sextile.

Love Spells: Leo, Sun, 5th, Libra, Venus, 7th, conjunction, trine, *sextile*, Juno.

Lover: 5th, Leo, Sun, Venus (female), Mars (male), Mercury (bi or same sex).

Low Magick: 6th, Virgo, Mercury, *3rd, Gemini*, Juno.

Luck: Jupiter, Venus, Sun, 9th, Sagittarius, Uranus, *11th, Aquarius*, trine, sextile, *conjunction*.

M

Magick in General: Pisces, 12th, Neptune, Cancer, 4th, Moon, Virgo, 6th, Mercury, Scorpio, 8th, Pluto, *Mars, Jupiter*, Ceres.

Male: Sun, Mars, Jupiter, Saturn, Chiron, fire, air.

Marriage: Libra, 7th, Venus, Moon in Taurus, Moon in Cancer, Moon in 7th, Waxing Moon, conjunction, trine, sextile, Juno.

Martyr: Virgo, 6th, Mercury, Chiron, Pisces, 12th, Neptune, Jupiter, Saturn.

Material Wealth: 2nd, Taurus, Venus, Jupiter, Pluto, Scorpio, 8th, Ceres.

Medium Work/Channeling: Cancer, 4th, Moon, Pisces, 12th, Neptune, *Jupiter*, sextile, semi-square, sesquiquadrate.

Memory: Moon, Mercury, 3rd, 9th, Gemini, Sagittarius, Cancer, Jupiter, Virgo, Chiron.

Metals in General: Mars, Saturn.

Metals, Specific: Gold—Sun; Silver and Aluminum—Moon; Quicksilver, Phosphorus and Mercury—Mercury; Copper, Brass and Bronze—Venus; Iron, Steel, Arsenic, Lodestone, Sulphur—Mars; Tin, Zinc—Jupiter; Lead, Antimony, Carbon, Coal, Salt, Rocks, Stones, Leather, Sulphur, Zinc—Saturn; Uranium, Lodestone, TNT, Nitrogen, Zinc, Radioactive and Multi-Colored Metals—Uranus; Neptunium, Oil and Petrochemicals, Iodine, Potassium, Rubber, Noble Gases—Neptune; Plutonium, Lava, Zinc, Tungsten, Nickel, Phosphorus, Volcanic Stones—Pluto.

Money: Taurus, 2nd, Venus, Jupiter, Scorpio, 8th, Pluto, trine, Juno.

Mother: Cancer, 4th, Moon, Taurus, Venus, 2nd, Ceres, Full Moon, *10th, Capricorn, Saturn.*
Morals: 8th, Scorpio, Pluto, Venus, 2nd, Taurus, Saturn, trine, sextile, conjunction.
Music and Song: Taurus, 2nd, Venus, Libra, 7th, Pisces, 12th, Neptune.

N
Naming: Aries, 1st, Mars, Leo, 5th, Sun, conjunction.
Necromancy: Neptune, 12th, Pisces, Pluto, 8th, Scorpio, Saturn.

O
Oaths: Saturn, 10th, Capricorn, Pluto, 8th, Scorpio, Vesta.
Occult: Neptune, Pisces, 12th, 8th, Pluto, Scorpio, Uranus, 11th, Aquarius.
Oils, Potions and Elixers: Neptune, Pisces, 12th, Jupiter.
Oracles: Neptune, 12th, Pisces, sextile, semi-square, sesquiquadrate.
Order: Saturn, Sun, Jupiter, Venus, fixed, non-void Moon, Pallas, Vesta, conjunction, trine, sextile.

P
Pagans and Paganism: Uranus, 11th, Aquarius, Neptune, 12th, Pisces.
Peace: Libra, 7th, Venus, Pisces, 12th, Neptune, Pallas.
Pets: 6th, Virgo, Mercury, Venus.
Power: Sun, Leo, 5th, Pluto, Scorpio, 8th, Uranus, 11th, Aquarius, Mars.
Prayer: 9th, Jupiter, Sagittarius, Vesta.
Prison: Pisces, 12th, Neptune, Pluto, Scorpio, 8th, Saturn.
Prosperity: Jupiter, 9th, Sagittarius, Taurus, 2nd, Venus, Sun, Leo, 5th, 8th, Scorpio, Pluto.
Protection: Saturn, Capricorn, 10th, Pluto, Scorpio, 8th, Sun, Leo, 5th, Virgo, 6th, Mercury, Pallas.
Poisons: Neptune, 12th, Pisces, Pluto.

Poppets: Libra, 7th, Venus, Gemini, 3rd, Mercury, conjunction.

Possession: 12th, Neptune, Pisces, Pluto, Uranus.

Psychism: Neptune, 12th, Pisces, Uranus, Pluto, 8th, Scorpio, Moon, 9th, sextile, semi-square, sesquiquadrate.

Q

Quiet: Saturn, Capricorn, 10th, 4th, Taurus, 2nd.

R

Reincarnation and Regressions: Cancer, 4th, Moon, Scorpio, 8th, Pluto, Pisces, 12th, Neptune, Retrograde Mercury, Ceres.

Religion: 9th, Jupiter, Sagittarius, 12th, Neptune, Pisces, Vesta.

Research: 8th, Scorpio, Pluto, Cancer, 4th, Moon, Saturn, Capricorn, 10th.

Results: 4th, Cancer, Moon, Saturn, Capricorn, 10th.

Robes: Virgo, 6th, Mercury, Venus, 7th, Libra, Leo, 5th, Sun.

Runes: Virgo, 6th, Mercury, Gemini, 3rd, sextile, Pallas, Chiron.

S

Satan: Saturn, Pluto, Scorpio, 8th, 12th, Pisces, opposition, square, *semi-square, sesquiquadrate.*

Saviour: Pisces, 12th, Neptune, Jupiter, trine, sextile.

Secrets: 12th, Pisces, Neptune, Pluto, 8th, Scorpio, 4th, Moon, Cancer.

Security: Jupiter, 9th, Sagittarius, Cancer, 4th, Moon, 2nd, Taurus, Venus.

Sex Magick: Scorpio, 8th, Pluto, Mars, Taurus, 2nd, Venus, conjunction, Vesta, Juno.

Shamans: Chiron, Virgo, 6th, Mercury, Neptune, Pisces, 12th, 8th, Scorpio, Pluto, Uranus.

Shielding: Saturn, Capricorn, 10th, Scorpio, 8th, Pluto, Pallas, *Aries, 1st, Mars.*

Siblings: Gemini, 3rd, Mercury, sextile.
Slaves and Slavery: 6th, Virgo, Mercury, Saturn, 12th, Pisces, Neptune.
Solitary Work: Saturn, Capricorn, 10th, Scorpio, 8th, Pluto, Pisces, 12th, Neptune, Aries, Mars, 1st, Mercury, Virgo, 6th, Chiron.
Soul: Moon, Sun, 5th, Leo, 8th, Scorpio, Pluto, Vesta.
Spirit Guides: Neptune, 12th, Pisces, Mercury, Virgo, 6th, Moon, Uranus, 11th, Aquarius, sextile.
Spirituality: Neptune, 12th, Pisces, Pluto, 8th, Scorpio, 9th, Sagittarius, Jupiter, Cancer, 4th, Moon, Uranus, 11th, Aquarius.
Spouse: 7th, Libra, Venus, 8th, Scorpio, Pluto, Mars, conjunction, opposition.
Status Quo: Saturn, Jupiter, Sun, Venus, earth, fixed.
Student: Gemini, 3rd, Mercury, 6th, Virgo, Chiron.
Success: 10th, Capricorn, Saturn, Jupiter, Sun, Venus.
Summoning: Venus, 7th, Libra, 2nd, Taurus, Jupiter, conjunction.
Sweetness and Light: Pisces, 12th, Neptune, Sagittarius, 9th, Jupiter, trine, *sextile, conjunction*.

T
Teaching: Chiron, Capricorn, 10th, Saturn, Virgo, 6th, Mercury, Gemini, 3rd, Cancer, 4th, Moon, Pallas, Chiron, *9th, Sagittarius, Jupiter*, sextile.

U
Underworld: Pluto, 8th, Scorpio, Saturn, Capricorn, 4th, Cancer.

V
Values: Taurus, 2nd, Venus, Jupiter, Sagittarius, 9th, Ceres, Juno.
Vampires: Pluto, Scorpio, 8th, Neptune, 12th, Pisces.
Victory: Jupiter, 9th, Sagittarius, 10th, Capricorn, Saturn, Venus, Mars.
Voudun: Scorpio, Pluto, 8th, 12th, Neptune, Pisces.

W

Wands and Staves: Mercury, Uranus, 3rd, Gemini, 11th, Aquarius, Pallas.

War: Aries, Mars, 1st, Libra, 7th, Venus, Pallas.

Water: Cancer, Scorpio, Pisces, 4th, 8th, 12th, Moon, Pluto, Neptune, Juno.

Weather: Moon, 4th, Cancer, Mercury, *Uranus*, *Neptune*, Juno.

Weight Gain: Waxing Moon, Jupiter, Sagittarius, 9th, Cancer, 4th, Moon, Taurus, Venus, 2nd, conjunction.

Weight Loss: Waning Moon, Saturn, Capricorn, 10th, Virgo, 6th, Mercury, Gemini, 3rd, square, opposition, *semi-square*, *sesquiquadrate*.

Will: Taurus, Leo, Scorpio (especially), Aquarius, fixed, Pluto, Sun, Saturn, Uranus, 1st.

Winning: Jupiter, 9th, Sagittarius, Sun, Leo, 5th, trine.

Wizards: Neptune, 12th, Pisces, Uranus, 11th, Aquarius, Pluto, 8th, Scorpio.

Working Partners: Virgo, 6th, Mercury, Gemini, 3rd, Pallas, Juno, Chiron, sextile, inconjunct.

Writing Spells Down for use Later: Sagittarius, 9th, Jupiter, Gemini, 3rd, Mercury, Virgo, 6th, sextile, Pallas.

X

Xerography: 3rd, Gemini, Mercury, Pallas, Chiron, sextile.

Y

Yoga: Virgo, 6th, Mercury, Chiron, Vesta.

Yogi: Neptune, 12th, Pisces.

Z

Zombies: Scorpio, 8th, Pluto, Pisces, 12th, Neptune, Saturn, Capricorn, 10th.

PART FIVE

AN ASTROLOGICKAL RITUAL

INTRODUCTION

This ritual was created in the summer of 1992 as a way to honor and acknowledge the energies of a powerful eclipse which was affecting my chart. It can be used as any circle is, but it is specifically recommended for those who are experiencing difficult transits or other stresses to their natal charts. It is a way of magickally acknowledging the energies at work, and letting you get in touch with the energies and possibly by using meditation within a circle to allow you to seek more constructive, less disruptive ways to handle the transits. You can also just use it as a "plainol" circle, for whatever use you have for a circle.

This circle can be used to acknowledge a difficult transit to your natal chart, or to get in touch with the energies of a particular transit in the sky. Using Sabian Symbols as meditation devices as part of the workings are especially effective. These are set out and explained in Dane Rudhyar's book, *An Astrological Mandala*. Briefly, they operate like an astrological tarot or I Ching. They are word-pictures and interpretations for each of the 360 degrees of the zodiac. You can use the symbols for the degree, or degrees, of the transit in question, and with meditation try to then formulate effective ways of working through the energies raised by the transit. You could also use them as a magickal focus for getting in touch with your own chart, taking the Sabian Symbol for the degrees of the planets and points in your chart, and meditating upon them for insight and guidance. It is recommended to try this with only a couple at a time. Doing your entire chart in one long ritual would take forever and also could

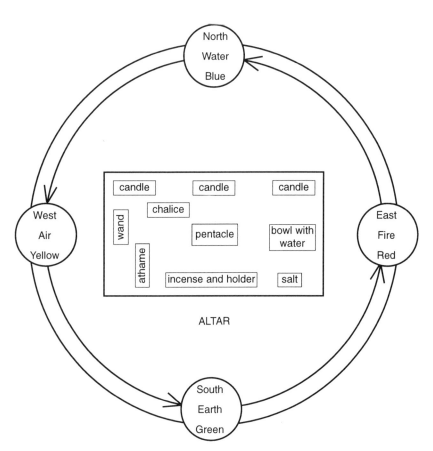

Figure 14.   Circle set-up and altar placement. The arrows indicate that movement in this Circle is in a moonwise/widdershins direction. Placement of items on the altar is approximate; use whatever arrangement fits the space available. The list of items on the altar is a suggestion which corresponds with the items used in the ritual as written here. Feel free to adapt/change/add items. Whatever makes you happy. If it works, then it is good. If it doesn't work, try getting back to the basics. Most people will want to add Goddess/God statues. Use whatever deities you normally use, or try using Ouranos and Gaia. This is not a hard and fast High Ritual Magick type of Circle. Changes are acceptable, and the thing should still work if you do your part.

be very wearying. And the validity of impressions of the latter meditations would probably be suspect. But as a personal growth project which lasts for a year or more, it could be valuable. If you also study astrology, during the time you are engaging in this project, it would be really effective.

Sabian Symbols are one of the more mystic tools used quite routinely in astrology today. There are other degree/symbol systems, all older than Sabian Symbols (which is also just another degree/symbol system, but the most thorough and well-done), but they seem to suffer from several faults. One is fatalism; they state that certain degrees are depraved or evil. Really nice if they are also the same as your Sun (or whatever). They also do not really agree very much. Most of these other degree systems depend upon such things as great conjunctions, fixed stars, exaltations of certain planets, dwads, and lunar mansions. The Sabian Symbols were derived from meditation and are also a symbolism of the cycle of the zodiac as a process of evolution. They relate each degree to the last and the next and take into account the symbolism of the degree opposite. The whole project was started by Marc Edmund Jones in 1925, and the original symbols were worked on and interpretations revised and updated several times through the publication of Rudhyar's book. Jones wrote books and articles based upon his interpretations of the degree symbols, but the book by Rudhyar is the one which survives and is used today.[1] They can be really wonderful when used to help gain deeper understanding of an eclipse or great conjunction or even your personal Ascendant. They are spiritual, yet non-denominational. I recommend them for the person

---

[1] I use Dane Rudhyar's *An Astrological Mandala* (New York: Vintage Books, 1973), but Marc Edmund Jones' book *The Sabian Symbols in Astrology* has been reprinted (Santa Fe, NM: Aurora Press, 1993). The reader might want to compare the two, though it is reported that Rudhyar's version is the more advanced and complete.

wanting to get in touch with the cycle of the astrological zodiac as a whole.

The people participating in this circle are left deliberately undefined. I have done this circle solo, both in a solitary setting and with others as observers/meditative participants. It could easily be adapted for use with a High Priestess/High Priest (perhaps substituting calling Ouranos and Gaia with invoking them). You could have a separate participant calling each quarter, ideally one who has the element or sign in question prominent in his or her chart. Or someone who is deficient in the sign/element in question, so as to allow this person to better get in touch with the energies which he or she lacks. As with most circles, it lends itself to many interesting adaptations. Try some, experiment, have fun! It does get the job done of raising energy, and was specifically created to work with astrological applications.

There is some explanation required. This circle is based upon the mundane astrological wheel. So the elements and quarters are corresponding as they would in the mundane chart, not as in magick as it is commonly practiced. Also, the direction you move for the entire circle is counterclockwise/widdershins/moonwise. That is to say, backward from the standard circle. Some say moving moonwise is used for banishing only, but I have used this circle, and it is just as effective as the "normal" circles I also use. Being an eclectic, I feel that intent and visualization are important, not necessarily the outward trappings of a ritual. This last statement is likely to cause controversy in some circles, but these are my opinions. If you object, that is your right, as it is your right to ignore this circle. As an astrologer, the mundane wheel has significance for me, perhaps moreso than the edict that moving moonwise is for banishing only. Whatever works.

The tools needed are pretty standard: quarter, altar and presence candles (exact colors are up to you)—personally, I use yellow for air, red for fire, blue for water, green for earth, white or natural beeswax for presence and altar candles; water, salt, fire and incense (and holders); athame and wand or staff; chalice with libation liquid (your personal choice, alcoholic or not—just so it is "live"); something to put all this stuff upon (an altar, portable or not). The altar placement is not important, wherever you feel it is appropriate (personally I use North, but that is where it fits best in my house. Saturn on my Ascendant makes me attuned to earth—"normal" North—and also very practical). East would be nice for the Ascendant symbolism, Center would be nice for the "person in the chart" symbolism, North would be nice for the "roots of magick" symbolism—whatever works. I am not a ceremonialist, so I am not really married to any specific hard-and-fast system of colors or altar placement or whatever. For me, variety is fun. I would be really bored if I had to stick to the same ritual time after time. And if you want to add stuff to this, either in word content or supplies, feel free.

THE RITUAL

Cast Circle as normal, using athame to create a circle of light, moving in a moonwise manner.

Cleanse Circle in your normal way, using water, salt, fire, and incense. Cleansing with a broom also works. Just remember to move moonwise.

Basically do whatever Circle you do up to the Calling of the Quarters.

Go to the East, raise the athame in greeting, make an Invoking Pentagram.

"The East is the Ascendant—where self is expressed. Aries lies naturally on its cusp. Creatures of Fire manifest in the signs Aries, Leo, Sagittarius, I welcome thee and ask that you witness this rite and guard this circle and all within. Hail and Welcome!"

Go to the North, raise the athame in greeting, make an Invoking Pentagram.

"The North is the Nadir—the base from which one's roots spring. Cancer lies naturally on its cusp. Creatures of Water manifest in the signs Cancer, Scorpio, Pisces, I welcome thee and ask that you witness this rite and guard this circle and all within. Hail and Welcome!"

Go to the West, raise the athame in greeting, make an Invoking Pentagram.

"The West is the Descendant—where each meets the other. Libra lies naturally on its cusp. Creatures of Air manifest in the signs Libra, Aquarius, Gemini, I welcome thee and ask that you witness this rite and guard this circle and all within. Hail and Welcome!"

Go to the South, raise the athame in greeting, make an Invoking Pentagram.

"The South is the Midheaven—the apex—where each faces the world at large. Capricorn lies naturally on its cusp. Creatures of Earth manifest in the signs Capricorn, Taurus, Virgo, I welcome thee and ask that you witness this rite and guard this circle and all within. Hail and Welcome!"

Go to the center of the Circle, raise the athame in greeting, make an Invoking Pentagram.

"Above is the sky and the stars themselves. Sky-Father Ouranos, I welcome thee and ask that you witness this rite and guard this circle and all within. Hail and Welcome!"

Staying at the center of the Circle, point the athame downward in greeting, make an Invoking Pentagram.

"Below is the Earth, our home and center of the Astrological Universe. Earth-Mother Gaia, I welcome thee and ask that you witness this rite and guard this circle and all within. Hail and Welcome!"

Take up the staff and "stir the paint," moving moonwise, mixing the energies and energizing the Circle.

Return to the center.

"The Circle is cast. As Above, So Below. So Mote It Be."

Do whatever working you have planned. (This would be the time for the meditations if you were using Sabian symbols.)

For an eclipse, you might try this working: (This would be most effective timed to coincide with an actual total solar or lunar eclipse. It is also effective if done within a week either way of said eclipse. If the eclipse is not visible where you live, then the timing is less critical. If it is visible, timing the ritual to get to this point just before totality is the optimum way to use it.)

"In various civilizations, it was believed that eclipses were caused by a great animal—frog, dragon, whatever—which was trying to devour the Sun (or Moon). You could clearly see the outline of its bite as it would consume the Great Orb. As this was happening, and especially during the period of complete darkness, the people on Earth would light bonfires, set off fireworks, make noise with cymbal, drum, rattle, or voice—make as much noise and commotion as they could in order to frighten the devourer into disgorging the Sun (or Moon), allowing the Light to return. Invariably it worked. The Light returned and all was well. Let us now celebrate this eclipse as those Old Ones did, with fire and noise and celebration of the Light." (Make noise, light fires, etc.)

When the leader of the Circle deems it appropriate (or the Sun or Moon has returned) all should cheer and then wind down and ground the energy.

Great Rite

Take the chalice and raise it up.

"Earth-Mother Gaia, You are with us always as we walk upon your sacred soil. Nourish us with your fertility, now and always."

Take the athame and raise it over the chalice.

"Sky-Father Ouranos, embodied in the stars above, watch over us and be with us in our lives, for yours is the seed of creation."

"As the cup is the female, and the athame is the male, together they are one."

Bring athame and cup together, and feel the power of the Goddess and God enter the wine.

Pass the cup around. Pour the last drops as a libation to the Goddess and God.

Dismiss the Goddess and God.

"Gaia and Ouranos, Mother and Father of us all. We thank you for your presence at this ritual. May we be ever mindful of your presence in our world, and may you ever watch over us, protecting and guiding us as we live our lives, from day to day, moon to moon, year to year. Together with your children Luna and Helios, you mark the times of our lives as they pass. May you be with us, now and always as we bid you Hail, and Farewell!"

Unstir the paint and ground the energy of the Circle.

Dismiss the Quarters.

Go to the East, raise athame in greeting, make a Banishing Pentagram.

"Creatures of Fire manifest in the signs Aries, Leo, Sagittarius, we thank you for attending this ritual, for guarding this Circle and all within. May we be ever mindful that your energies operate in each of us, and as you leave, we bid you Hail and Farewell!"

Go to the North, raise athame in greeting, make a Banishing Pentagram.

"Creatures of Water manifest in the signs Cancer, Scorpio, Pisces, we thank you for attending this ritual, for guarding this Circle and all within. May we be ever mindful that your energies operate in each of us, and as you leave, we bid you Hail and Farewell!"

Go to the West, raise athame in greeting, make a Banishing Pentagram.

"Creatures of Air manifest in the signs Libra, Aquarius, Gemini, we thank you for attending this ritual, for guarding this Circle and all within. May we be ever mindful that your energies operate in each of us, and as you leave, we bid you Hail and Farewell!"

Go to the South, raise athame in greeting, make a Banishing Pentagram.

"Creatures of Earth manifest in the signs Capricorn, Taurus, Virgo, we thank you for attending this ritual, for guarding this Circle and all within. May we be ever mindful that your energies operate in each of us, and as you leave we bid you Hail and Farewell!"

Cut the Circle open and say:

"The Circle is open and yet unbroken. Merry meet, and merry part, and merry meet again."

It is done.

AFTERWORD

Well, there it is. Sure has a lot of stuff. I wanted to touch on a lot of different topics, without actually teaching how to do the math or intense interpretation. If you have read all this and absolutely hunger for more, there are some books I would recommend. First and foremost is *Secrets from a Stargazer's Notebook*, by Debbi Kempton-Smith. It is an excellent general introduction to astrology, easily available, and fun to read. It also has planetary placement tables so you can work out your chart yourself. If you actually want to learn how to do it, I recommend Marion March and Joan McEvers' series, *The Only Way to Learn Astrology, Vols. 1–5*. They are the definitive primers. A good self-interpretation workbook is Douglas Bloch and Demetra George's *Astrology for Yourself*. Services like Astrolabe or Astro Communications Services (ACS) will do computer charts and have other computer interpretations and such available for those who don't want to learn the math, but want their own chart done so they can use it. (See p. 325 for more information on these resources.) ACS also offers Ephemerides and Tables of Houses along with other astrological books. They made their reputation on computer accuracy in Ephemerides and the like.

Other books to read are: *An Astrological Mandala*, by Dane Rudyhar, which delineates and explains the Sabian Symbols, sort of the Astrological tarot. Joseph Rigor's *The Power of Fixed Stars* is my favorite book on Fixed Stars. *Horary Astrology* by Anthony Louis is the newest and one of the best books on Horary for those insane/interested enough to want to take up that madness/discipline. And

The Encyclopaedia of Medical Astrology by Cornell, is the best all around encyclopaedia and arcane tome of obscure information on astrology in general, the title notwithstanding. Demetra George's *Asteroid Goddesses* is the best book on the big four asteroids, and *Chiron, Rainbow Bridge to the Outer Planets* by Barbara Hand Clow is my favorite Chiron book (as long as you don't take the Nibiru stuff too seriously.) Other good books are *The Inner Sky* and *The Changing Sky* by Steven Forrest and *Skymates* by Steven and Jodie Forrest. These books would make up a fairly complete astrological library, if you were to take up the discipline. They are all in print, as far as I know.

The bibliography lists these and other books, but do not assume that if a book is in the bibliography that I recommend it. Some are more useful and wonderful than others. And there are a couple of real clunkers. But I read them all (at least partially) for research, so they need to be listed. And many are not in print and quite difficult to find. Crowley's *Astrology* for one. That's a shame because that is a really good astrology book, even though his focus is mainly on Uranus and Neptune. He was one hell of an astrologer, and the book was decades ahead of its time. It reads as very contemporary, (unlike his other books), despite it being written in 1914 and revised in 1947. Maybe someone will reprint it. Some of the really old books, Lilly and Al Biruni and Ptolemy, are good, but are not slanted for a modern astrological practitioner, so they are more useful for research or horary and electional work. And some of the older books written in the 1940s and earlier are more fatalistic and negative than we are used to in modern astrology books.

Hopefully this book has given you a good introduction and overview to astrology as well as giving interpretations and techniques for using astrology in magick and spiritual growth. If you understand that the Moon in different signs has different effects, and there are quite a few astrologickal techniques you can use to enhance your magickal workings, and everyone has some sort of psychic potential, then you have gotten quite a bit from this book. If it all seems a hopeless jumble, be patient, take it bit by bit and work slowly with what you do understand. I have been doing all of this for quite a few years and it is difficult to remember back when I was still learning all of this. But I do remember that I just kept at it, and read and read and did it and did it and eventually I realized that I actually KNEW this stuff. Scary, but heady and empowering.

Thank you for reading this far and keeping with it. I hope you enjoyed reading this as much as I enjoyed writing it. Support your local astrologer, and may your magick be effective and rewarding. Blessed Be.

RESOURCES

Ordering Charts—If you are unable to calculate your own natal chart, you can send away for a computer generated version. For a natal chart, you will need to provide the following information:

day, month, and year of birth
time of birth (A.M. or P.M.)
place of birth (city and state, or if you were born outside the USA, city and country)

Reputable sources for charts include Astrolabe and ACS. The addresses and information follow.

Astrolabe
Box 1750
Brewster, MA 02631

To request a copy of your natal chart, call the Astrolabe Chart Service Order Line at 1–508–896–5081. You can also get information and place orders for Astrolabe's computer programs by calling 1–800–843–6682. One program, *The Astrologer's Companion*, is a DOS program that includes phases of the Moon and planetary days and hours. It's a memory resident program, which means you can either use the program by itself or pop it up on the screen when you're doing something else like word processing. When you open the program, it gives you the horoscope of the present moment, set for wherever you live (or any other place you want.) To determine a good time for a magickal ceremony, you can move the chart forward in time, looking for propitious aspects and the proper Moon phase, planetary day and planetary hour. Another program, *Printwheels*, allows you to print charts in a variety of styles, including "oldtime" styles used by ancient or Medieval astrologers.

I have not tried any of these programs myself, as I am one of the last astrologers working by hand. (Proof that you do not need a computer to begin your own study.) However, computer whizzes or math-phobes may enjoy investigating the various programs that are out there.

> Astro Communications Services
> 5521 Ruffin Road
> San Diego, CA 92123

You can order your natal chart from ACS by phone toll free at 1–800–888–9983. You can also send a fax to 1–619–492–9917.

Chart Styles—There are two basic chart styles. One is made with houses that are the same size, sometimes known as "pieces of pie." The other chart style shows proportional houses. You will have to choose which style you prefer. Beginners will probably be happiest with the old-fashioned system of same-size houses.

House Systems—There are many. Most of the charts in this book use Placidus Houses. You might also like Koch houses. As you can see from looking at Aleister Crowley's charts (charts 1–3 on pages 26-28), the house system you choose changes the chart.

Project Hindsight—For those interested in the really old astrology, the stuff written before the split between astrology, science and magic, Project Hindsight is undertaking to translate (and also re-translate) ancient, medieval and Renaissance manuscripts of interest to astrologers. Much of this material has never been translated into English. It is difficult and not for the casual reader, but there is a wealth of astrological, magical, philosophical, alchemical, and other information contained in the volumes. Booklets are available individually or by subscription. They have translations from Greek, Latin, Hebrew and will be starting Arabic translations also. For a list of volumes and further information, write them at:

Project Hindsight
The Golden Hind Press
P.O. Box 002
Berkeley Springs, WV 25411

This is the cutting edge of astrology, going back to our roots. Look for contemporary books published disseminating some of this knowledge in a more modern context. Rob Hand, Robert Zoller and Robert Schmidt are the three principle astrologer/translators working on the project.

BIBLIOGRAPHY

Titles listed with an asterisk are revised or reissued editions of older original manuscripts. Dates of original publication are given when available.

Adler, Margot. *Drawing Down the Moon*. Boston, MA: Beacon Press, 1986.

Allen, Richard Hinkley. *Star Names: Their Lore and Meaning*. New York: Dover Publications, 1963 (originally published 1899).

Al Biruni, Abu'l-Rayhan Muhammad Ibn Ahmad. *The Book of Instruction in the Elements of the Art of Astrology*.* Translation by R. Ramsay Wright. London: Luzac & Co., 1934 (from original manuscript written in Ghaznah, 1029).

Ashmand, J. M. Ed. *Ptolemy's Tetrabiblos*.* North Hollywood, CA: Symbols & Signs, 1976 (original ca. 140 C.E., English edition, "Waverly," ca. 1850's).

Barker, Stan. *The Signs of the Times*. St. Paul, MN: Llewellyn Publications, 1984.

Bills, Rex E. *The Rulership Book*. Richmond VA: Macoy Publishing, 1976 (Reprinted Tempe, AZ: American Federation of Astrologers, 1993).

Bloch, Douglas, and Demetra George. *Astrology for Your Self*. Berkeley, CA: Wingbow Press, 1987.

Buckland, Raymond. *Buckland's Complete Book of Witchcraft*. St. Paul, MN: Llewellyn, 1986.

Bulfinch, Thomas. *Bulfinch's Mythology*.* (original ca. 1850's) Feltham, Middlesex, England: The Hamlyn Publishing Group, 1968.

Calverley, Roger Anthony. *The Healing Gems*. Oyyawa, Ontario, Canada: Bhakti Press, 1983.

Carter, Charles E. O. *An Introduction to Political Astrology*.* London: L. N. Fowler, 1969.

Charubel. *The Degrees of the Zodiac Symbolized*.* Chicago: Aries Press, 1985 (original 1898).

Clow, Barbara Hand. *Chiron: Rainbow Bridge Between the Inner & Outer Planets*. St. Paul, MN: Llewellyn Publications, 1987.

Cornell, H. L., M.D. *Encyclopaedia of Medical Astrology*.* St. Paul, MN: Llewellyn Publications, and New York: Samuel Weiser, 1972.(Original 1932 with additions and updatings 1960's.) Reprint York Beach, ME: Samuel Weiser, 1992.

Cozzi, Steve. *Generations and the Outer Planet Cycles.* Tempe, AZ: American Federation of Astrologers, 1986.

Crowley, Aleister. *Astrology.** (Original from manuscripts ca. 1914, updated with additions, 1947) Jersey, Channel Islands: Neville Spearman, 1947.

Crowley, Aleister. *777 and Other Qabalistic Writings.** York Beach, ME: Samuel Weiser, 1973 (Originals from manuscripts 1907 and later, updated and revised by Israel Regardie after Crowley's death.)

Cunningham, Scott. *Cunningham's Encyclopedia of Crystal, Gem & Metal Magic.* St. Paul, MN: Llewellyn, 1987.

De Long, Sylvia. *The Art of Horary Astrology in Practice.* Tempe, AZ: American Federation of Astrologers, 1980.

Denning, Melita and Osborne Phillips. *Planetary Magick.* St. Paul, MN: Llewellyn, 1989.

Devore, Nicholas. *Encyclopedia of Astrology.* New York, NY: Philosophical Library, 1947.

Dobyns, Zipporah Pottenger, Rique Pottenger, Neil F. Michelsen. *The Asteroid Ephemeris.* Los Angeles, CA: TIA Publications, 1977.

Donath, Emma Belle. *Asteroids in the Birth Chart.* Tempe, AZ: American Federation of Astrologers, 1979.

Ebertin, Reinhold. *Fixed Stars and their Interpretation.** Translated by Irmgard Banks, Melbourne Australia, Aalen, Germany: Ebertin-Verlag, 1971. From original book *Sternenwandel und Weltgeschehen,* by Elspeth Ebertin, 1928, expanded and additions in 1971 edition.

Forrest, Steven. *The Changing Sky.* New York: Bantam Books, 1986.

Forrest, Steven. *The Inner Sky.* New York: Bantam Books, 1984.

Forrest, Steven and Jodie Forrest. *Skymates.* New York: Bantam Books, 1989.

George, Demetra. *Asteroid Goddesses.* San Diego, CA: ACS Publications, 1986.

George, Demetra. *Mysteries of the Dark Moon.* San Francisco: Harper-Collins, 1992.

George, Llewellyn. *A to Z Horoscope Maker and Delineator.** St. Paul, MN: Llewellyn Publications, 1972. (Original edition, 1910.)

Gettings, Fred. *Dictionary of Astrology.* New York: Routledge & Kegan Paul, Inc. 1987. (See also Gettings' *The Arkana Dictionary of Astrology.* New York: Viking-Penguin, 1990).

Graves, Robert. *The Greek Myths 1 & 2.* London: Penguin, 1986. (Original edition, 1935?)

Hall, Manly P. *Astrological Keywords.** Los Angeles: Philosophical Library, 1959. (Original, ca. 1940?)

Hall, Manly P. *Magic.** Los Angeles: Philosophical Research Society, 1978. (Original, ca. 1935.)

Hope, Murry. *Practical Greek Magic*. London: Aquarian Press, Harper-Collins, 1985.

Jacobson, Ivy M. Goldstein. *All Over the Earth Astrologically*. Pasadena, CA: Pasadena Lithographers, 1963.

Jacobson, Ivy M. Goldstein. *Simplified Horary Astrology*. Alhambra, CA: Frank Severy Publishing, 1960.

Jacobson, Ivy M. Goldstein. *The Way of Astrology*. Pasadena, CA: Pasadena Lithographers, 1967.

Jansky, Robert Carl. *Interpreting the Eclipses*. Van Nuys, CA: Astro-Analytics Publications, 1977.

Johari, Harish. *The Healing Power of Gemstones*. Rochester, VT: Destiny Books, Inner Traditions, 1988.

Kempton-Smith, Debbi. *Secrets from a Stargazer's Notebook*. New York: Bantam, 1982.

Lee, Dal. *Dictionary of Astrology*. New York: Warner Books, 1974.

Leo, Alan. *The Complete Dictionary of Astrology*. Rochester, VT: Destiny Books, Inner Traditions, 1989. (Original 1949 from partial manuscript and notes and edited by Vivian Robson after Alan Leo's death.)

Leo, Alan. *Esoteric Astrology*. Rochester, VT: Destiny Books, Inner Traditions, 1989 (Original, 1940's?)

Lilly, William. *Christian Astrology*. Issaquah, WA: Justus & Associates, 1986. (Original 1647, revised 1659.)

Lofthus, Myrna. *A Spiritual Approach to Astrology*. Sebastopol, CA: CRCS Publications, 1983.

Louis, Anthony. *Horary Astrology*. St. Paul, MN: Llewellyn Publications, 1991.

Manning, Al G. *Helping Yourself with White Witchcraft*. W. Nyak, NY: Parker, 1972.

Marks, Tracy. *Your Secret Self: Illuminating the Mysteries of the Twelfth House*. Sebastopol, CA: CRCS, 1989.

McEvers, Joan, Ed. *Spiritual, Metaphysical and New Trends in Modern Astrology*. St. Paul, MN: Llewellyn, 1988.

Michelsen, Neil F. *Tables of Planetary Phenomena*. San Diego: ACS Publications, 1990.

Monaghan, Patricia. *The Book of Goddesses and Heroines*. St. Paul, MN: Llewellyn, 1990.

Morford, Mark P. O. and Robert J. Lenardon. *Classical Mythology*. New York: David McKay, 1971.

Mountainwater, Shekina. *Ariadne's Thread: A Workbook of Goddess Magic*. Freedom, CA: Crossing Press, 1991.

Reinhart, Melanie. *Chiron and the Healing Journey*. London: Arkana, Penguin, 1989.

Rigor, Joseph E. *The Power of Fixed Stars*. Hammond, IN: Astrology &
   Spiritual Publishers, 1979.

Robertson, Marc. *Not a Sign in the Sky but a Living Person*. Tempe, AZ:
   American Federation of Astrologers, 1975.

Robson, Vivian E. *The Fixed Stars and Constellations in Astrology*.* York
   Beach, ME: Samuel Weiser, 1984 (originally published 1923).

Rudhyar, Dane. *An Astrological Mandala*. New York: Vintage Books, 1973.

Ryan, Anne. *Planets in Mutual Reception*. South Euclid, OH: The House of
   Astrology, 1980.

Scofield, Bruce. *The Timing of Events: Electional Astrology*. Orleans, MA:
   Astrolabe, 1985.

Sepharial. *Transits and Planetary Periods*.* London: Aquarian Press; and
   New York: Samuel Weiser, 1970 (originally published 1920).

Simmonite, W.J. *Arcana of Astrology*.* North Hollywood, CA: Symbols
   and Signs, 1977 (original 1847; revised and updated by John Story,
   1890.)

Starhawk. *Spiral Dance*. New York: HarperCollins, 1989.

Ungar, Anne and Lillian Huber. *The Horary Reference Book*. San Diego,
   CA: ACS Publications, 1984.

Walker, Barbara G. *The Book of Sacred Stones*. San Francisco: Harper San
   Francisco, 1989.

———. *The Secrets of the Tarot*. New York: HarperCollins, 1984.

———. *The Woman's Encyclopedia of Myths and Secrets*. New York: Harper-
   Collins, 1983.

Weinstein, Marion. *Positive Magic*. Eugene, OR: Earth Magic, 1992.

Wilson-Ludlam, Mae R., *Horary, the Gemini Science*. Richmond, VA:
   Macoy Publishing Co., 1973. Also available from Tempe, AZ: American Federation of Astrologers, 1973.

Zain, C.C. (Elbert Benjamine). *Horary Astrology*.* Los Angeles: Brotherhood of Light, 1973 (original 1930).

Zolar. *Zolar's Encyclopedia of Ancient and Forbidden Knowledge*. New York:
   Prentice Hall, 1970.

INDEX

Achernar, 264
air, 17, 45
Alcyone, 257
Aldebaran, 255, 258
Algol, 257
Algorab, 261
Almach, 257
almanac, 3, 67
Alnilam, 259
alphabet, 15
Alphard, 261
Alphecca, 262
Alpheratz, 256
Altair, 263
altar, 312
Antares, 255, 262
Aquarius, 18, 56, 153
Arcturus, 262
Aries, 18, 54, 148
Ascendant, 168
ascendant/midheaven degrees, 117
aspects, 16, 38, 67, 72, 106, 113
asteroids, 34, 264, 274
astrocartography, 9
astrology
    agricultural, 12
    Chinese, 228
    electional, 11
    esoteric, 7
    exoteric, 7, 8
    financial, 12
    heliocentric, 13
    Hindu, 228
    horary, 5, 10
    medical, 11
    mundane, 12
    natal, 3, 9
    natural, 12
    siderial, 13
    tropical, 13
    Uranian, 8
    vocational, 9
    Western, 228
astro-meteorology, 12
Bach, Eleanor, 266
Bailey, Alice, 8, 211
Bellatrix, 258
Beltane, 46, 286, 287
Betelgeuse, 259
Bills, Rex, 41, 295
birthstones, 226
Cadua Draconis, 198
caduceus, 227
Cancer, 18, 54, 149
Capella, 258
Capricorn, 18, 56, 153
Caput Draconis, 198
cardinal, 17, 45
Castor, 260
Ceres, 34, 265, 267, 275, 277
Chiron, 34, 278, 280
conjunction, 39, 106
constellations versus signs, 247
contra-parallel, 40, 107
Cornell, H. L., 294
cycle
    solar/lunar, 282
days of the week, 89
declination, 40
Dee, John, 14
Deneb, 263
Deneb Adige, 264
Deneb Algedi, 263
Denebola, 261
detriment, 108
Dobyns, Zipporah, 266
Donath, Emma Bell, 266
earth, 17, 44
eclipses, 234
ecliptic, 192
electional charts, 67, 120
elements, 16
ephemeris, 3, 67
Esbats, 281

esoteric rulers, 211, 217
    Aquarius, 221
    Aries, 218
    Cancer, 219
    Capricorn, 221
    Gemini, 218
    Leo, 219
    Libra, 220
    Pisces, 222
    Sagittarius, 221
    Scorpio, 220
    Taurus, 218
    Virgo, 219
exaltation, 108
fall, 108
final dispositor, 183
final signature, 130
fire, 16, 44
fixed, 17, 46
fixed stars, 253
Fomal haut, 255, 263
Gauquelin, Francoise, 9
Gauquelin, Michel, 9
Gemini, 18, 54, 149
genetheliacal astrology, 3
George, Demetra, 266
George, Llewellyn, 223
Goddess, 164, 287
Great Year, 251
Heindel, Max, 232
Herschel, 21
house systems, 230
houses, 16, 30, 148
    angular, 30, 31
    cadent, 30, 31
    succedent, 30, 31
Hyades, 257
Imbolc, 46, 52, 285, 288
inconjunct, 40, 107
Jones, Marc Edmund, 313
Juno, 34, 265, 271, 276, 277
Jupiter, 19, 89, 96, 171
King George III, 21
Koch houses, 25
Lehman, Lee, 266

Leo, 18, 55, 150
Libra, 18, 55, 151
Lilly, W., 41
Lughnasadh, 46, 51, 286, 287
Mabon, 51, 286, 288
Magick
    houses, 46, 47, 48, 49, 128
    planets, 46, 57
    potential, 58
    membership list, 297ff
    signs, 46, 53, 128
    timing, 63
magick and astrology, 41, 128
Markab, 264
Mars, 19, 89, 95, 170
Mercury, 19, 89, 95, 166
Mercury retrograde, 66, 79, 80
Midsummer, 51, 286, 287
Mirach, 256
Moon, 19, 64, 89, 163
    balsamic, 293
    crescent, 292
    disseminating, 291
    full, 291
    house placement, 117
    in houses, 100
    in signs, 82–87
    last aspect, 103, 104
    new, 293
    next aspect, 103, 105
    phases, 281, 290
    planting by, 12
    void-of-course, 66, 76, 77
    waxing/waning, 66, 74
mundane wheel, 23
mutable, 17, 46
mutual reception, 66, 110, 183
natal charts, 127
Neptune, 20, 97, 178
Nodes of the Moon, 192, 199
    North Node, 200
    North Node Aquarius/11th, 209
    North Node Aries/1st, 201
    North Node Cancer/4th, 203

North Node Capricorn/10th, 208

North Node Gemini/3rd, 202

North Node Leo/5th, 204

North Node Libra/7th, 206

North Node Pisces/12th, 210

North Node Sagittarius/9th, 208

North Node Scorpio/8th, 207

North Node Taurus/2nd, 202

North Node Virgo/6th, 205

South Node, 201

Nostradamus, 14

Oestarra, 285, 287

opposition, 39, 107

orbs, 230

outer planet cycles, 240

Pallas, 34, 265, 270, 276, 277

Paracelsus, 14

parallel, 40, 106

Pisces, 18, 56, 154

planetary correspondences, 36

planetary definitions, 160

planetary hours, 66, 88ff, 99

    sample table, 90

planetary stations, 234

planet

    of the day, 89

planets, 16, 18, 33

    magickal nature, 154

    outer, 176

Pleiades, 257

Pluto, 20, 97, 180

Polaris, 259

Pollux, 260

poppet, 295

Praesepe, 260

Procyon, 260

psychic potential, 58

qualities, 16

quincunx, 40, 107

reading ephemeris, 67ff

Regulus, 255, 261

Rigel, 258

ritual, 315

Rudhyar, Dane, 311

rulerships, 36, 37, 66, 108, 109, 294, 297ff

Sabbat cycle, 282

Sabbats, 281

Sabian symbols, 232, 313

Sagittarius, 18, 56, 152

Samhain, 46, 51, 286, 288

Saros cycle, 232

Saturn, 19, 89, 96, 173

Saturn Return, 174

Scorpio, 18, 55, 152

semi-sextile, 39, 107

semi-square, 39, 107

sesquiquadrate, 40, 107

sextile, 39, 107

Sidum Georgius, 21

signs, 30, 148

    type, 130

Sirius, 259

Spica, 122, 261

square, 39, 107

Sun, 19, 89, 94, 162

synastry, 10

syzygy, 235

Taurus, 18, 54, 148

timing tools, 63

    secret, 101

transits, 232, 233

Transpluto, 34

trine, 39, 107

Trismegistus, Hermes, 14

Uranus, 19, 96, 178

Uranus-Neptune conjunction, 240

Venus, 19, 89, 95, 169

Vesta, 34, 265, 272, 276, 277

Via Combusta, 254

Virgo, 18, 55, 150

water, 17, 45

Wega, 263

widdershins, 23

Witte, Alfred, 8

Yule, 52, 285, 288

ABOUT THE AUTHOR

Estelle Daniels began her astrological studies in 1967 and has practiced professionally since 1972, working with natal, synastry, horary and electional astrology. Presently an initiate of Wicca and member of a Wiccan church, she avidly subscribes to the Arhat project and helps publicize the translations in the pagan community. A native of Minneapolis, Minnesota, Estelle lectures on astrological and pagan topics.